THE LAST HEADBANGERS

ALSO BY KEVIN COOK

Titanic Thompson: The Man Who Bet on Everything

Tommy's Honor: The Story of Old Tom Morris and Young Tom Morris,
Golf's Founding Father and Son

Driven: Teen Phenoms, Mad Parents, Swing Science,
and the Future of Golf

THE LAST HEADBANGERS

NFL Football in the Rowdy,
Reckless '70s — the Era That Created
Modern Sports

KEVIN COOK

W. W. NORTON & COMPANY

New York • London

For information about permission to reproduce selections from this book,
write to Permissions, W. W. Norton & Company, Inc.,
500 Fifth Avenue, New York, NY 10110

For information about special discounts for bulk purchases, please contact
W. W. Norton Special Sales at specialsales@wwnorton.com or 800-233-4830

Manufacturing by Courier Westford
Book design by Chris Welch
Production manager: Julia Druskin

Library of Congress Cataloging-in-Publication Data

Cook, Kevin, 1956–
The last headbangers : NFL football in the rowdy, reckless '70s, the era that created
modern sports / Kevin Cook.
p. cm.
Includes bibliographical references and index.
ISBN 978-0-393-08016-2 (hardcover)
1. National Football League—History—20th century. 2. Football—United States—
History—20th century. 3. Nineteen seventies. I. Title.
GV955.5.N35C66 20102
796.332'6409047—dc23
                              2012020568

W. W. Norton & Company, Inc.
500 Fifth Avenue, New York, N.Y. 10110
www.wwnorton.com

W. W. Norton & Company Ltd.
Castle House, 75/76 Wells Street, London W1T 3QT

1 2 3 4 5 6 7 8 9 0

Contents

This book isn't meant to glorify the uglier aspects of NFL football in the 1970s and early '80s: the drugs, the booze, the cheating and head-hunting, the occasionally seamy sex, and the risks the game posed to players' health. There may be no greater cruelty in modern sports than the toll pro football has taken on the bodies and brains of its players.

This book is meant to inform and entertain, but I also want to celebrate the courage of those men, who by the 1970s had an inkling of the risks and took them anyway. They played for their families, for money, for their teammates, for love of the game. The risks paid off for some of them and ruined others' lives. Some went on to coach, while others analyzed the game on TV or found jobs that allowed them to shake hands and reminisce for a living. Others struggled with injuries that hobbled them or withered their brains to the point that they were senile at fifty. Others died before they turned fifty.

Was it worth it?

This book is dedicated to the players who took the risks.

THE LAST HEADBANGERS

Prologue

END OVER END

Phil Villapiano's helmet didn't fit. The Oakland Raiders' lantern-jawed linebacker stuck his head inside, gave the helmet a whack, and felt it rattle around his ears. Plastic piece of junk! How's he supposed to stop Franco and Bradshaw with his helmet bobbing around on his head?

While Villapiano fussed with his helmet, other Raiders paced and fretted, stretching, cracking their necks and knuckles. The visitors' locker room at Pittsburgh's Three Rivers Stadium smelled of Brut and Right Guard and Hai Karate, liniment, and nervous sweat. The players—big men but not giants, averaging six-two and 219 pounds—adjusted their pads, guzzled water from squirt bottles, spat on the floor. Fred Biletnikoff, a scrawny receiver with thinning blond hair and a wispy mustache, stopped chain-smoking long enough to trudge to the can and loudly puke. His teammates mumbled what might have sounded like prayers in any other locker room, but not a room full of Raiders. The Raiders were pro football's Hells Angels, and their mumbles were mostly curses. Safety George Atkinson stood in a corner, scratching the tight, shiny coils of his

1

beard. Then Atkinson sprang forward, throwing a forearm shiver at a phantom opponent. Biletnikoff, returning from the can, sat on a wooden stool and tied the laces of his cleats. Tied and retied them. Ten times. Eleven times. They still didn't feel right. He retied them again, looking around to see if anybody was going to give him shit about it. No, the others were deep in their own routines, pounding each other's pads, grinding their teeth, making their own toilet trips in the minutes before they took the field for their American Football Conference divisional playoff against the Pittsburgh Steelers. The Raiders were 4-point underdogs. Winner goes to the 1972 AFC title game, one step from the Super Bowl.

John Madden ran a beefy pink hand through his hair. Madden stood six-four, weighed 270, and sweated like the offensive tackle he used to be. His black polo shirt clung to an ample belly over polyester Sansabelt slacks. The youngest head coach in the league at thirty-six, he wasn't the rah-rah type. Madden had one rule: Show up on time and play hard on Sunday. He treated his players as professionals who didn't need pep talks. Pacing a locker room littered with socks and towels, Ace bandages, paper cups, and squirt bottles, studying his players' faces, Madden thought his team looked ready.

Villapiano, for sure. As Madden watched, the linebacker yanked the silver helmet off his head. He took a breath, then reared back and smacked his forehead into the cement-block wall. *Bam. Bam bam.* Now he paused as if waiting for the wall to crumble. But that wasn't it—he was waiting for something else.

A moment later, Villapiano pulled his helmet back on. There, better. Knocking his forehead against the wall had made his head swell a little. Now the helmet fit.

A few yards away in the stadium's lower concourse, the Steelers sweated in their more spacious home locker room. They were less growly than the Raiders, more like a construction crew than a biker gang. Veterans Ray Mansfield and Andy Russell, who were among the better-paid Steelers, making $22,000 a year, carpooled to the stadium to save on gas that cost fifty-five cents a gallon. Quarterback Terry Bradshaw sold used cars during the off-season. Fullback Franco Harris, a rookie with Fred Astaire feet and the chiseled features of Hercules, sometimes hitchhiked to home games. Fans who lingered after the game might pull out of the parking lot to see Harris standing on the curb in jeans and a dusty jacket, flagging a ride home. Now Harris sat with his hands folded, staring at the green linoleum floor. A few feet away Roy Gerela, alone as usual, as a kicker was supposed to be, picked at the extralong sleeves of his jersey. Defensive end L. C. Greenwood stubbed out a pregame cigarette.

John "Frenchy" Fuqua picked his helmet off a hook beside his cubicle. Off the field, Fuqua sported a feathered Three Musketeers hat, a cape, and a gold cane. His favorite pair of platform shoes featured hard-plastic heels with live goldfish swimming around inside. Claiming to be a French count "turned black" by fallout from a nuclear test, he warned opponents that he would deliver "the coop de grah on 'em." Steelers coach Chuck Noll, passing between players, nodded to Fuqua, who was checking his helmet for smudges and his uniform for lint, tapping his toes to some internal music. That was Frenchy, off in his own world.

Noll, forty, was even less rah-rah than Madden. On the first day of training camp he'd told the Steelers, "If I have to motivate you, I'll get rid of you." Noll and Madden were part of coaching's younger generation, men who rejected the old-fashioned image of the NFL coach as a World War II general throwing fits and barking orders. They were more modern than that. They were space-age coaches who saw their jobs as similar to that of the lead engineer on a NASA mission: Manage your personnel, draw up a game plan, anticipate surprises, and create multiple responses to possible setbacks, including last-ditch options. When the game starts, let your men execute the mission.

Noll scanned the room. This was the time when old-school coaches delivered rousing pregame speeches.

Terry Bradshaw could have used a little rousing. The Steelers' third-year quarterback was this crew's gawky country boy, a Bible-reading Forrest Gump with a secret. Despite his rifle arm and aw-shucks manner, Bradshaw suffered moods as black as his helmet. He wanted approval, even love, from a coach who saw open emotion as a sign of weakness. (Later, when Marianne Noll ran to hug her husband after a Steelers' Super Bowl victory, Noll shook her hand.) Alone with his worries, Bradshaw sat at his cubicle clenching and unclenching his throwing hand.

The coach cleared his throat. A few players looked up. Noll spoke without raising his voice, almost as if he were talking to himself.

"Play the way you've been taught," he said.

That was all. It was time to line up in the tunnel that led to the field.

Twenty miles south of Pittsburgh, in the town of Monongahela, sixteen-year-old Joe Montana flipped on the TV. The screen showed a blimp shot of Three Rivers Stadium, a cement bowl set down where the Allegheny and Monongahela Rivers met to form the muddy Ohio. The stadium's five decks shuddered with the thudding feet of fifty thousand fans hungry for a win. "Here we go Stilll-ers, *here we go!*" (Stomp, stomp!) This spot on the north bank of the Allegheny was a stone's throw from the site of the first pro football game, a scrum between the Pittsburgh Athletic Club and the Allegheny Athletic Association in 1892. The Steelers, born forty-one years later, were still looking for the first postseason victory in their long, lousy history.

Montana, the second-string quarterback at Ringgold High, recalls the early '70s as a time when "everything was changing fast. You'd turn on TV and you couldn't believe what you were seeing. In sports, politics—*life.*"

In the first months of what would be known as the Me Decade, National Guardsmen broke up an antiwar rally at Ohio's Kent State University by firing into the crowd, killing four students and wounding nine others. The students were protesting the American invasion of Cambodia, President Richard Nixon's escalation of a Vietnam War that would claim fifty-eight thousand US soldiers' lives and kill more than 2 million Vietnamese. The civil rights movement of the '60s begat war protests and an emerging women's rights movement in a time when every civic and social tradition seemed up for grabs.

In 1972 a Supreme Court featuring one of Franco Harris's predecessors in the Pittsburgh backfield, ex–football star Byron "Whizzer" White, was asked to legalize abortion in *Roe v. Wade*. The Court agreed, hizzoner dissenting. Antiwar actress Jane Fonda straddled a North Vietnamese antiaircraft gun, flashing peace signs, and Bobby Fischer humbled Boris Spassky in the Chess Match of the Cold War. At the Summer Olympics in Munich, Palestinian terrorists calling themselves Black September ushered in a new age of international terrorism, killing eleven Israeli athletes and coaches. The Watergate scandal, triggered by a burglary of the Democratic National Committee headquarters, couldn't stop Nixon's landslide reelection victory over George McGovern, despite mounting fury over the president's role in the burglary and cover-up. But Watergate would trigger impeachment hearings—only the second such hearings in US history—and the first presidential resignation. When it was over, Nixon boarded a helicopter on the White House lawn, flashing peace signs that he claimed meant victory.

In 1972 comic George Carlin got arrested in Milwaukee for uttering the Seven Words You Can Never Say on Television, "shit, piss, fuck, cunt, cocksucker, motherfucker, and tits." Other advances brought the first artificial heart, the first digital watches, the first e-mail. Atari introduced arcade-style Pong machines, with digital paddles batting a square, gray "ball" in what seemed the height of

high-tech entertainment. Eli Lilly discovered Prozac. Clint East-
wood chased psycho scum across movie screens in *Dirty Harry*, while
Francis Ford Coppola put the finishing touches on *The Godfather*.
On the radio, Don McLean's mournful "American Pie" led a Top 40
whose variety still astounds: soul from Al Green, pop from Sonny
and Cher, rock from Three Dog Night, early metal from T. Rex, Helen
Reddy's anthem "I Am Woman," and Neil Young's "Heart of Gold,"
plus the O'Jays, the Chi-Lites, and the Moody Blues. The past was
represented by Elvis Presley's new hit "Burning Love," the future by
fourteen-year-old Michael Jackson's "Rockin' Robin."

On December 14, astronaut Gene Cernan became the last man
to walk on the moon. Cernan and Harrison Schmitt left behind a
stainless-steel plaque: *Here Man completed his first explorations of the
moon. December 1972 AD*. When their Apollo 17 capsule splashed
down in the Pacific five days later, the Steelers and Raiders were
already practicing at Three Rivers Stadium for the AFC playoffs.

The night before the game, more than a hundred beery Steelers
supporters marched on the Pittsburgh Hilton, where Madden's
Raiders were staying. The fans hurled bottles at the hotel, hoping
to piss off the Raiders or at least disturb their sleep. Many of the
bottles fell short, exploding on the sidewalk in bursts of glass and
suds that drew cheers from the crowd. Around midnight a tall man
claiming to be a hotel guest tried to slip into the lobby. Cops tackled
him and clubbed him, opening a head wound that would require six
stitches, only to discover to the mob's delight that he was Raider
tight end Bob Moore.

An omen for Oakland?

The first half of the Raiders-Steelers playoff may as well have been
'60s football. Three yards, a cloud of dust (or Tartan Turf—the Steelers' strain of AstroTurf), and a punt. The halftime score was nothing
to nothing. Gerela kicked a third-quarter field goal that brought his
fans, Gerela's Gorillas, to their feet, hooting as they tried to see the

field through the eyeholes in their *Planet of the Apes* monkey masks. Madden kicked a water bottle. Noll, wearing a hooded sweatshirt and an early Motorola headset—clamps and wires connecting hard-plastic earpieces—stood by the Steelers bench with his arms crossed. Noll liked a 3–0 score. This was the run-first, block-hard, chew-dirt football he championed: "Before you can win the game you have to not lose it."

In the fourth quarter, another Gerela field goal made it 6–0. Gerela's kickoff pinned the Raiders deep in their own territory. Madden pulled Daryle Lamonica aside. "I'm sending Stabler in," he told his quarterback. Lamonica, who liked to throw deep, would have no chance to pull out a miracle win against the Steelers' prevent defense. His backup, Ken "the Snake" Stabler, who owed his nickname to his slithery scrambles, could sneak inside passes and short runs under the defense. Lamonica was a clean-cut '60s pocket passer; Stabler with his shaggy locks and rock-star mustache looked like the counterculture in shoulder pads, a hell-for-leather gambler.

"I was scared," recalls Stabler. "I felt like I was gonna throw up. But I was ready, too. In those times when the moment's right there in front of you . . . you gotta grab it."

A Steelers substitution helped. A few plays after Stabler began moving the Raiders into Pittsburgh territory, Steelers pass-rusher Dwight White limped off with a sprained calf muscle. White's backup, Craig Hanneman, replaced him at right defensive end for one play.

The Raiders lined up at Pittsburgh's 30-yard line with 1:13 on the clock. Stabler, calling signals, saw Hanneman in a three-point stance where White should have been.

"You notice anything new. A possible weakness. You file and remember," Stabler says. As the play began, he made a mental note of Hanneman's location, across the line a couple of yards to his left.

Moments after the snap, Stabler scrambled left. Hanneman's

prime task now was to contain him—to stay between the quarterback and the sideline. He didn't have to tackle Stabler, just funnel him toward the middle of the field, where other Steelers would converge to take him down. According to White, "We'd gone over that a billion times in practice. *Contain him*. And guess what? Craig doesn't contain."

Stabler rolled left. He pump-faked, and when Hanneman went for the fake, Stabler ducked around him to the outside. Weaving like a drunk in an earthquake, the Raider quarterback snaked forty yards to gain thirty and dived into the end zone.

Craggy George Blanda, forty-five, the oldest player in league history, booted the extra point in a stadium so quiet you could hear his foot hit the ball. Raiders 7, Steelers 6.

"We outplayed them all day. Then we screwed up one play," recalls Pittsburgh linebacker Russell, who chased Stabler in vain. "If you're a Steeler fan at that moment, you can't help thinking we're still losers."

Bradshaw couldn't move the Steelers. Stalled at their own 40, they were down to their last snap. The clock told the story: 00:22 left to play. DOWN: 4. TO GO: 10. In his owner's box upstairs, Steelers founder Art Rooney headed for the elevator. The game was lost; he wanted to get downstairs in time to intercept his players on their way to the locker room, to thank them for trying.

In the second-deck red seats, Pittsburgh baker Tony Stagno, wearing a combat helmet festooned with an Italian flag, pulled an inch-tall ivory figure of a man, a voodoo fetish, from a little wooden box. Stagno was a cofounder of Franco's Italian Army, fullback Harris's fan club. According to Steelers broadcaster Myron Cope, "Stagno . . . extracted from a small case an ivory fetish and fixed the Oakland Raiders defense with the Italian evil eye."

In the Steelers' huddle, Bradshaw called, "Sixty-six circle option." A pass to rookie Barry Pearson, with halfback Fuqua as a safety valve.

"Aw, not that play," said Harris. His role was to block. Coming out of the huddle he was thinking, *Okay, it's been a great year. This is probably the last play, so play it hard to the end.*

Here's the radio call by Jack Fleming: *Hold on to your hats, here come the Steelers out of the huddle. It's down to one play . . . Terry Bradshaw at the controls. Twenty-two seconds remaining, and the crowd is standing.*

Bradshaw took the snap from center Mansfield. Otis Sistrunk and Art Thoms led Oakland's charging front four, while the corners and safeties stayed back in what the Raiders called a nickel prevent (pronounced *PREE-vent*)—*nickel* because there were five defensive backs behind the linebackers, *prevent*, of course, because the DBs stayed deep to allow a short strike but nothing lethal. Safety Jack Tatum, aka the Assassin, played deepest; he was Oakland's last line of defense. Linebackers Gerald Irons and Villapiano keyed on Pittsburgh's running backs, with Irons responsible for Fuqua, Villapiano for Harris.

Bradshaw backpedaled six steps. Then hell broke loose: "Raiders to the left of me, Raiders to the right."

"I was chasing Bradshaw," says Sistrunk. "Almost had him—I got a hand on his arm."

Bradshaw leaned to his right, peering downfield, dodging Sistrunk and Thoms, who slipped past, grabbing air. "I shoved another Raider away with my left hand. Another came flying at me; I ducked."

Bradshaw running out of the pocket, looking for somebody to throw to . . .

Looking for Pearson, but the rookie receiver was covered. Twenty yards downfield, Frenchy Fuqua peeked over his shoulder. "I was open," Fuqua remembers. "I'm thinking, 'Bradshaw, throw it!'"

The clock ticked down to 00:16. Franco Harris saw his quarterback scrambling. Abandoning his blocking assignment, he turned downfield to give Bradshaw another target. "I wasn't supposed to be out there," he said after the game. "I saw Terry in trouble. But then he threw deep."

. . . He fires it downfield!

With a snap of his wrist, Bradshaw gunned the ball toward Fuqua. Harris took a step in the same direction, as players are trained to do—to make a tackle if the ball's intercepted or maybe grab a deflection. Flashing back to his college days at Penn State, Harris remembered what coach Joe Paterno told players to do on busted plays. Four words: *Go to the ball.*

Tatum, the safety, closed in on receiver Fuqua.

"I swear I could hear Tatum breathing," Fuqua would say. "I'm hauling ass to get to a point, he's coming to destroy whatever's at the same point."

Tatum might have intercepted the ball, but he wasn't out to catch it. He wanted to deal a punishing blow, separating Fuqua from ball, helmet, consciousness. That was Tatum's style. Closing fast, he drove his shoulder into Fuqua, who flew two yards sideways and crumpled on the 35-yard line.

The football caromed upfield. Bradshaw, tackled, banged his hands on his helmet, thinking the pass was broken up, game lost, season over. But the ball was still in the air. Only a few players knew it, but the game wasn't over yet. One of those players, Harris, moved toward the Fuqua-Tatum collision without breaking stride. Another, Raiders linebacker Villapiano, looked up in time to see the ball.

"Franco's my man on the play!" Villapiano recalls almost forty years later. "I left him and went toward contact when Bradshaw threw the ball. Next thing I know the ball's flying back over my head, going end over end, and I might be on the wrong fucking side of football history."

1

HUP

George Stanley Halas was born to hit. The jug-eared son of a Chicago tailor, Halas grew up knocking baseballs around sandlots and butting heads in industrial-league football games. In the summer of 1915 he was playing ball for Western Electric when the company hosted an employee picnic. More than twenty-five hundred workers boarded the Great Lakes steamer SS *Eastland* for a ride to the picnic grounds, but the twenty-year-old Halas was running late that morning. He missed the boat. And the worst shipwreck in Great Lakes history. The *Eastland* capsized when hundreds of passengers crowded one side of the deck to watch a canoe race. "As I watched, a steamer as large as an ocean liner slowly turned over on its side as though it were a whale going to take a nap," an eyewitness wrote. The ship sank in water twenty feet deep, its stern only fifteen yards from shore, its bow even closer. Eight hundred and forty-four passengers drowned. Rescuers carried their bodies to a makeshift morgue, an icehouse on the future site of *The Oprah Winfrey Show*. Halas lived on to play football for the University of Illinois and right field for the New York Yankees in 1919. A year later, Babe Ruth arrived from Boston to play the same position for the Yankees, and Halas moved on to represent his next employer, the Staley Starch Company of Decatur, Illinois, at the 1920 founding of the National Football League.

History is like football. Each player has his role; some are interchangeable while others decide the outcome, and it's not always clear which is which. Each play is a differential equation (or, for the Redskins, a mess) that affects the next play and the next, creating a pattern that may make sense in hindsight but could not have been predicted from the start. Like a good story.

Suppose Halas went down with the *Eastland*. At the very least, the Chicago Bears would look different. Today's Bears wear navy blue and orange because those were the colors of Halas's alma mater, Illinois. But Halas's contributions went beyond style. Without one of the pioneers who shaped its beginnings, today's NFL might be unrecognizable, or might not exist.

The story of the NFL in its 1970s heyday starts in Canton, Ohio, in 1920. Ralph Hay's Hupmobile showroom occupied the ground floor of the Odd Fellows Building, a gabled and turreted brick hulk in downtown Canton. A balding, glad-handing car dealer, Hay owned the Canton Bulldogs, one of four Ohio teams that had been scrumming for beer money since pro football's dark ages at the turn of the century. Hay and his friend George Halas, then player-coach of the Decatur Staleys, thought they could make a few dollars staging football games around the Midwest. Their summit with football men from four states lasted through the evening of September 17, 1920. Along with Hay's Bulldogs and Halas's Staleys, nine other teams were represented: the Akron Pros, Cleveland Indians, Dayton Triangles, and Massillon Tigers from Ohio, the Chicago Cardinals and Rock Island Independents from Illinois, the Hammond Pros and Muncie Flyers from Indiana, and the Rochester Jeffersons from upstate New York, 250 miles from Canton. As the sticky night wore on, several of the men left the Odd Fellows Building to go hunting for refreshment. They returned with buckets of ice-cold beer. Halas and the other founders sat on the running boards of Hay's Hupmobiles, dipping ladles into the buckets. Thus cooled and illegally fortified—defying Prohibition, which banned alcohol earlier that year—they drew up a schedule for the first season of a new league.

Two of their teams still exist. In 1922 the Staleys moved to Chicago and became the Bears, named as a nod to baseball's Cubs, who let them share Wrigley Field. Halas considered calling them the Cubs, but chose Bears because football players are bigger than baseball players. The other original club, the Cardinals, would flit from Chicago to St. Louis to Arizona. Over the league's first eighty-eight years the Bears and the Cardinals faced off ninety times, with the Bears leading the survivors' series, 57-27-6.

Nobody faced the Massillon Tigers, who dropped out before league play began. But by then the Buffalo All-Americans, Chicago Tigers, Columbus Panhandles, and Detroit Heralds had signed up. That fall, Dayton's Triangles manhandled the Panhandles in the first league game, 14–0.

Halas, Hay, and the other originals chose football's first hero as their president. Jacobus Franciscus Thorpe, whose Native American name, Wa Tho Huk, means "path lit by lightning," stood six-one and weighed 195 pounds. Jim Thorpe, thirty-two, had an upswept thatch of black hair, a square chin, and dark, hooded eyes. The best athlete the world had yet seen, he had won gold medals in the Olympic decathlon and pentathlon before signing with Hay's Bulldogs for $250 a game, an eye-popping sum at a time when Henry Ford's Model T's sold for $290 and Hay's Hupmobile road yachts cost $1,000. In a brief fling with pro baseball, Thorpe batted .327 for the 1919 Boston Braves while twenty-four-year-old Ruth hit .322 for the crosstown Red Sox. But Thorpe was born to run and kick the melon-shaped football of his day. As a collegian, leading tiny Carlisle (Pennsylvania) Indian Industrial School against mighty Army, he ran 92 yards for a touchdown only to see the play called back on a 5-yard penalty. So he took the next handoff 97 yards for a touchdown. With linebacker Dwight Eisenhower spraining his knee in a failed attempt to catch him, Thorpe's Carlisle Indians upset Army, 27–6.

Thorpe and the rest of the pro league's pioneers were player-coaches, owner–equipment managers, and street-corner ticket-hustlers. In 1923, the new league's fourth season, Bears player-owner Halas stripped the ball from Thorpe and ran it 98 yards for a touchdown, setting a record that stood for fifty years. By then the American Professional Football Association (APFA) had rechristened itself the National Football League, a grand title for an eighteen-team outfit with no outposts south of Washington, DC, or west of Chicago, where Papa Bear Halas hawked tickets on Clark Street outside Wrigley Field. He charged extra for a few special tickets: They allowed fans to sit at the end of the visiting team's bench.

In a stunt designed to grow the game, Thorpe jumped from the Bulldogs to an all-Indian team based in LaRue, Ohio, population 802. The Oorang Indians were named after owner Walter Lingo's prize Airedale, King Oorang, and starred Native American players including league president Thorpe, Peter Black Bear, Baptiste Thunder, Xavier Downwind, and strongman Nick Lassa, known as Long Time Sleep, who wrestled a bear at halftime. A barnstorming troupe promoting Lingo's kennels, the Indians went 4-16 over two seasons. Their prime contribution to league history was inventing the halftime show. Rather than rest on the sideline or retreat to a locker room between halves, they entertained the crowd by racing Lingo's Airedales, showing off their target-shooting skills, and flinging flaming tomahawks.

The Indians were among more than two dozen early NFL franchises to fold before the league started making money. Pro football was overshadowed by the "purer," far more popular college game and dwarfed by baseball, the national pastime that was thought to reflect American efficiency and fair play better than the mud-and-guts NFL. Red Grange proved fans would turn out to see pro football—Grange signed with Halas's Bears and drew crowds of more than sixty thousand on a 1925 tour that helped establish the NFL—but the Galloping Ghost was a beloved collegiate hero. Nobody doubted which brand of football the country preferred. The 1926 Army-Navy game drew one hundred thousand fans to Chicago's Soldier Field, where the professional Cardinals played before crowds of less than ten thousand despite giving tickets away. By the end of the first NFL decade, only ten teams survived. They were led by Halas's bruise-colored Bears, the Monsters of the Midway, who lost games as grudgingly as their owner spent money.

In 1940 Halas avenged a bitter regular-season loss to the Redskins—he thought the refs had cheated his Bears—by tattooing the Skins in the championship game, 73–0. His hair was now thin and so was he, sunken eyes magnified by black-framed glasses always trained on the bottom line. He picked pennies off sidewalks long after he was a millionaire. Hall of Fame linebacker Dick Butkus tells a latter-day Halas story that's as irresistible as it is apocryphal: "We're side by side at a urinal when he sees a quarter in there by the drain. Halas reaches into his pocket and flips another quarter in and says, 'I'm not reaching in there for a quarter, but for fifty cents . . .'"

Art Rooney doubled his money at the track. The brawling son of a Pittsburgh saloonkeeper, Rooney had been one of the town's best young athletes. Knute Rockne offered him a Notre Dame football scholarship, but Rooney opted for professional boxing and local politics. In 1933 he bought an NFL franchise after getting a tip that the Pennsylvania legislature was about to repeal blue laws that banned Sunday sports. It was at a racetrack that Rooney met Philadelphia's De Benneville "Bert" Bell, the raccoon-coated black sheep of a prominent political family. Together, the blue blood and the barman's son would bring decades of lousy football to the Keystone State. Both were fervent horseplayers, but Bell never had a hot streak like the one Rooney enjoyed in 1936, when he parlayed a $300 stake at New York's Empire City Race Track into $21,000, equal to $250,000 in 2012 dollars. A devout Catholic who believed that earthly events hold higher meanings, Rooney did what he thought Eligius of Chaptelat, the patron saint of horses, would do. He let it ride. He took his $21,000 straight to Saratoga, where, on an ominous day that saw a lightning bolt kill several horses in the paddock, he put $2,000 on a nag that won a photo finish, and $10,000 on an eight-to-one shot that won by a nose, and left with a profit of $256,000, worth $3 million today.

Rooney's Pittsburgh Pirates, founded in 1933 and named as usual in honor of the local baseball club, never had a winning season. In 1940 they became the Steelers, but the new name did nothing to temper their fortunes. The Bears and Green Bay Packers would claim a combined seventeen league titles over the next forty years while Pittsburgh's steel doormats won none.

During most of those years even the Midwestern monster teams played a rudimentary sort of football. The Packers' founder/coach/halfback Earl "Curly" Lambeau threw his franchise's first forward pass out of the single wing, a formation in which the center lateraled the ball to one of the backs. A precursor of today's shotgun and wildcat formations, the single wing predominated until Halas's Bears began attacking out of a T formation, with the quarterback under center. Single-wing quarterbacks spent most of their time blocking; in the T, quarterbacks could hand off to one of three running backs or drop back to pass. Halas liked to put one of his runners in motion out of the backfield, a plan that led to the "pro set," featuring two running backs and a flanker. Amid these mutations the game retained the gnarl of its roots in soccer and rugby. Players fought before, during, and after games. Kicking and biting, they broke fingers and teeth on dusty fields that turned to bogs when it rained. They wore leather helmets until inventor John Riddell, former coach of the Evanston (Illinois) High School football team, introduced the first plastic helmets, which had a disconcerting tendency to shatter on impact. Much like Bulldog Turner's nose.

During his thirteen-year career, Bears center Turner set an unofficial league mark by getting his nose busted five times by a single fist, the uppercutting right of Packers lineman Big Ed Neal, who would come out of his three-point stance and immediately punch Turner in the face. This was semipro ball: Rank-and-file players worked construction or in factories during the week and then earned an extra $50 or $100, which might double their pay, by suiting up for the local NFL club on Sunday. Coaches diagrammed plays for them to run, but the roughnecks in the trenches often ran wild instead. The Redskins had a "bootsie play" that called for all eleven defenders to "hit one man and try to tear him to pieces."

The melon-shaped ball they chased and drop-kicked—but seldom threw—was known as a pigskin because its granddaddy, the original English soccer ball, was a pig bladder blown up like a balloon. The early American football, all leather except for its cotton laces, leaked, sometimes audibly. It had a little nozzle under the laces. Players reinflated it by blowing into the nozzle between plays. Knute Rockne helped develop a thinner, less leaky ball that aided the passing game Rockne helped pioneer at Notre Dame, and in the late '30s and early '40s one of the first great pro passers, Washington Redskins quarterback "Slingin'" Sammy Baugh, used the new, streamlined ball to riddle lumbering defenses with bullets and bombs, launching what might have become a high-scoring, crowd-pleasing era if not for World War II.

With millions of able-bodied men enlisting or getting drafted, the league limped through World War II with rosters full of rejects. The lowly Pennsylvania clubs found themselves on the brink of bankruptcy. They survived only by joining forces. In 1943 Rooney and Bell combined their rosters to create the green-and-gold-clad Phil-Pitt Steagles, who shocked the league by going 5-4-1 with co-coaches Earle "Greasy" Neale and Walt Kiesling feuding all the way. Neale was almost comically nasty to Kiesling's ex-Steelers. When one of them limped off the field, saying, "Coach, I think my leg's broke," Neale barked, "Get back in there and find out for sure!"

Despite their winning record, the Steagles upheld their towns' NFL traditions. They set a league record that still stands by fumbling ten times in a single game. Running back Jack Hinkle lost the league rushing title by a yard when a careless official scorer credited a 37-yard run by Hinkle to a teammate who never touched the ball. A season later, with Bell's Eagles back in business at Philadelphia's Shibe Park, Rooney's Steelers merged with the Chicago Cardinals for a year. The Card-Pitts dropped a hard-fought opener against the Cleveland Rams, with Card-Pitts quarterback Coley McDonough firing touchdown passes of 40 and 67 yards. A week later the Army drafted McDonough. The other Card-Pitts passers went on to throw eight touchdown passes and 41 interceptions for a club sportswriters dubbed the Carpets. After their encouraging debut the league's doormats lost nine straight to finish 0-10. Rooney called his bastard club "the worst in NFL history," quite a distinction given the Pittsburgh franchise's history to that point: 32 wins, 75 losses, 6 ties, and 0 postseason victories. Rooney would have to wait twenty-eight more years, until 1972, for his Steelers to move that last number from 0 to 1.

After the war the upstart All-America Football Conference planted franchises in the booming California markets of Los Angeles and San Francisco. The AAFC's Cleveland Browns, named after their legendary coach, Paul Brown, upstaged NFL owner Dan Reeves's Cleveland Rams. Reeves asked his fellow owners to let him move to LA, where 103,000 fans had seen the 1945 USC-UCLA game while the Rams drew 11,000 to their opener in Cleveland. The other owners voted him down.

"And you call this a national league!" Reeves said, storming out of a league meeting. "Well, you can consider the Cleveland Rams out of pro football."

Halas, Cardinals owner Bill Bidwell, and Redskins chief George Preston Marshall chased Reeves to his hotel suite, where the miffed Rams owner shut himself in the bathroom. "It's either Los Angeles or Dallas," he called through the door. "Or nothing!" When Halas objected that the other clubs couldn't afford thousand-mile train trips to play his team, Reeves offered to add $5,000 a game to visiting teams' customary 40 percent of the gate. They shook hands on it, and in 1946 the Rams beat baseball's Dodgers to the West Coast. Three years later the AAFC disbanded, with the profitable Browns, San Francisco 49ers, and Baltimore Colts joining the NFL. But it would take more than new blood to invigorate the NFL, according to *Sport* magazine. "Professional football is a dying sport," the magazine's editors wrote with the wisdom of sportswriters in all ages. "Pro football never has been able to sell itself completely to fans who are so wild over the collegiate version."

NFL attendance began rising that year and never stopped. One reason was pro teams' near parity on the field, which kept games and conference races close. "On any given Sunday, any team in our league can beat any other team," said Commissioner Bert Bell, who'd been kicked upstairs after winning 10 games and losing 46 as the Eagles' owner-coach. But another factor would play an even bigger role in pro football's evolution from minor sport to national obsession. Like most football factors, it can be expressed in a number:

In half a dozen crucial years, the number of television sets in the United States rose by 14,500 percent. In 1948 there were 172,000 TV sets in America. Six years later there were 25 million.

The officials whistled seven penalties for a total of fifty yards in the '48 title game. It was the first year the league's referees all used whistles rather than horns to blow plays dead, and also the first year the NFL championship was televised. Red Grange huddled in a fur coat in an open-air TV booth at Shibe Park, calling play-by-play for a TV audience of less than one hundred thousand. A decade later 45 million viewers, including President Eisenhower, still a little tender in the knee he'd hurt chasing Jim Thorpe forty-six years before, tuned in the '58 title game between the Giants and Colts. They saw Baltimore's Johnny Unitas throw for a record 349 yards in an overtime thriller that is still called the Greatest Game Ever.

The Colts and Reeves's Rams were each hauling in more than $100,000 a year for local TV rights in the early 1950s. NFL attendance averaged forty-five thousand a game, then fifty thousand. Soon it was sixty. Baseball was still a bigger draw overall, but the NFL drew far more fans per game. Americans were embracing a cold-weather sport that was better suited to the nation's Cold War soul. Or maybe it was simpler than that. Maybe pro football just made better TV.

Ex-Steagle owner Bert Bell, sixty-four, spent the third Sunday of the 1959 season at the Steelers-Eagles game at Philadelphia's Franklin Field. Commissioner Bell sat in the cheap seats as usual, rubbing elbows with loud, beery fans. Late in the fourth quarter, with his beloved Eagles leading 28–24, Bell suffered a massive heart attack. He died in his seat, Eagles fans cheering all around him.

The search for his successor led to a man who did more than anyone else to create the modern NFL. And just as it had done fifteen years before, when Rams owner Reeves hid from Halas and company, the league's history made its way through a hotel bathroom.

When the owners convened at the Kenilworth Hotel in Miami Beach to choose Bell's successor, they planned to pick a league insider, either acting commissioner Austin Gunsel or 49ers executive Marshall Leahy. Twenty-three ballots later, they were deadlocked. It was January 1960, the first month of a watershed decade. Eisenhower was about to cede the Republican Party to Vice President Richard Nixon, a rabid Redskins fan who'd warmed the bench for the Whittier College football team a quarter century before and would face Massachusetts senator John F. Kennedy, known for photogenic touch-football romps on his family's Hyannis Port estate, to see who would be the next president. At the same time, almost unnoticed, several dozen U.S. military advisers in South Vietnam were reinforced by hundreds more. Soon the army had Vietnam casualties to announce: sixteen dead in 1961.

At the Kenilworth Hotel, Steelers owner Rooney exhaled a puff of cigar smoke. "This voting's going nowhere. We need another candidate," he said.

Rams owner Reeves saw his general manager as a compromise candidate. Pete Rozelle was only thirty-three, a PR man with just three years in the club's front office. But no one doubted his intelligence, and unlike older league hands the smiling, Coppertone-tanned Rozelle had no enemies in other front offices. The Mara brothers, Wellington and Jack—sons of New York bookie Tim Mara, the Giants' founder—liked the kid. Even the Machiavellian Paul Brown liked Rozelle, or at least saw him as potentially malleable enough to gain Brown's vote.

The Compromise Kid excused himself from the conference room while the owners discussed his nomination. As the door clicked shut behind him, he looked up and down the corridor. Where should he wait? The hotel's lobby was a hundred yards away. He couldn't wait there—what if they chose him and couldn't find him? On the other hand, he didn't want to lurk. It wouldn't do for them to choose him only to find him with his ear pasted to the conference-room door. So Rozelle went to the men's room across the hall, where he waited. And waited. Fifteen minutes passed. A hotel guest came in, did his business, and washed and dried his hands while Rozelle stood at the mirror, trying to look casual, patting down his thinning hair, washing his own hands. Years later Rozelle guessed that he washed his hands at least twenty times in that half hour. At last the Colts' owner, Carroll Rosenbloom, came through the door. He smiled and said, "Hello, Mr. Commissioner."

Following Rosenbloom back into the conference room, the young commissioner began the Rozelle era by announcing, "I can honestly say I come to you with clean hands."

The "Child Czar," as one headline tabbed him, soon chaired a league meeting to outline his plans for the 1960 season, including the division of TV rights and the relocation of NFL headquarters to New York from Bell's tacky digs outside Philadelphia. He was interrupted by Redskins owner Marshall, barging into the meeting wearing slippers and a bathrobe. The sixty-three-year-old Marshall, a West Virginia–born laundry mogul, may have been testing Rozelle's nerve. After Rozelle finished addressing the owners, Marshall launched a tirade against "the boy," waving his hands and swearing his brother owners were ruining the league by entrusting its future to a PR smoothie. All the while Rozelle sat beside him, listening politely. After all, Marshall was one of the owners, his new bosses. Rozelle nodded. The commissioner's job was already his; he could afford to let the old man vent. It was one of the moments when the imperturbable Rozelle proved himself to his thirteen employers— including Marshall, who supported him after that.

Pete Rozelle saw the potential of televised football, but as the '60s began, his league lost a step to yet another start-up circuit. The American Football League was the brainchild of Lamar Hunt, the clever, bespectacled son of oil billionaire H. L. Hunt. Lamar Hunt, twenty-eight, had bid for an NFL franchise only to be rejected, so he and Houston's Bud Adams, another spurned NFL suitor, rounded up half a dozen well-heeled, like-minded men and founded the AFL. The league debuted in 1960 with eight teams: the Boston Patriots, Buffalo Bills, Dallas Texans, Denver Broncos, Houston Oilers, Los Angeles Chargers, New York Titans, and Oakland Raiders. Owners paid $25,000 each for franchises that would be worth around $1 billion apiece half a century later. Sportswriters quickly dubbed them "the foolish club," but the AFL owners weren't fools. Hunt in particular recognized that sports—particularly colorful, violent professional football—was a form of unscripted TV drama. He and his fellow "fools" were creating a phenomenon that wouldn't have a name for another thirty years: reality TV.

The AFL employed a Spalding JV-5 football, a quarter-inch longer and a quarter-inch thinner than the older league's Wilson ball. Quarterbacks such as George Blanda, who doubled as a placekicker, Len Dawson, and Jack Kemp loved the more-throwable AFL ball. By the time they tossed the first tight spirals of the AFL's opening weekend, Hunt had hammered out a five-year, $8.5 million television deal with ABC. He left most of the hammering to MCA president David "Sonny" Werblin and one of Werblin's hardheaded agents, Jay Michaels. ("I ate a bowl of cereal beside the typed-up contract on our kitchen table," recalls sportscaster Al Michaels, Jay's son.) But the deal was Hunt's idea, as was the way the AFL divvied up its $8.5 million in TV revenue. While the NFL remained a patchwork of television fiefs, with the popular Colts raking in $600,000 a year while the small-town Packers settled for an annual $35,000, the AFL divided TV money evenly. Each club got the same $266,000 per year. As a result, all eight AFL teams instantly earned more from TV than five of the thirteen established NFL clubs.

With pockets full of TV loot, junior-loop scouts and executives signed up half the NFL's first-round draft picks, including Heisman Trophy winner Billy Cannon. Along with other signees, mostly lesser college stars and NFL retreads, the newcomers helped make the AFL a reasonable facsimile of professional football, faster-paced and often more fun than the grind-it-out NFL. The AFL introduced two-point conversions to the pro game, along with putting players' names on their jerseys.

Still, the new league's lowlights played like *Candid Camera*. Even with their streamlined ball, AFL quarterbacks threw thirty-one more interceptions than touchdown passes in the league's first season. The AFL-champion Oilers, who played home games on a Houston high school field, starred flanker Charley Hennigan, a Louisiana biology teacher who left the classroom long enough to try out for the team. Hennigan scored the first touchdown in Oilers history. He did it while playing with his last school-district pay stub—$270.62 for a month's work—stuck inside his helmet, between his hair and the helmet's foam lining. The pay stub, he said, reminded him "to run fast and stay in the league." Hennigan went on to make the All-AFL team in 1961, '62, and '64, the year he earned $7,000 and led the league with 101 receptions, a pro record. The Oilers defended their title in 1961. The rest of the AFL made them look like a well-oiled franchise: After a losing 1960 season, the stumbling, fumbling Oakland Raiders allowed 99 points before scoring a single point in '61 and drew fifty-three thousand fans. All year. New York's Titans weren't much more popular. Owned by Harry Wismer, the Redskins' plummy radio voice and Grange's partner in the ABC booth at the '48 NFL title game, the AFL Titans went 7-7 in their first season at the weedy Polo Grounds, which had sat empty in the two years since baseball's New York Giants fled for San Francisco. Players' paychecks bounced. When the 1961 draft came around, the Titans' only guide to college talent was a newsstand copy of *Street & Smith's Football Yearbook*. When a PR man asked for photos of the Titans' stars, Wismer sent pictures of himself. Fortunately for Hunt and the other owners, Wismer went broke. In 1963 he sold the team for $1.3 million to a group led by Werblin, who gave the Titans a new name evoking the La Guardia–bound air traffic zooming over its new home at Shea Stadium, a name that rhymed with that of baseball's Mets, born the year before, and matched that of the balletic street gang in *West Side Story*. The New York Jets would soon be the sexiest team in football.

Rozelle intended to crush the AFL by imitating it. With help from Browns owner Art Modell, who had worked at ABC, the NFL commissioner convinced a dozen of America's leading capitalists to pool their TV revenue the way Hunt and his so-called fools' club did, "for the good of the league."

"That was crucial," says TV and league executive Dennis Lewin. "There was a football war on, and Pete Rozelle got those big-money boys—Halas, Dan Reeves, Rosenbloom, and the Mara brothers—to split TV rights with the small-market teams. That's the moment when NFL dominance began."

There was a legal hurdle. Hunt's AFL had slipped under the radar of government trustbusters, but the NFL's plan to share TV money attracted the scrutiny of Kennedy's Justice Department. Attorney General Robert Kennedy, the president's brother and a former Harvard football letterman, threatened to nix the NFL's "communistic" revenue-sharing plan. Lucky for the league, Colts owner Rosenbloom had close ties to the Kennedy clan. The Baltimore owner, a major donor to JFK's 1960 presidential campaign, had once brought a couple of Colts to play as ringers in one of the Kennedys' famous touch-football games. Now Rosenbloom lobbied the administration on the league's behalf. A season later, President Kennedy signed the Sports Broadcasting Act of 1961, granting the National Football League an antitrust exemption that ensured the league's stability. Within three months, Rozelle capitalized on the Kennedys' support by signing the NFL's first national television contract: two years for $9.3 million, a jaw-dropping sum at the time. The league's TV revenue would grow a thousandfold in the next half century.

The '60s began with staticky, black-and-white TV images and

ended with bright, smeary color. Football came in styles as distinct as Johnny Unitas's crew cut and Buck Buchanan's Afro. Despite the occasional bomb from the Redskins' Sonny Jurgensen to Charley Taylor or from Dallas's Don Meredith to "Bullet Bob" Hayes, the NFL came across as slower and more earthbound than the jazzy AFL. The Minnesota Vikings used a grand total of two offensive sets, with no shifts and nobody in motion. As the decade progressed the dominant Packers steamrolled opponents with an attack consisting almost entirely of nine plays, most of them off-tackle runs. "Run to daylight" was Packer coach Vince Lombardi's mantra—he wanted Green Bay runners to find four or five yards in the trenches. In the off-tackle run or Lombardi's favorite variant, the Packer Sweep, offensive linemen sealed off a lane for a running back. On off-tackle runs, quarterback Bart Starr handed off to the fullback, who moved to a spot between the tackle and the tight end and followed the one who set a better block. During sweeps, the two guards pulled left or right to create a hole, with the center and run-side tackle walling off defenders as Starr pitched the ball to the halfback, with the fullback blocking. If it sounds complicated, it wasn't. Compared to today's game plans it was tic-tac-toe.

The AFL, like its ragtag cousin the American Basketball Association, offered a show that was faster, bolder, and blacker than the establishment brand. The AFL's Dallas Texans, coached by motormouth Hank Stram, featured multiple sets and shifts, men in motion, and a triple-stack defense that hid linebackers behind linemen. Chargers coach Sid Gillman, the son of a movie-theater owner, cut game film a hundred different ways and spliced it into minimovies that isolated particular players or parts of the field. Sitting in a smoky screening room, he'd say, "Look! When we do this, they do that." Along with assistant coaches Chuck Noll and Al Davis, Gillman used insights gleaned from his films to develop a pass-happy attack that would remake the game. "God bless runners.

They get you first downs and keep your defense off the field," he said. "But if you want to ring the cash register, pass." Passers such as the Chargers' John Hadl, the Texans' and Chiefs' Len Dawson, and the Raiders' Daryle Lamonica would gun the AFL's sleek JV-5 ball downfield, while Starr, the NFL's ideal quarterback, handed off to Jim Taylor for another 4-yard Packer Sweep.

The NFL had integrated in 1946, a year before Jackie Robinson broke baseball's color line. Still the Browns' black players, Marion Motley and Bill Willis, stayed in Cleveland that year while their white team-mates made a road trip to Miami. Florida law still banned integrated sports. Washington owner Marshall, who saw his Redskins as the South's team, kept his club lily-white for another five years and had a band play "Dixie" before home games. "We'll sign Negroes when the Harlem Globetrotters sign whites," Marshall said. His comeup-pance came when Kennedy's secretary of the interior, Stewart Udall, reviewing plans for Marshall's proposed new stadium in the District of Columbia, asked Attorney General Robert Kennedy if it was lawful for a football team to practice racial discrimination on federal land. Kennedy, smiling, said, "Go get him."

To build his new ballpark—now called Robert F. Kennedy Stadium—Marshall was forced to integrate his Skins. He used the number-one pick in the 1962 draft to make Syracuse's Ernie Davis the first black Redskin, then shipped Davis to Cleveland for the Browns' equally black Bobby Mitchell, who led the league with 72 catches and 11 touchdowns that season while the luckless Davis, who had rejoiced at the news that he'd be joining his idol Jim Brown in Cleveland's backfield, suddenly found himself too weak to carry the ball. When Davis died of leukemia a year later, the Browns retired his number, 45. Ernie Davis is the only NFL player to have his number retired without playing in the league.

By then the Browns' number 32 was only two years from retirement. Like Thorpe, Jim Brown had starred at lacrosse and doubled as a running back and kicker in college. Six-two and 232 pounds with 4.5 speed, Brown was the prototype of the bigger, faster modern athlete. He took handoffs the old-fashioned way, forearms parallel in front of him, a football and a half apart, a cradle for the ball. He pulled the ball close, shifted it to his hip, and cut toward the edge of the TV screen, leveling defenders who got in his way. As a rookie, Brown annoyed white teammates by sounding "militant" and tooling around training camp in a lavender Cadillac. "We'll play hard, dress right, carry ourselves with class, and be team people," he said of black players. "But we don't have to kiss any ass." Early that season he won over the whitest Browns by running through the Giants' feared Sam Huff. "I hit that big sucker head-on," Huff recalled. "He broke my nose, broke my teeth, and knocked me cold." In 1964 Brown crossed over to the big screen as an action-movie star. Soon he was upstaging Lee Marvin and John Cassavettes in *The Dirty Dozen*. He quit football in '65, "before it could humble me."

The other towering figure of '60s pro football was Brown's opposite—a plump, Jesuit-trained former altar boy prowling the Green Bay sideline in a camel-hair coat. Vince Lombardi, now the patron saint of rock-ribbed right-wing NFL fans, was a Democrat who warned his team, "If I ever hear 'nigger' or 'dago' or 'kike' around here, you're through." Lombardi may have learned tolerance from his brother, Harold, who was homosexual. Not openly—hardly anyone was—but Vince and Harold knew, and his brother's struggles to forge an identity in '60s America shaped the coach's worldview. Only one kind of identity mattered to Lombardi. "Son," he asked recruits, "are you a Green Bay Packer?" Meaning: are you brave, disciplined, clean-shaven, and tough enough to endure constant abuse? According to tackle Henry Jordan, "Lombardi was color blind—he treated us all like dogs." Lombardi's drill-instructor methods worked: After a 17–13 loss to the Eagles in the 1960 league championship game—

Jim Taylor dragged down at the gun with the goal line in sight—his Packers never lost another postseason game.

If Lombardi was the old NFL's idol, the younger league's version was the grandson of a Hungarian miner who settled in Pennsylvania coal country. In his school days, Joe Willie Namath was known for his speed. A basketball star at Beaver Falls High, Namath led the team in dunks. As an All-American quarterback for Bear Bryant at Alabama, he came out of college in 1965 dreaming of a $100,000 pro contract. That was what he would have gotten from the St. Louis Cardinals, who chose him with the twelfth pick in the NFL draft. At that point, Sonny Werblin jetted into the picture, luring Namath to New York with the richest deal in team-sports history: $427,000 over three years, including a $7,000 '65 Lincoln Continental and $30,000 to pay for hiring three new Jets scouts, two of whom were Namath's brothers. The third was his brother-in-law.

This was war, and AFL owners were gaining ground. They elected Al Davis, the Raiders' fierce, combative coach and general manager, to be their new commissioner. "We need a ruthless bastard to take the fight to the NFL," said Oilers owner Adams. The thirty-seven-year-old Davis fit the bill. Brooklyn-born and, according to a legend that amused him, raised by wolves, Davis took it as a compliment when people called him devious. His first official act was to add the words *dynamic young genius Al Davis* to a press release announcing his selection. Editing that press release was also one of his last official acts, for Davis underestimated the sneakiness of his AFL allies.

Without telling Davis, several AFL owners had met with Rozelle and the NFL. In July 1966 they reached an agreement: The leagues would merge, with Rozelle as commissioner. Davis was apoplectic. "I was the general who won the war," he said. "We knocked the hell out of the NFL." If there was to be a merger, he expected to be the new league's commissioner. Instead his brother owners asked him to run the AFL as a lame duck until the merger took effect four years later. So

Davis quit. He bought a stake in the Raiders and returned to owners' meetings as Rozelle's implacable enemy. But not even the Wrath of Al stemmed the NFL's progress. When Davis fought the divisional realignment that followed the merger, Vince Lombardi cornered him coming out of a meeting. The fifty-three-year-old Packers coach grabbed the younger, taller Davis by his checkered lapels and shoved him against a wall. "If you're going to cause trouble, you'll be run out of here. We don't need you!" Lombardi rasped. And for once, Davis backed down.

The merger brought instant benefits to the newly betrothed NFL and AFL. Television revenue tripled to $28.2 million over two years. The AFL's Dolphins and expansion Falcons and Saints stretched NFL territory deep into Dixie. Bubba Smith, the top pick in the leagues' first shared draft, signed for half Namath's pay, and soon the owners discovered a way to save money on the grass under the players' feet.

In 1967's Summer of Love, sixty thousand flower children flocked to the Monterey Pop Festival to hear Jimi Hendrix, Janis Joplin, and the Grateful Dead. An hour up the coast, the 49ers played on grass at Kezar Stadium, where pot smoke wafted down from the cheap seats. Elsewhere the prediction in *The Graduate*, released that fall, was coming true: "*Plastics*. There's a great future in plastics." AstroTurf, a nearly maintenance-free layer of nylon blades over layers of rubber and concrete, appeared in Houston's air-conditioned Astrodome and spread weedlike from there to stadiums around the league. The bluish Poly-Turf in Miami's Orange Bowl was endorsed by the NFL Players Association, which got a cut of Poly-Turf's profits. "There is every indication that synthetic surfaces cut down on casualties," Rozelle announced, "particularly of the knee type." He was wrong. Seventies players would wish they'd never heard of the stuff. Artificial turf increased knee-wrecking injuries and caused turf toe, an excruciating bruising at the base of the big toe. Fake turf would also rub skin off your arms and legs. Players dreaded going into the shower after games. Their skin got so raw that trainers treated it with burn ointment. After enough turf burn, the hair on their limbs grew back thicker, more like chin whiskers.

If they loathed the new turf, many players loved other synthetics. The '60s added anabolic steroids to the amphetamine "pep pills" pro jocks had taken for decades. Steroids first appeared on the training table of Gillman's Chargers in 1963, in cereal bowls brimming with pink pills. Those pills were Dianabol, the first widely used sports steroid. Gillman's strength coach, Alvin Roy, had learned about the stuff from Russian coaches at the 1960 Rome Olympics. Now Gillman told the Chargers, "Take your pills, boys." The pills were legal; pro football wouldn't ban steroids for another twenty years. A decade later, farther up the California coast, Madden's Raiders would supplement steroid pills with horse testosterone—in doses meant for horses—and primitive human growth hormone culled from cadaver brains. "We were reckless. Stupid. It probably killed a bunch of us," an ex-Raider says. "But you've got to remember the times we were in. Everybody wanted the new drug."

In the late '60s the newly allied leagues concocted a season-ending match between their champions, the AFL-NFL World Championship Game. Lamar Hunt, whose children loved a fad toy from Wham-O, the high-bouncing Super Ball, sent Rozelle a letter: *I believe we should 'coin a phrase' for the Championship Game. . . . I have kiddingly called it the 'Super Bowl,' which obviously can be improved upon.* Rozelle thought the nickname lacked class, but it proved as resilient as a runaway Super Ball. The game itself took longer to catch on.

The first Super Bowl wasn't a sellout. There were sixty thousand fans and forty thousand empty seats at the Los Angeles Coliseum on January 15, 1967. For pregame festivities, league officials released a flock of pigeons. The Coliseum's natural grass was painted a garish green to look brighter on television, more like AstroTurf. How far would Rozelle's NFL bend to accommodate TV? The answer came when the Packers' Don Chandler kicked off to open the second half. NBC, still running a halftime interview with Bob Hope, missed the kickoff. League officials radioed referee Norm Schachter, who waved his arms and blew the play dead. A moment later, play resumed with another kickoff by Chandler, the only do-over in Super Bowl history.

Lombardi's NFL Packers thumped the AFL Chiefs that day, 35–10. A year later they dismantled Davis's Raiders in Super Bowl II. A year after that, the NFL-champion Baltimore Colts were 18-point favorites over Namath and the Jets. Another mismatch. Pundits joked about the Stupor Bowl, a boring sequel to the real championship, the NFL title game.

Coach Don Shula's 15-1 Colts had demolished Cleveland 34–0 for the right to play the Jets. The Colts rumbled into Miami for the third Super Bowl with not one but three crew-cut stars, quarterbacks Unitas and Earl Morrall and bruising halfback Tom Matte. The 12-3 Jets got there by slipping past Davis's Raiders 27–23, with Namath heaving three touchdown passes despite a wicked hangover. "That *hippie*," Halas called Namath. At least Broadway Joe had made bed check the night before the game. "I grabbed a girl and a bottle of Johnnie Walker Red and stayed in bed with them all night," he said. During Super Bowl week the Colts drilled a rigid game plan while shaggy playboy Namath lounged by the pool at the Jets' hotel, running his mouth. "We're gonna win the game. I guarantee it," he said.

Namath's poolside boast changed the world. Not only the sports world but the real world, too, as the walls between news, sports, and gossip began to crumble. Namath's line was as famous as the year's other great quote, Neil Armstrong's "That's one small step . . . " That Namath's prediction came true in a 16–7 game in which the out-manned Jets controlled the ball with short passes, a style of offense that would eventually spell the end of '70s football, mattered less than the way he said it. Grinning, half-kidding, great-looking. All that mattered was that the hippie won. Namath's guarantee was the unofficial end of '60s football, the end of Packer dominance and crew-cut sports heroes, a giant leap toward the next decade. The Jets' shaggy quarterback set the stage for pro football's raging, reckless, hairy, hormonal adolescence, the dawn of the NFL era.

At Three Rivers, the ball flew over Phil Villapiano's head, turning end over end.

Franco Harris gathered it off his shoe tops at the Oakland 43. Raiders linebacker Villapiano gave chase, only to fall short when the Steelers' John McMakin, trailing the play, dove into his legs, a blatant clip that would have canceled the play if any of six officials had seen it.

Raiders center Jim Otto, standing near Madden on the sideline, wasn't sure what just happened. "I saw Franco reach down for the ball. I thought, 'Where'd he come from? Is that a live ball?'"

Play-by-play man Fleming shouted on the radio: *It's caught out of the air! The ball picked up by Franco Harris. Harris is going for a touchdown for Pittsburgh . . . . Five seconds left on the clock. Franco Harris pulled in the football. I don't even know where it came from. Fuqua was in a collision! There are people in the end zone. Where did it come from?*

Raider cornerback Jimmy Warren had a last shot at Harris. Warren's fingers scratched the 32 on Harris's right-shoulder pad as Harris dipped his right shoulder, escaping, and loped down the sideline without breaking stride.

Bradshaw, facedown on the artificial turf, thought he heard cheering. Or maybe he was just concussed.

Raiders safety Jack Tatum, his right shoulder ringing from the hit he'd put on Frenchy Fuqua, saw Harris nearing the end zone. "I didn't know he had the ball. I thought, 'He's sure in a hurry to get to the locker room.'"

Madden's assistant Tom Flores, sitting in a coaches' booth upstairs, blinked. "It's one of those times when you're not sure what you're looking at," Flores recalls. "Our guys are stunned. Tatum's jumping up and down, going crazy. Madden's going crazy, chasing officials around. The Pittsburgh crowd's going crazy. We're all thinking, *What the hell was that?*"

It wasn't a touchdown. Not yet. Back judge Adrian Burk signaled touchdown, but referee Fred Swearingen could overrule him. Swearingen huddled with Burk and the other officials. As he recalled it later, they gave him "four 'I don't knows' and two 'I thinks.'"

Swearingen jogged to the dugout at the edge of the stands. Fifty thousand fans were cheering the biggest play in Steelers history. Hundreds of them stormed the field to celebrate.

In the dugout, someone handed Swearingen a telephone, the same phone Pirates manager Bill Virdon used to call his bullpen during baseball season. The ref put the receiver to his ear. He covered his other ear and heard a scratchy voice in the phone.

"Who's this?" the voice barked.

"Swearingen."

"McNally here." It was NFL supervisor of officials Art McNally, who was sitting in the press box upstairs. McNally had seen the instant replay. There was no precedent for replay reviews; the officials were on their own. McNally chose not to reveal what he'd seen on the monitor. He asked, "How do you rule?"

"Touchdown," Swearingen said.

McNally let out his breath. "That's right."

On the field, Tatum charged Fuqua for the second time in a minute. "Tell them you touched it!" he shouted. Tatum knew the rule: If two offensive players in a row touch the ball, it's no catch. No touchdown; Raiders win.

Referee Swearingen jogged back to the field. He raised his arms: touchdown.

In the Steelers' chaotic locker room, Fuqua told a hometown reporter, "The guy hit me and the ball bounced off my chest."

Linebacker Russell spun Fuqua around. *"No,"* he said. "What you mean is, the ball hit Tatum."

Fuqua nodded. "Oh, yeah. *That's right,*" he told the Pittsburgh writer, who never reported Fuqua's first quote. "That's right, Tatum hit the ball."

Maybe. Or maybe Fuqua, slightly concussed, wasn't sure.

2

DINGS, DOLPHINS, AND THE BACK OF GOD'S HAND

When Pittsburgh fans recall their team's glory years, they usually start with the Immaculate Reception in 1972. But memory can play tricks. The Steelers didn't win the Super Bowl that year, or the year after that. In fact Noll's men had to wait two more years for the "Steeler Decade" to begin, two years in which Franco Harris's touchdown was often called the Miracle Catch.

Hours after the play, a Steelers fan named Sharon Levosky phoned WTAE-TV, Pittsburgh's ABC affiliate. Sportscaster Myron Cope was shuffling papers, scribbling a few lines to describe that day's playoff game with its crazy finish. Cope had a minute to spare before he went on the air. He reached for the ringing phone.

"Myron," Levosky said, "I've got a friend who's calling it the Immaculate Reception. Isn't that perfect?"

Cope used the term on the air that night, but it didn't catch on right away. At first Harris's catch was still the Miracle Catch, or occasionally the Miraculous Reception. Only over time, like the shift from beatification to sainthood, did the Miracle become Immaculate.

"We didn't call it either one of those in Oakland," says the Raiders' Villapiano. "We called it the Piece-of-Shit Reception."

After the game, Noll told the Steelers to "get out of here and celebrate. But only till Monday." The stone-faced coach looked around at his sweaty, happy, half-naked Steelers and almost smiled. "We've got another game next week!"

Seven days later the Steelers faced the unbeaten Miami Dolphins in the AFC title game. Winner goes to Super Bowl VII. (The championship game had acquired its Roman numeral two years earlier, with Super Bowl V, largely for what Rozelle considered its "classy" look but also to avoid calendar confusion, since the 1971 season led to the 1972 Super Bowl, etc.) It was New Year's Eve, the last gasp of bloody, bumpy 1972 and the birth of '73, ushered in on TV by *Dick Clark's New Year's Rockin' Eve*. Bandleader Guy Lombardo and his Royal Canadians had owned the holiday for decades, ringing in each new year with a lugubrious rendition of "Auld Lang Syne," but times were changing. Clark's new *Rockin' Eve* was counterprogramming for the younger generation, starring Al Green, Helen Reddy, and Three Dog Night, who began tuning their electric guitars in Times Square a few hours after Shula's Dolphins marched through confetti onto the field at Three Rivers Stadium in Pittsburgh. The Dolphins' 15-0 record didn't earn them home-field advantage; in those days the home field during playoffs was awarded on a rotating basis, and '72 favored the AFC Central–champ Steelers.

The AFC Championship matched two former assistants of Paul Brown, the Ohio legend who had founded his namesake Cleveland Browns before taking over the Cincinnati Bengals in 1968. "Paul Brown changed football forever," says Shula. "Before Paul, it was more physical: 'Let's beat 'em up, destroy the other team.' He made coaching more like teaching." Like Brown, Shula and Noll believed in running the ball first, second, and usually third. Both men liked to quote the old saying that three things can happen when you pass, and two of them are bad. So far in 1972, Shula's unbeaten Dolphins had passed the ball only 259 times while running 613 times, by far the most in the league. Quarterback Bob Griese kept opponents honest with an occasional deep ball to wideout Paul Warfield, who averaged more than 20 yards per catch, but Warfield caught only 29 passes all year while fullback Larry Csonka ran the ball 213 times. "My Hunky," Shula called Csonka, referring to their shared Hungarian heritage. Csonka and Dolphins halfback Eugene "Mercury" Morris hit holes bored in defensive lines by Pro Bowl linemen Larry Little, Jim Langer, and Norm Evans. The hulking Csonka, whose U-shaped noseguard gave him the look of a rodeo bull, played football like a bully. On one play he kayoed a tackler with a vicious forearm to the chin and became the only player in modern history to get flagged for unnecessary roughness while carrying the ball. Csonka thudded his way to 1,117 yards in '72, while Morris gained exactly 1,000. The first duo in NFL history to gain 1,000 apiece was supported by third wheel Jim Kiick, whose 571 yards gave the trio a league-record 2,688 yards gained on the ground, more than a mile and a half of hard-won NFL turf, and more than 1,000 yards over the league average.

Some of that mileage was an unintended consequence of a rule meant to increase passing. This would be a theme of the '70s: more and more rules designed to help quarterbacks light up the scoreboard. "Defenses got too stifling in the early seventies. There were too many ten-to-three games," says former Ravens coach Brian Billick. "The league wanted *points*." But sometimes the league's efforts backfired.

The NFL's powerful Competition Committee had reconfigured the field before the '72 season. To make room for more passing, the committee moved the hash marks—where balls downed near the sidelines were spotted—toward the middle of the field. And not just a little: The new hash marks were only eighteen feet six inches apart, the width of the goalposts. They were (and still are) less than half the width of the hash marks in college football. The idea behind the change was to widen the short side of the field, giving offenses more room to operate. "This will make the game exciting," said Oilers coach Bill Peterson, picturing his quarterback, Dan Pastorini, hitting wideouts flying untouched down the field.

"The next thing they'll do," Lions linebacker Wayne Walker griped, "is have mechanical fields, so they can tilt them and the offense can always go downhill."

Few spectators noticed the difference. Even today, how many fans notice that NFL hash marks are less than half the width of NCAA hash marks? But in football evolution as in any other kind, small variations can have game-changing effects. Narrowing the hash marks gave receivers more room to maneuver, but also broke open the running game. "When the hash marks were wide, there was no room to run on the short side," Noll explained. "With the hash marks in, you could run either way. They were thinking passing game, but now the running game had the whole field to work with."

In 1972, the so-called Year of the Runner, a record ten running backs gained 1,000 yards or more. The Bills' O. J. Simpson led the way, slashing to a league-best 1,251. "Trying to arm-tackle O.J. was like grabbing a truck," says a defender. "It took two or three guys to bring him down. Then he bounces up and gives you this crazy-eye stare, like, 'Who the fuck are you, tackling *me*?' We called it the death stare." Simpson was joined in the 1,000-yard club by runner-up Larry Brown of the Redskins, the Giants' Ron Johnson, Miami's Csonka, Raiders steamroller Marv "Mother" Hubbard, Steelers rookie Franco Harris, Dallas's Calvin Hill (whose wife, Janet, was Hillary Rodham Clinton's college roommate and whose son, Grant, became an NBA star), Chargers skitterer Mike Garrett, the Packers'

John Brockington, and Csonka's backfield mate Mercury Morris, who finished with 991 yards, but got credit for 1,000 when the league reversed a 9-yard loss on a lateral.

Dave Hampton was less lucky than Morris. On the season's final Sunday, in the fourth quarter of a Falcons-Chiefs game at Atlanta Stadium, Falcons fullback Hampton gained a yard to reach 1,001. The officials handed him the game ball. Hampton squeezed it to his chest. He was the first Falcon ever to reach 1,000 yards in a season. But only for a couple of minutes. With the clock ticking down, quarterback Bob Berry slipped while handing off to Hampton, who got gang-tackled for a 6-yard loss. Those 6 negative yards dragged his season total down to 995. A year later, a last-ditch tackle in the season's final game would leave the snakebitten Hampton at 997 yards. After a year lost to injuries, Hampton rehabbed and returned in 1975. The final moments of *that* season's final Sunday found him stuck on 998. The Falcons were out of the game, trailing the Packers at Lambeau Field, 22–13. There was time for one more play. He crashed the line. When the yardage was announced—4 yards, giving him 1,002—players from both teams embraced Hampton, who got a standing ovation from the Packers' fans. He won the Comeback Player of the Year award.

Shula's Dolphins ran more than ever after Griese broke his ankle in '72. Griese's backup was Earl Morrall, a creakier version of the Morrall who had piloted Shula's "unbeatable" Colts into Super Bowl III against Namath and the Jets. At thirty-eight, his flattop going gray, Morrall was still useful enough to earn the $90,000 the Dolphins were paying him, more than twice Terry Bradshaw's salary and triple the league average. Handing off to Csonka, Morris, and Kiick, he'd kept Miami's unbeaten season going after Griese's injury. At high noon on December 31, 1972, the day of the '72 AFC Championship, the 15-0 Dolphins came into Three Rivers as 3-point favorites.

The 12-3 Steelers came in with a grudge. Madden and the Raiders had spent the week griping about the Immaculate Reception, dismissing it as a homer call. "There's no way they'd call it our way in Pittsburgh," Madden sputtered to reporters. "There woulda been a riot. Somebody woulda been killed!" When reporters pressed Noll for a reply, the Pittsburgh coach shook his head: "No comment." But the writers kept coming back. Wednesday, Thursday, Friday, the same questions: Was Harris's catch illegal? Were the Raiders better, and the Steelers just lucky?

Finally Noll responded, "The rulebook doesn't cover the hand of God."

On the last day of 1972, eight days after the Miraculous Reception —and long before the play became forever "Immaculate"—God would show Pittsburgh the back of his hand.

Bradshaw got lit up early. Concussed by a first-quarter blow to the helmet, he fumbled inside the Dolphins' 10-yard line. The ball bounced toward the end zone while Bradshaw, seeing stars, groped for it like a blind man. The Steelers got lucky when guard Gerry Mullins fell on the ball for a Pittsburgh touchdown. Steelers 7, Dolphins 0.

Late in the half, Dwight "Mad Dog" White anticipated Morrall's snap count and burst through the line. He charged, snarling, but White was too late. Morrall got the pass off. Linebacker Jack Ham intercepted, but the play was erased—White had stepped offside. The penalty seemed not to matter because the Steelers held, bringing Miami punter Larry Seiple into the game. But in the same way rules tweaks can backfire, producing outsize, unexpected results, White's misstep affected the Dolphins' series of downs, which affected the half, the game, and the season. If White doesn't step offside, Ham's interception gives the Steelers the ball. But with Ham's interception nullified, Shula sent the Dolphins' punting unit onto the field.

Linebacker Russell recalls thinking, "We stopped 'em. Here comes the punter. We're up seven, and we get the ball at the end of the half. So we might go up fourteen-zip. Or ten-zip. At worst, we're up by seven."

On the Dolphins' bench, Csonka thought, "Somebody's got to do something to make us win."

Larry Seiple was versatile for a punter. Teammates paid him the ultimate punter compliment by calling him a real football player. A crew-cut redhead out of Kentucky, where he doubled as a wide receiver, he'd played enough flanker to catch 41 passes for the Dolphins back in 1969, averaging more than 14 yards per catch. Now, with the clock running down, Seiple snagged the long snap. He cradled the ball at waist height and went into his punting motion. The Steelers turned their backs and ran, dropping deep to pursue punt-return blocking assignments.

Seiple had to make a split-second choice. A fake punt? He and Shula had discussed it in training camp, but not lately. Not in this context, with the Dolphins down by 7 in the AFC Championship, with a trip to the Super Bowl and an undefeated season on the line. Still he could hear Shula's gravelly voice back in training camp, on a sun-baked gridiron at St. Thomas University in Miami Gardens.

"If you see that you can run it, run it," Shula had told him. "Just don't get caught."

Seeing the numbers on the black-clad Steelers' backs, Seiple held the football. He stopped midpunt, tucked the ball under his arm, and took off. ("I couldn't resist," he said after the game.) Seiple would always remember those moments as the weirdest of his career. Sneaking downfield, crossing the 50, he was startled to find himself gaining on several Steelers. Noll and his assistants yelled at the oblivious Steelers, pointing at the punter, who scampered all the way to Pittsburgh's 12-yard line. A Morrall-to-Csonka touchdown pass tied the game.

"Of course we were shocked," Steeler linebacker Russell recalls. "We still felt okay at the half. Tie game. But seven to seven looks a hell of a lot better if you're the guys who just got seven."

Before the second half began, Shula put his tanned right hand on Griese's shoulder. The Dolphins' quarterback hadn't played in eleven weeks. His right ankle was still tender after two months in a cast, the skin on that leg even paler than the rest of "Vanilla Bob" Griese.

"Can you go in?" Shula asked.

Griese said, "I'm ready."

The son of Sylverious Griese, an Evansville, Indiana, plumber, Bob had dedicated himself to football after Sylverious died in 1955, when Bob was ten years old. Griese threw pipe-straight passes with an overhand motion at Purdue, where he finished second to the stronger-armed Steve Spurrier in voting for the 1966 Heisman Trophy. As a pro he was Shula's on-field avatar. "Griese was efficient but a little boring, like the team. People thought the Dolphins were a little effete," recalls *Sports Illustrated*'s Mark Mulvoy. Both Shula and Griese were ardent Catholics, as was Dolphins owner Joe Robbie. The Dolphins hedged their metaphysical bets by inviting ministers and rabbis to locker-room services, but the ministers and rabbis couldn't help feeling like a spiritual taxi squad when the team flew Miami archbishop Coleman Carroll to Pittsburgh for the AFC Championship. The halftime score might have been 7–7, but Miami led the priest gap, with Archbishop Carroll trumping Pittsburgh's chaplain, Father Dan Rooney, the Steeler owner's brother.

Shula and Griese believed in old-fashioned hammerhead football, lulling opponents to sleep with the running game, springing an occasional surprise. They had a second-half surprise for the Steelers. "We didn't expect Griese to come in," Russell says, "but it shouldn't have mattered. Our defense was the same either way." Warfield lined up in the slot on a play designed to gain ten or twelve yards. He slanted over the middle and Griese hit him in full stride. Warfield head-faked Russell, and their eyes met. This is football's lion-and-gazelle moment, the linebacker drawing a bead on the ballcarrier, who can choose his flight path—and Russell froze. "That's my play," he remembers. "I'm supposed to shut off the inside, and I was *right there*, but I . . . hesitated." On grainy game film, Warfield races past Russell for a 52-yard gain. Jim Kiick runs the ball in for a Miami touchdown. Dolphins 14, Steelers 7.

In the upper deck, Gerela's Gorillas peered down at the field through their monkey masks, shaking their fists at the Dolphins. With Bradshaw watching from the Pittsburgh bench, still woozy, backup quarterback Terry Hanratty moved the Steelers into field-goal range. But the Dolphins blocked Gerela's kick. Noll may have had the better team on both sides of the ball, but Shula was killing him on special teams. Griese led Miami to another score. Dophins 21, Steelers 7. The Dolphins had scored three touchdowns against a Pittsburgh defense that had allowed exactly one touchdown in the previous twenty quarters.

With Griese racking up yardage and points, Bradshaw sat. He blinked, trying to shake the sand and stars out of his head. A tough guy at Louisiana Tech, the six-three, 220-pound quarterback had bowled over college linebackers, but after three years of NFL contact he considered himself "a cross between a fullback and a sissy." In college, he put his head down and broke tackles. "In pro football that's like trying to run over an angry building. I can't remember how many times I got hit so hard I lost my memory."

Gerela's third-quarter field goal cut the Dolphins' lead to 21–10. Hanratty sat beside Bradshaw on the Steelers' bench, asking questions: "Brad, what's the score? Who are we playing?"

"I was pretty loony," Bradshaw admitted later.

Hanratty tried again. "What day is it?"

Bradshaw stared at the field. He saw a football game going on. "Sunday?" A good guess.

"Well, Brad, you got one right." Hanratty waved to Noll. Thumbs-up—Terry Bradshaw was ready to play.

Bradshaw reentered the game on the Steelers' next series, wobbling a little on his way to the huddle. "That would never happen today," says one '70s player. "Everybody's too scared. But in our day, nobody got 'concussed.' You never heard that bullshit. You got 'dinged.' You got 'blown up.' You got 'thumped.' You got 'your bell rung.' You got 'smoked.' You got 'your clock cleaned.' You got 'your head handed to you.' Fine, you got hit. Get back in the game."

Bradshaw came out throwing. He completed four passes in a row, including a touchdown strike to Al Young. Dolphins 21, Steelers 17. A hundred thousand thudding feet rocked Three Rivers Stadium, the twelve-acre bowl of steel and cement reverberating to the standing-room crowd's chant of *Here we go Still-ers, HERE WE GO!* A series later, with time running out, the rumble grew louder as Bradshaw faked to Harris, who slipped into the flat looking for a miracle.

The Dolphins' Nick Buoniconti picked off Bradshaw's wobbly spiral and that was that. Noll yanked the Motorola headset off his ears. The 16-0 Dolphins were going to the Super Bowl. The home-field Steelers were losers again. Three Rivers was quiet as fifty-nine thousand fans shuffled toward the exits. Greene, Ham, and Russell started down the tunnel into the dark. Franco Harris, his helmet under his arm, took a last look up at the emptying stands. "It was tough," he recalls. "Our fans had forty years in the doldrums. That was Pittsburgh pro football. Then we gave them a miracle, but we didn't make the Super Bowl."

"I missed Warfield on a big play," Andy Russell says. "We fell asleep on the fake punt. But there was something more than our mistakes going on. I think Miami won because they thought they deserved it. They believed more than we did. We played the game hoping to win. The Dolphins *expected* to win."

Jack Ham said, "We learned something about playoff football today. Don't screw up."

In the Dolphins' locker room, Shula hugged punter Seiple. "That fake punt got us started," he said. Shula hugged creaky quarterback Morrall, who'd piloted the offense to nine victories in his nine starts, and Griese, who came off the bench to beat the league's best defense. Then, kneeling on the champagne-soaked floor of the visitors' locker room, the Dolphins prayed. "Not to say God helped us win," Shula says. "No. We said thanks for our families, our friends, our teammates, and the chance to compete."

That evening a propeller plane carrying Roberto Clemente, the Pittsburgh Pirates' star outfielder, flew emergency supplies from Puerto Rico to earthquake victims in Nicaragua. A previous shipment had been looted. This time Clemente, a national hero in Puerto Rico, went along to keep the food and medicine safe. It was three months since he'd doubled off the Mets' John Matlack at Three Rivers Stadium to reach 3,000 career hits in his last at bat of the season. Clemente's 3,000th hit set off celebrations in Pittsburgh and San Juan, Puerto Rico. Three months later, at 9:23 p.m. on December 31, 1972, while the Steelers were clearing their gear out of the Three Rivers locker room they shared with the Pirates, Clemente's plane crashed after takeoff from San Juan International Airport. The news came just before midnight, turning forty years of Pittsburgh doldrums into something worse.

3

BRAD'S BAD

Don Shula's phone rang at one thirty in the morning. "Must be some nut, calling at this hour," Shula told his wife as he reached for the bedside phone.

Dorothy Shula heard her husband say, "Who?" He sat up straight in bed. "Oh. Hello, Mr. President."

Richard Nixon was calling to talk about a pass play. Nixon had played a little football for the Fightin' Poets of Whittier College in the early 1930s; a teammate described him as "fearless" and "ineffectual." Forty years later, after his beloved Washington Redskins lost in the playoffs, Nixon switched his allegiance to Shula's Miami Dolphins in Super Bowl VI. "You should try a down-and-in pattern to Warfield," he told the coach. "I think it would work."

"Yes, sir, Mr. President," Shula said. "We like that play, too." And why not? The Dolphins ran some sort of slant to Warfield half a dozen times a game. On Super Sunday, sure enough, Warfield went down-and-in against the Cowboys in the first quarter. Incomplete. Cliff Harris, Dallas's ornery safety, sneered, "Some football genius Nixon is." The Cowboys went on to win, and Shula, the first coach to take two different teams to Super Bowls—his Colts had lost to Namath's Jets—was the first to lose two.

A year later the Dolphins beat Pittsburgh to advance to their second straight Super Bowl. The Steelers' playoff share was $5,500 per man, while the Super Bowl champs would bank an additional $15,000 apiece on Super Sunday, more than half the average NFL salary, on top of their bonuses for the first two rounds of the play-offs (a more potent incentive than the 2011–12 champion Giants' $172,000 per man in postseason bonuses, about a fifth the league average). By then Nixon, reelected in the biggest landslide ever, had been caught by his own hidden microphones as he watched the Redskins on TV with his daughter Julie. *"Goddamn!"* the president was recorded shouting. "Son of a bitch!" For Nixon, watching the 1972–73 Redskins in Super Bowl VII would be a welcome distraction from the Watergate scandal seeping in around his wingtips. The First Fan had switched his allegiance back to the Skins—he was pulling for Washington against Miami.

The seventh Super Bowl opened like the first: A thousand pigeons flew over the field. The rest of the festivities, overseen by Rozelle and Dallas's Tex Schramm, the sport's premier showman, attested to the game's growth. Twenty-six golf carts, each festooned with a giant helmet representing one of the NFL teams, sped along the sidelines. The crew of Apollo 17 recited the Pledge of Allegiance. A choir of orphans sang the national anthem, and the University of Michigan's marching band puzzled the crowd with tunes that only hard-core NFL fans could possibly name—the two conferences' theme songs, "The AFC's for You and Me" and "It's the NFC."

Late in the fourth quarter, with the Dolphins leading 14–0, they lined up for a 42-yard field goal. Three points would ice the game, assuring Miami the first perfect season in NFL history. "I was thinking, 'If we kick a field goal, we'll be up seventeen to nothing,'" Shula recalls. "A seventeen-oh score and a seventeen-and-oh perfect season."

Miami's placekicker wasn't tricky like punter Seiple. Garabed "Garo" Yepremian could only do one thing: boom a football with his strong left foot. He hailed from the Mediterranean island of Cyprus, where his parents were so poor they burned olive pits in the fireplace for heat. Yepremian followed his older brother Krikor to America, where Krikor played soccer at Indiana University. Garo, too, was a soccer player, known for his powerful kicks. They were watching football on TV one day when he saw the placekicker boot a field goal. "I can do that," he said. Krikor pestered the Detroit Lions into giving his brother a tryout, and Garo's blasts led Lions coach Harry Gilmer to take a flier on him. Moments before his first NFL kickoff in 1966, the story goes, Yepremian heard Gilmer say the Lions had lost the coin toss. So Garo ran onto the field to hunt for the lost coin. After Gilmer told him to kick off "and then run to the bench before you get hurt," Garo hustled to the other team's bench and sat among the hulking Bears until they ran him off.

The balding, five-eight Yepremian sometimes sounded a little like Latka, the fuddled immigrant Andy Kaufman played on TV's *Taxi*. Early in his career Garo would jog off the field saying, "I keek a touchdown," a line *Tonight* show host Johnny Carson repeated for years. Meanwhile Yepremian was revolutionizing the way points were scored in the NFL. The league's first Cypriot wasn't its first soccer-style kicker—Hungary-born Pete Gogolak had already scandalized purists by approaching the ball from a forty-five-degree angle rather than straight on, kicking with his instep rather than his toe. But Garo was better than Gogolak. As a rookie he connected on a record six field goals in a single game, dispatching the ball with a *thoomp* that was audible in the upper deck. After joining the Dolphins he led the league in scoring in 1971 but may have been more famous for "I keek a touchdown"—fans loved to quote the line back to him. Opponents, too.

Standing at midfield on Super Sunday '73, fists clenching and unclenching, Yepremian waited for the snap.

"Keek a touchdown!" somebody yelled.

Thoomp. The kick took off like a dart, a 42-yarder to clinch the Super Bowl and complete the league's only perfect season. Except that Redskins rusher Bill Brundige, slicing between blockers, got his hand up. The football caromed off Brundige's paw and floated back toward the startled Yepremian, who could have preserved the Dolphins' perfect season by falling on it, protecting a two-touchdown lead at the two-minute warning. Instead he had a brainstorm: throw a pass!

"My mind, it went blank," Yepremian said later. He tried to heave the football downfield. The ball slipped straight up off his fingers as if he were serving a volleyball. When it came back down, he tried to swat it out of bounds, but the ball bounced to Redskins cornerback Mike Bass. While Shula gaped and President Nixon, watching the play on a White House TV, jumped up and down, Bass took the ball 58 yards for a Washington touchdown. Yepremian's blunder turned a coronation into a barn burner. Instead of 17–0, the score was 14–7, with 2:07 to play.

Rather than try an onside kick, the Redskins kicked deep. They held, came within a whisker of blocking Seiple's punt, but to Yepremian's everlasting relief, time ran out on the president's team. Shula's game plan had worked: the Dolphins had closed the Year of the Runner by winning a ground-based Super Bowl, with Griese completing 8 of 11 passes—a record-low 11 passes in an entire Super Bowl—while handing off 37 times. Corralling Yepremian in the champions' locker room, the coach told him, "Garo, I forgive you. But if we lost, I would have killed you."

Shula had a word for Richard Nixon, too. "I want to thank the president for not sending in any plays."

Nixon's favorite sport was on the rise. That off-season, André Laguerre, the top editor of *Sports Illustrated*, called Roy Blount Jr. into his office. "Roy," he said, "I want you to spend a year with an NFL team and write about it." Laguerre's tastes ran more toward tennis and yachting, but his readers loved pro football above all else. *SI*'s NFL coverage had more than tripled since the '50s. As Laguerre told his boss, Time Inc. kingpin Henry Luce, "I'm developing a strong hunch that pro football is our sport."

Baseball had been the country's top sport for a century but was now the national pastime by reputation only. No one knows the precise moment pro football surpassed the older game—Namath's poolside guarantee may have been the turning point—but the switch was thrown in the late '60s. Back in 1961, a Gallup Poll found that 34 percent of Americans called baseball their favorite sport, while 21 percent favored football. Eleven years later the numbers had practically reversed: in a new Gallup Poll, 36 percent preferred football, versus 21 percent for baseball. The NFL was a better fit for a faster, rougher post-Vietnam America, a difference comedian George Carlin captured in an immortal bit:

Baseball is a nineteenth-century pastoral game. Football is a twentieth-century technological struggle. In football you wear a helmet. In baseball you wear a cap! Football has clipping, spearing, piling on, late hitting, and unnecessary roughness. Baseball has . . . the sacrifice. Football is played in rain, snow, sleet, hail, fog, mud. In baseball, if it rains, we don't go out to play. "I can't come out to play, it's raining out!" Baseball has no time limit: We might have extra innings! Football is rigidly timed and will end even if we have to go to sudden death. And the objectives of the games are different: In football the object is for the quarterback, also known as the field general, to be on target with his aerial assault, riddling the defense by hitting his receivers with deadly accuracy in spite of the blitz, even if he has to use the shotgun. With short bullet passes and long bombs, he marches his troops into enemy territory, balancing this aerial assault with a sustained ground attack that punches holes in the forward wall of the enemy's defensive line. In baseball the object is to go home . . . I'm safe at home!

Laguerre gave writer Blount his choice of NFL teams to cover. Blount chose the Steelers partly because the Immaculate Reception made them seem touched by destiny, partly because a team with Bradshaw, Harris, Mean Joe Greene, and Count John "Frenchy" Fuqua was sure to be good copy, and partly because he liked their cornerback's name: Mel Blount. The two Blounts were no relation, though they joked that Roy's white grandfather might have owned Mel's black one.

Noll hated the idea. After five years as head coach he had assembled a roster he believed was talented and disciplined enough to win the next Super Bowl. Sure, the lowly Steelers wanted all the press they could get. Each fall a team PR man gave reporters a photocopied sheet of all the players' home phone numbers. But a national-magazine writer poking around the locker room might gum up the works. Even so, Steelers owner Art Rooney and his son, club executive Dan Rooney, gave Blount their all-access okay. "If we're careful, and we don't speak out of turn," Dan Rooney told Noll, "Blount's presence might contribute to the team's closeness."

It was a big if. As it turned out, the gimlet-eyed Blount revealed the team's feuds, drinking binges, drug use, and racial tensions in magazine stories that became a book, *About Three Bricks Shy of a Load.* Blount told of a Steeler trying to shoot down a police heli-copter, and a Steeler wife stripping off her clothes at a party, lying naked on the carpet, and asking, "Who's first?" His warts-and-all account introduced readers to a band of flawed, driven, horny men trying like hell to make a living in a sport that broke strong men every day. Many of their elders—men such as Unitas, Huff, Ray Nitschke, Night Train Lane, a thousand others—were hobbled if not crippled, trying to buy groceries and pay medical bills with dimes left over from premodern salaries and whatever goodwill their names still commanded. The Steelers of the '70s were better paid but they weren't getting rich. Some rode a Pittsburgh city bus to practice. They were the last generation of NFL players who weren't set for life after five years in the league. The Steelers' average salary in 1973, $25,000, was equal to about $120,000 in 2012 dollars. At $35,000, Bradshaw was earning only $5,000 more than the Jets had paid Namath's brother and brothers-in-law for being related to Broadway Joe. Bradshaw's $35,000 salary was less than two-tenths of 1 percent of the $18 million the Patriots paid Tom Brady in 2010.

"The league wasn't modern yet," recalls Blount. "Not like today, when players have gotten so rich they employ squads of friends and hangers-on, with Ben Roethlisberger's paid bodyguard standing by while he takes a young woman into the bathroom. In the '70s, it was still football on a human scale." Blount's portrait of the '73 Steelers cast Noll as a chilly professor trying to teach an almost-great team how to quit beating itself. Bradshaw wished the coach would get fired and replaced by someone who'd give him an occasional smile and a pat on the butt. "Bradshaw and Noll were never going to love each other," Blount says, "but Noll wasn't after love. He knew a lot of the players disliked him. He didn't care as long as they listened."

Linebacker Russell hasn't forgotten his first meeting with Chuck Noll in 1969. "He'd just gotten hired. I'd just made my first Pro Bowl. Noll calls me in and I figure he wants to congratulate me. But, no, he rips right into me. 'Russell, I've been watching a lot of game film,' he says, 'and I don't like the way you play. One, you're too aggressive. You miss tackles. Two, you switch off assignments and try to make the big play. You want to be the hero, but you're interfering with the larger defensive scheme. And three, your techniques are flawed. I'm gonna teach you how to play this game.'"

Noll didn't hire a linebackers coach that season. He tutored the linebackers himself, interrupting practice to point an accusing finger at Russell's right foot. "You're out of position! Move that foot two inches."

Russell could have pulled rank. The Steelers' veteran captain could have spat on the ground, pretended not to hear, asserted himself at the coach's expense. Instead he moved his foot two inches. With the captain's acquiescence, Noll took control of the team's future. Soon he introduced aerobic workouts that made the Steelers feel like guinea pigs. Each player would run five 350-yard laps, then rest and put two fingers to his neck, checking his pulse while a coach counted to ten. The proper rate was thirty beats in those ten seconds. Any faster meant you were pushing too hard; slower meant you weren't going hard enough. Control your heart, control your performance. They felt themselves toughening up. Outside Noll's purview they started a team tradition: any player who loafed or quit got the Bleeding Pussy Award, a tampon.

When Russell got beat on a play-action pass during a 47–10 loss during Noll's first year, he expected a scolding. Instead the coach asked, "What was your thought process on that play?" Weak-side linebacker Russell had done his homework. He said, "I watched a lot of film. They only showed that formation ten times in the last five years, and five of those plays went the other way, away from me. Of the five that came my way, only one was a pass. The other four were off-tackle runs. So if they're coming my way, why would they play-action without setting me up with an off-tackle run?"

Noll said, "Maybe they thought, 'Russell's smart, so let's *not* set him up.' But if you pay attention you can see their thinking. Watch your postsnap keys—if the tackle doesn't fire out with the snap, he's staying back to protect the quarterback. That's a pass, not a run. But you were so invested in your tendency chart, you missed the key."

Forty years later, Russell says, "I thought I was smart, but this guy was two or three steps ahead of me. Two or three steps ahead of the game as we knew it. I thought, 'I want to play for this guy.'"

Jockeying in Pittsburgh traffic, Joe Greene honked his horn. Greene and Mel Blount carpooled to Three Rivers Stadium, Blount laughing as Greene cut off Bradshaw's pickup truck. They parked and shot Brad the bird, grinning, and shouldered their gear, striding to a spacious home locker room where Russell and Fuqua played Frisbee golf, sailing disks at a towel bin. When Mean Joe walked past, the Frisbee-throwers held their fire. Sometimes Noll would walk through looking straight ahead, seemingly lost in thought, a Frisbee zipping toward the back of his head, until he leaned an inch sideways to let the Frisbee fly by. Noll saw more than he let on. This was in keeping with a plaque on his desk that quoted Pope John XXIII: SEE EVERYTHING. OVERLOOK A GREAT DEAL. IMPROVE A LITTLE.

Greene, esteemed by his teammates and feared by opponents, supported Noll through three years in which the team went 12-30. "Chuck Noll didn't put his arms around us and hug us, and he didn't celebrate when we came off the field after a good play," Greene said. "But he knew *we* knew he had a good plan." Noll had told Rooney from the start that the Steelers would lose before they started winning. It would take years to reshape the roster, weeding out players who were physically or mentally weak, retraining those like Russell who had bad habits. By 1972 Noll thought his team was ready to win the Super Bowl, but that was the Dolphins' season. A year later he considered the Steelers the best team in the league. When a reporter asked if Noll worried about the team's rugged '73 schedule, he clenched his jaw as if chewing a bullet. "No. We have an easy schedule," he said. "We don't have to play the Pittsburgh Steelers."

But he was worried about his quarterback. Was Bradshaw teachable? "There was never any question about his ability. It's about dedication," Noll said. Yes, Bradshaw had as much raw talent as any passer alive. He could throw the ball sixty yards on a line. His short passes traveled so fast and spun so hard that the ball sometimes cut the skin on his receivers' hands. Gloves didn't always help. Catch one of Bradshaw's bullets point-first on the numbers and you woke up the next day with a Rorschach bruise on your chest. Receivers called those bruises cancer shots. They expected Bradshaw's game-calling and leadership skills to improve enough to complement that arm. Noll doubted it would happen.

"Chuck would like a guy who catches on quickly, understands defenses," running back Rocky Bleier told sportswriter Bill Chastain years later. "That wasn't Bradshaw. Brad was a gunslinger. He dealt from emotion."

Oil and vinegar, head and heart, opera and Opry, Noll and Bradshaw. The coach, a symphony buff and amateur chef, never connected with the country-boy quarterback who kept his pickup truck's radio tuned to WEEP, Pittsburgh's country-western station. Noll got so annoyed with Bradshaw that he'd grab his face mask and chew him out in front of the team. Soon the moody quarterback was second-guessing himself before the coach had a chance to do it. The rip on him had always been that he was worth the proverbial $1,000,000.10, a million-dollar arm and ten-cent head. Bradshaw's worst fear was that it was true.

He'd grown up feeling dumber than the other kids in Shreveport, only to discover years later that he suffered from attention deficit disorder as well as depression. As a high school senior Bradshaw considered playing college ball at Baylor, he recalled in his book *It's Only a Game*. "Baylor is a fine Baptist university whose motto is *Pro Ecclesia, Pro Texana*, which roughly translates, 'Terry can't even understand the motto, so no way is he going there.'" Instead he starred at Louisiana Tech, whose unofficial motto was *Throw, Terry, throw.* The Steelers hoped to make him the top pick in the 1970 NFL draft—their booby prize for going 1-13 in 1969. But first they had to win the most important coin flip in football history. This coin toss wasn't for possession of the ball or home-field advantage. It was for Bradshaw. After the Steelers and Bears both went 1-13 in '69, giving them equal claim to the top pick in the 1970 draft of college players, Rozelle announced that they would break the tie with a coin toss. The flip took place at the Fairmont Hotel in New Orleans, two days before Super Bowl IV. The Steelers were represented by Coach Noll and team president Dan Rooney, while Bears owner Halas dispatched his son-in-law, Ed McCaskey. Commissioner Rozelle pulled a coin from his pocket: a 1921 silver dollar, as old as the league. He tossed it into the air. They all watched the coin spin.

McCaskey called, "Heads."

How do the '70s play out if that coin comes up heads? That question hangs in the air with Rozelle's silver dollar. Suppose the silver dollar spins one turn more or one less—does that make the Bears the team of the '70s while Terry Hanratty or Joe Gilliam looks downfield for the Steelers? If Bradshaw goes to Chicago, do the '70s belong to the Dolphins or Raiders or Cowboys . . . ?

Rozelle let the coin fall. He wasn't about to let either team claim he interfered with fate. Like a referee, he let the coin fall, then stepped toward it and announced the result: "Tails." Noll and Rooney shook hands and exchanged one word: "Bradshaw." They took their wives to dinner together that night, and Rooney said he had a surprise for the coach. He handed Noll the coin Rozelle had flipped, the silver dollar that meant Terry Bradshaw was going to be a Steeler. "Chuck," he said, "this is the start of something big."

"This guy's going to be our Moses," center Mansfield announced after the Steelers took Bradshaw with the first pick in the 1970 draft. He couldn't have known how long it would take Pittsburgh to reach the promised land.

The first trouble came when Mansfield invited Bradshaw to a team party. Several of the cursing, farting, shot-and-a-beer veterans mocked the dimple-chinned rookie. "They looked on me as a Bible-toting Li'l Abner," Bradshaw recalled. And those were the white teammates who were supposed to be his buddies on a roster that ate, drank, and partied along racial lines, as most pro teams did, with the whites laughing with Archie Bunker in *All in the Family* on a bar TV at one end of town while the blacks cracked up watching *The Flip Wilson Show* at the other. Bradshaw didn't fit in anywhere. One day at his first training camp he whistled and said, "I never seen so many colored guys in one room!" It was an ignorant thing to say but not malicious. He'd had no black teammates in Louisiana and *colored* was about the nicest word he'd heard for blacks. But his good intentions wouldn't have mattered if not for Greene, who had watched Bradshaw bring his lunch tray to a "colored" table at camp one day and plop down with a friendly "How y'all doing?" He was the first white Steeler to do so. Mean Joe didn't speak up, but he noticed. After that, if someone called Bradshaw a cracker or worse, Greene glared at the guy. That was all it took.

Bradshaw vomited before his first pro game. Early in the first half he called receiver Ron Shanklin's number. Shanklin, whose puffy Afro barely fit under his helmet, liked to growl while running patterns to psych out defenders. *Grrr*ing his way through the Oilers' secondary, he got open. Bradshaw saw him, but the ball slipped from the rookie's clammy hand and floated toward Shanklin, who backtracked to gather it in. Instead of a touchdown, he got drilled on contact. Nine incompletions and an interception later, Bradshaw dropped into his own end zone for a desperation pass and stepped on the end line for a safety. He had scored the first two points of his NFL career—for the other team. Noll yanked him, and backup

Hanratty finished up. After the game Bradshaw sat in his truck in the players' parking lot, weeping.

"I was unprepared for pro ball," he admitted years later. He recalled being amazed to see Steeler defenders practicing a fake fake-blitz. They would show blitz, bouncing up to the line more or less rabidly, depending on their acting chops. Mel Blount, for one, deserved an Oscar for selling the fake fake-blitz. The idea was to make the other team's quarterback think they were pretending. To make him think they were faking blitz. Then they blitzed.

Bradshaw rubbed his prematurely thinning hairline. "Make him think *you* think *he* thinks . . . " It gave him a headache.

The lonesome quarterback worried that he'd never master Noll's playbook. He looked to his coach for moral support, but Noll had none to give. One day Bradshaw spent the first couple of minutes of a team meeting chatting with Steelers owner Art Rooney. Noll fined him for it.

Mean Joe Greene saw that Bradshaw was big for his position— six-three, 215. Like Greene he was big and quick and a gamer. A fighter. In his worst college game he threw five interceptions—and made the tackle after four of them. On a busted play in his rotten rookie year with the Steelers, he scrambled, fighting off a rusher who grabbed his throwing arm. The lineman looked as if he were doing a chin-up on Bradshaw's arm. The rookie didn't get the pass off, but he held on to the ball.

Bradshaw completed 83 of 218 throws his rookie year—38 percent—with 6 touchdowns and 24 interceptions. When punter Bobby Walden got hurt in the season's last game, Noll punished Bradshaw by sending him in to punt. Swarmed by Eagles, Bradshaw got his kick blocked for a Philadelphia touchdown, a fitting bookend to his opening-day safety.

Li'l Abner slunk home to Louisiana. "Did I deserve the team's support?" he asks today. "I don't know. Football is a tough-ass business, and I was immature." Back in Shreveport, he told his father he was going to "show 'em" in his second year. Which he did, sort of, connecting on 203 of 373 passes, fourth best in the league, for 13 touchdowns. He was still the league's leading dyslexic, as he joked years later, throwing into coverages he couldn't read. Twenty-two more interceptions gave Terry Bradshaw 46 picks and only 19 touchdown passes in his first two years as a pro. Afraid of Noll, sick of being sneered at in front of the team, he went to owner Rooney and spilled out his troubles to the kindly Chief, who said, "Terry, hang in there. We're all on the same side."

When Rooney was away, Bradshaw avoided Noll by ducking into the owner's empty office. Rooney's secretary just smiled. The boss's pet Steeler had the run of the place. He would sit in there alone, smoking one of the Chief's cigars.

To Noll, Bradshaw was a project at best. At worst, the failing quarterback was a wasted number one draft pick. But Joe Greene saw a different sort of project. The more he watched Bradshaw flounder, the more determined he was to help him.

Fans and reporters called the six-four, 275-pound, electric-quick tackle Mean Joe. The Steelers just called him Mean. Greene grew up hating the sweaty fieldwork he did as a ten-year-old, picking cotton near Temple, Texas. As a tackle at North Texas State he tossed opposing linemen aside as if they were scarecrows. After the Steelers made him the fourth pick in the 1969 NFL draft (USC's O. J. Simpson went first), a Post-Gazette headline asked, "Who's Joe Greene?" Greene, miffed, held out before signing and reported to camp twenty pounds overweight. Noll promptly introduced him to the Oklahoma, a drill that pitted a rusher against a blocker, man-to-man. In the Oklahoma, also called the nutcracker, the rusher and blocker line up in a space walled off by tackling dummies. The walls are a yard apart, creating a lane three feet wide and nine to ten feet long, a space the size of a toilet stall. The players take their stances. When a coach blows his whistle, they launch themselves forward. The drill ends when one of them hits the ground.

On Greene's first day, Noll matched him against All-Pro center Ray Mansfield. "A bunch of us hung around to see Mansfield beat the fat rookie in his first Oklahoma," says Russell. "Well, at the whistle Greene picked Ray up and just threw him aside. Our jaws dropped. Now Bruce Van Dyke, a guard, another All-Pro, goes in to try Greene, and Greene destroys him. I'm standing there thinking, 'What'll we do with this monster?'"

They'd make history. But not yet. The '69 Steelers beat the Lions in their opener and then ran the table in reverse to finish the season 1-13. That was the year *Pittsburgh Press* columnist Roy McHugh advised rookies, "The first thing a Steeler must learn is how to lose." But Greene loathed losing even more than picking cotton. In Chicago he spat on the Bears' fierce Dick Butkus, an eight-time Pro Bowler, and dared him to fight. Butkus, an inch shorter and thirty pounds lighter than the wild-eyed rookie, pretended not to hear. During a season-ending loss in Philadelphia, riled at being held on every play, he knocked two Eagles linemen out of the game. When the third-stringer held him, Greene grabbed the football and chucked it off the field. If the referee didn't stop the holding, he said, "I'll stop the game." The ref shrugged and gave the center another ball. Greene, steaming, took the new ball and fired it into the second deck at Franklin Field.

Greene's fire helped forge the famed Steel Curtain defense. His "get-offs"—first steps after the snap—changed the sport. So quick that opponents had to double-team him, Greene eased the blocking on the rest of Pittsburgh's front four. Not that double-teams stopped him. Sacks wouldn't be an official statistic until 1982, but nobody doubted that Greene led the league, just as he unofficially led the Steelers without challenging Noll or Russell, without a vote, without a word from anyone. Mean never sought a captaincy; he didn't give a damn about titles or hierarchy. He led by actions and attitude. As Dan Rooney recalled, "Greene's influence with the other players cannot be overestimated. While Noll tried to figure out which quarterback should have the job, Greene saw the potential in Bradshaw. When he took Bradshaw under his wing, it seemed clear to everyone who our quarterback would be."

Says Bradshaw, "Joe was the leader of our team. Hell, he felt sorry for me. I never got the respect a quarterback deserved, but he supported me. And it mattered."

In October of '73, the 5-1 Steelers hosted their division rivals, the 4-2 Bengals. It was a pivotal game enhanced by Cincinnati's being Paul Brown's team. A graying icon in a gray fedora, the great Brown had built dynasties at every level of the game while barely setting foot outside Ohio: at Massillon High School, where his record was 80-8-2; Ohio State University, where he led the Buckeyes to the 1942 national championship; and Cleveland, where his eponymous Browns won three NFL titles. Now Brown was coaching the Bengals. He also owned the team. His coaching tree already featured Shula, Sid Gillman, Weeb Ewbank, Blanton Collier, Otto Graham, Lou Saban, Ara Parseghian, Bill Walsh, and others, including Noll, who had spent six years as a messenger guard for the 1953–59 Browns, relaying plays from the coach to the huddle. Some of Brown's protégés strayed far from the tree—Noll in particular rejected Brown's old-school methods and relished any chance to beat the old man. When reporters asked Coach Noll why he didn't use messenger guards, he said Brown's system "emasculates the quarterback." In case anyone missed the dig at his old boss, he went on to mock the sixty-five-year-old Brown as "the oldest quarterback in the league."

Noll, forty-one, was less master and commander, more of a '70s guy. The militaristic approach of old-guard coaches such as Halas, Lombardi, and Brown was losing ground as football evolved from the raccoon-coated, pennant-waving days of the single wing into a more modern, multifaceted game. Younger coaches saw players as more than X's and O's. Me Decade coaches such as Noll and Bill Walsh hoped to unlock each player's potential. *That* was modern leadership. Noll, recalling how he resented being a cog in Brown's offense, wanted to outhit Lombardi's X's and outrun Brown's O's by nurturing his Steelers' talents. At least that's what he claimed when he wasn't browbeating them for footwork that was off by an inch.

When Fuqua popped off before the Cincinnati game, warning the Bengals to watch their tails in the three-river valley of the coop de grah, Pittsburgh writers cornered Noll. Wasn't Frenchy providing bulletin-board fodder for the enemy? Shouldn't the coach shut him up? Noll shrugged. "I want our players to be themselves."

All except the quarterback. Too loose a goose even for Noll, Bradshaw came in for withering criticism after almost every game. The fourth-year flop was booed at home by fans who preferred his backup, Pennsylvania native Hanratty. Early in the Cincinnati game, with the Steelers trailing 6–3, Bradshaw stumbled to the sideline clutching his throwing arm. He had a separated shoulder. He was done for the day, maybe the season. And the home crowd at Three Rivers loved it! Hoots, whistles, and applause rose from the stands as more and more fans saw that Bradshaw was hurt. They stood to cheer Hanratty, who connected on 4 of 7 passes for 127 yards, including a 51-yard touchdown strike, in the Steelers' 20–13 victory.

The fans were "vicious," Greene said. "They don't know what it's like to bust your ass out there. To hear people *cheering* when a guy gets hurt . . . " He shook his proud, massive head. From that moment on, the two primary Steelers were paired up, one on each side of the ball, one black, one white. Together they would prove those cheering, jeering fans wrong and bring the Vince Lombardi Trophy into their locker room. Not for the fans. For the team, the doormat Pittsburgh Steelers. That would be the sweetest payback.

The doctors said Bradshaw might be back in time for the playoffs. Meanwhile second-stringer Hanratty broke a rib, leaving snaps in the hands of *his* backup, Joe Gilliam. That was rotten news for the Steelers, but a veritable cornucopia of consequence for Howard Cosell, star of the greatest show in sports.

4

THREE FOR THE SHOW

*T*err-y Brad-shaw. Quarterback. Pittsburgh Steelers. Injured! Shoulder sep-a-ration.*"

Howard Cosell was setting the stage for the game of the year. It was December 3, 1973.

"Terry Han-ratty. Backup man from Note-ra-Dame. Injured! Just a week ago."

TV screens from coast to coast showed NFL mayhem, '70s-style: Bradshaw and Hanratty getting pummeled in film clips. The two quarterbacks would spend this Monday night as spectators, just like 20 million other viewers.

"Thus this young man, Jefferson Street Joe Gilliam, black quarter-back!" Cosell's nasal drone, one of the best-known voices in America, was milking the moment for all it was worth. Cut to psychedelic screen graphics with neon bubble letters spelling *Monday Night Football*. The sound track was a funky keyboard riff that made the conferences' theme songs sound as square as John Philip Sousa.

Cosell, fifty-five, was in his element. He'd distinguished him-self as a '60s sportscaster who championed black athletes such as

Muhammad Ali. Ali had refused to fight in the Vietnam War in '66, famously saying, "I ain't got no quarrel with the Viet Cong. No Viet Cong ever called me nigger." Then came the assassination of Martin Luther King Jr., the rise of the Black Panthers, and a resurgence of the Ku Klux Klan. Race was the hottest hot-button issue, and Cosell knew his color-blindness put him at odds with millions of his viewers. He knew that many if not most of them were scared of men who looked like Joe Gilliam. Scared or worse. Judging by the hate mail Cosell got each week, some of it threatening the "nigger-loving Jew," quite a few Americans would have joined a lynching party for Gilliam *and* Cosell. And that delighted Cosell. If parts of America still hated to see a black man succeed, if the NFL still doubted athletes such as the Rams' James Harris and the Steelers' Gilliam, Cosell would be happy to rub their noses in tonight's top story.

"Joe Gilliam, getting his shot in the wake of all the talk through all the years about black quarterbacks in the National . . . Foot . . . ball . . . League!"

In a sweltering production truck parked outside the Orange Bowl, director Chet Forte watched a bank of twenty staticky monitors. Forte was a chain-smoking, cola-guzzling bundle of nervous energy. Once the game started, he sometimes skipped bathroom breaks. Rather than miss a play he would unzip his fly, fill a plastic cup, and stow it in a corner, saying, "Nobody drink that." Now he pointed at a monitor, selecting a pregame two-shot of Cosell and Gilliam. America saw Cosell in his canary-yellow blazer, a dot of sweat below his black toupee, holding a mic to the tip of Gilliam's goatee.

"Do you feel an almost overwhelming pressure? Will it affect your performance adversely?" Cosell asked.

Gilliam had the half smile of a man who knew what question to expect. "You know, pressure is a state of mind," he said. "There's enough rigamarole and razzmatazz in the press and news media. We let them take care of the pressure because we got other things to do."

Like making up for forty years of losing football in Pittsburgh. Starting now, with this late-season bout against the Super Bowl champion Dolphins, a game Cosell said "needs *abso-lutely* no buildup." With sore-shouldered Bradshaw watching from the bench beside Hanratty, Gilliam was about to get his chance.

"Look at him!" Cosell said. "Jefferson Street Joe Gilliam!"

The nickname came from the potholed road that ran past the campus at Tennessee State University. Nashville's answer to Broadway Joe Namath, Jefferson Street Joe had quarterbacked Pearl High in the city's first season of integrated high school football, getting cursed and spat at before, during, and after games. Then he led Tennessee State to black-college national titles in 1970 and '71. Steeler coach Noll and his scouts, who specialized in overlooked black collegians such as Joe Greene (North Texas State, 1969) and Ernie Holmes (Texas Southern, '71), claimed Gilliam in the eleventh round of the '72 draft, the 273rd pick overall. At his first training camp, Gilliam deliberately held back in the 40-yard dash. He didn't want to get shifted to receiver or defensive back, the fate of many other black quarterbacks who were thought to be too dumb or undisciplined to play the position in the pros. He made the roster as a third-string quarterback, and when Bradshaw and Hanratty went down, Gilliam became the fourth black quarterback in NFL history after the well-named Willie Thrower, who played a single game for the 1953 Bears (eight passes, three completions); Marlin Briscoe, who threw five passes for the Bills and Dolphins from 1970 to '73 after two seasons in the AFL; and James Harris, who'd joined the '73 Rams as John Hadl's backup and thrown one pass all year. That meant that Gilliam's first throw tonight would be the fifteenth pass by a black quarterback in the league's fifty-three-year history.

"Look at him!" Cosell said, daring viewers to behold the changing face of American sport. What he didn't know was that Gilliam embodied more than one trend. While other Steelers stuck to shots and beers after practice, Gilliam, according to several accounts, had begun sampling the heroin and cocaine that would eventually kill him. By all accounts he was troubled, mistrusting Noll, who he thought favored Bradshaw, acutely aware of the pressure he bore as a black man passing. On *Sports Illustrated*'s cover he was "Pittsburgh's Black Quarterback."

"A confident young man! A superb athlete," Cosell said, racking up ratings while he pushed social justice. Controversy? Bring it on. It was no accident that a *TV Guide* poll had just named Howard Cosell the most-hated sportscaster in America. Such was the hegemony of *Monday Night Football*, the most popular sports show in TV history, that the same poll named Cosell America's *favorite* sportscaster, followed closely by his boothmates Don Meredith and Frank Gifford.

Prime-time football was as modern as the brand-new World Trade Center. The show was one of Commissioner Pete Rozelle's masterstrokes. Starting in the late '60s, Rozelle pitched the idea to all three networks. (There were only three, dividing 70 million TV households.) Number one CBS turned him down flat. CBS already owned Monday evenings with the top-rated *The Doris Day Show* and *The Carol Burnett Show*, both aimed toward women. Everybody knew the prime-time audience was mostly female, and women wouldn't watch football. Even male fans would surely tune out the blowouts and boring games that were an unavoidable consequence of broadcasting sports, so where was the upside? Even if a few million men would watch the popular Dolphins, Cowboys, Packers, Bears, Jets, and Giants, who would miss Doris Day to see the hapless Oilers play the Saints?

Second-place NBC gave Monday-night football a one-game tryout, but to Rozelle's dismay the game ran late that night, delaying Johnny Carson's *Tonight* show. Carson paced his soundstage in a fury, cursing his bosses, and that was the end of NBC's interest.

Which left third-place ABC, often mocked as the "Almost Broadcast-ing Company," to launch an experiment produced by a redheaded dynamo who got his start babysitting a sock puppet.

When the young Roone Arledge was producing a kids' show starring ventriloquist Shari Lewis and her puppet, Lamb Chop, for WPIX-TV in New York, he was known for throwing fits over how the bobble-eyed puppet was lit. By the early '70s, after moving to ABC, where he produced college-football games and helped create *ABC's Wide World of Sports*, Arledge was president of the last-place network's sports division. With confidence as Trump-like as his swoop of reddish-blond hair, he decided to remake sports TV. "I'm tired of football being treated like a religion," he announced in a memo, vowing to dramatize "all the excitement, wonder, jubilation and despair that make this America's number-one sports spectacle. In short—we are going to add show business to sports!"

He started with what you might call techtainment. Each week, during *Monday Night Football*'s famed opener, director Forte counted down: "Fifteen seconds to air . . . stand by all cameras . . ." Funky electric-piano theme music and a bubble-letter logo led into a cutting-edge broadcast featuring split-screen shots of the action, slow-motion replays, and shotgun microphones that picked up coaches' instructions, quarterbacks' snap counts, linemen's on-field grunts, and pad-to-chin collisions in the trenches. There were new on-screen graphics and jiggly in-your-face shots provided by portable cameras, which in those predigital times were about as portable as a Dumpster. Each "handheld" camera was shouldered by a camera-man with a ninety-pound pack on his back, the cameraman trailed by a cable-puller lugging an antenna and dragging inch-thick wires along the sideline.

"We totally changed the way football was covered," says Dennis Lewin, one of *MNF*'s early producers. "Up to then, you'd have three to five cameras. We used nine. We had two cameras on the fifty-yard line, one on each side of the field, and one on each side of the twenty- or twenty-five-yard lines. We had at least one high end-zone camera, and a handheld on each bench, and another one mounted on a golf cart zipping up and down the sideline. We did isolations—a split screen showing the quarterback and the middle linebacker, or iso's on two receivers. All of this was *new*."

Arledge told director Forte to emphasize the garish Vegas beauty of football *at night*, helmets glistening under stadium lights. "That sealed it," says future *MNF* color man Dan Dierdorf. "I mean, if you think about baseball, basketball, hockey, or boxing, you can't beat a front-row seat. But football's actually better on television than from even the best seat on the fifty-yard line. It's easier to follow. It's more dramatic. It's the game that's most enhanced by TV. When they put it on at night, it was like inventing money."

As a final enrichment, Arledge hired football's first three-man announcing team. Keith Jackson was the show's first play-by-play man, but Arledge dumped him after a season of what he saw as Jackson's bland competence. To replace Jackson, Arledge hired former Giants hero Frank Gifford. The blond, square-jawed Gifford, forty-three, the only NFL player ever to make All-Pro at three positions, was one reason *Monday Night Football* drew a record-setting female audience—an astounding 40 percent of the millions who tuned in every week. "My mom was one of them," recalls future NFL coach and *MNF* announcer Jon Gruden. "Mom had a little crush on Frank Gifford." Like plenty of other ten-year-old boys in those days, Jonny Gruden got sent to bed at halftime—Monday was a school night— but sneaked back downstairs to watch over his parents' shoulders.

Former Cowboys quarterback "Dandy Don" Meredith sat beside Gifford in the booth. Meredith, thirty-five, had retired at age thirty at least partly because he loathed Dallas's imperious coach, Tom Landry. Like Bradshaw he was a country boy whose quick grin hid a brooding spirit. As a player he'd been wounded by losing year after year to Lombardi's Packers, most painfully in the Ice Bowl of 1967, when Bart Starr's last-second quarterback sneak gave Green Bay its third straight league title and left Meredith weeping in the locker room. Six years later he was the most popular color man in TV history, crooning, "Turn out the lights, the party's over," when a game got clinched. Meredith kept the party going with a lively taste for '70s substances. Decked out in pink jeans, Hawaiian shirts, and a white Stetson, he was smoking pregame joints by '73, the year he welcomed viewers to Denver with a jolly "We're in the Mile High City, and I sure am!" When a close-up revealed Dandy Don's bloodshot eyes, Forte cut away.

Cosell, the journalist in the booth, saw himself as the cure for TV talk by ex-jocks. "I'll destroy the parrots who have been providing us with their fatigued litany for years," he predicted in the show's first season. Vain, insecure, brilliant, determined to right every wrong from racism to cliché-ridden commentary, he was "a genius," says Lewin. Don Ohlmeyer, another of Arledge's lieutenants at the time, calls Cosell "a lawyer with a photographic memory who saw what he called the 'jockocracy' taking over TV sports." Cosell would buttonhole the producers and rip Gifford and Meredith for their work habits and grammar, dismissing them as handsome lunks who wouldn't know a story if it bit their muscular butts.

As if to prove his brainpower, he narrated the show's famous halftime highlights off the top of his head. The highlights were another Arledge innovation. Ditching the usual halftime coverage of marching bands in favor of a highlight reel set to music, Arledge created the most hotly anticipated four minutes in the sports week. Football fans weren't yet inundated with highlights; wall-to-wall highlights were still in the future. ESPN wouldn't beam its first *SportsCenter* to several dozen viewers for another six years. Sports fans of the '70s hadn't seen Sunday's big plays a dozen times by dinnertime—they hadn't seen them at all. Now they saw O. J. Simpson in his Buffalo red, white, and blue, slashing his way to the first 2,000-yard season by a running back; the Rams' dashing Roman Gabriel launching one of his 460 passes that year; the Oilers' Dante Pastorini in a circle of hell called the Houston huddle, calling plays that broke down behind a diaphanous offensive line, Pastorini fumbling 17 times in the third year of a career in which he would break his nose a dozen times, break thirty-eight ribs, and pose unblocked in *Playgirl*; Oilers coach Oail Andrew "Bum" Phillips stalking a sideline in rhinestone-studded cowboy boots; the Cowboys' pinch-faced Landry under his fedora; Shula's Dolphins winning again to leave Madden's mangy Raiders, the NFL's Klingons, gnashing their teeth. All spliced together at the last minute, all narrated in Cosell's urgent honk.

If Arledge and his *MNF* team made it look easy, it wasn't. Footage of Sunday's games—celluloid tape on bulky reels—had to be carried by hand from NFL stadiums to taxis, rental cars, and the occasional bus, then flown to Philadelphia and driven fifteen miles to the Mount Laurel, New Jersey, headquarters of NFL Films. If a blizzard shut down the airports, a gofer such as Bob Goodrich drove the tapes through snowdrifts to Mount Laurel, where video technicians turned the celluloid clips into a satellite feed transmitted to a production truck parked outside the stadium at that week's *Monday Night* venue. "Those highlights determined what mattered that week," says Goodrich, who rose from gofer to producer. "It wasn't just fans watching. All the players who'd played on Sunday tuned in to see if they made the highlights. Coaches, agents, executives—everybody watched. And what I'll never forget is how amazing Howard was. I'm a production assistant, bringing him notes on all the plays we had on film—linemen's names and numbers, down and distance, the teams' records. All of which he already knew. He'd say, 'Young man, just show me the footage.'"

"No one else could have done what Howard did," producer Lewin says. "We'd boil the highlights down to four minutes—that's a lot of TV time. We had a shot sheet, but there wasn't much on it. A phrase or two. 'Fumble . . . twenty-yard pass, Griese to Warfield.' But Howard knew all the players, their stats, their biographies. He would narrate the highlights without a cut: 'Out of Purdue University, he married his highschool sweetheart. . . .' Usually on the first take. Not always—he was human—but he'd usually do it in one take. Four straight minutes of perfect narration. And I ask you: then or now, who else could do that?"

Middle schooler Joe Montana saw a future in those highlights. "*Monday Night Football* was *it*, man," Montana recalls. "Howard, Frank, and Dandy Don, those guys were pretty dang entertaining. You'd turn on the TV and feel the momentum, like, *this is gonna leave baseball and basketball behind.* I watched every week, thinking, 'If I could just get on there . . .'"

Monday Night Football was only the eighteenth-rated prime-time program of 1973, but its pull, particularly among male viewers, made news. *Variety* fretted that movie attendance on Mondays was "in a real nosedive as a result of ABC's pro football." Newspapers noted that X-rated movie theaters—still viable two decades before Internet porn—were closing on Monday nights. Crime rates dropped as criminals stayed home to watch the game. "The whole country was talking about it," says the Raiders' Villapiano. "It was like a Super Bowl every week. If you played on Sunday, you probably still had some painkillers working Monday morning, but they'd be wearing off that night, so you're feeling every bruise on Monday night, lying on the couch with a drink in your hand, hoping you made the halftime highlights."

His Raiders were one of Monday's marquee attractions, going 10-3 in '70s matchups the league scheduled to pit the best teams against each other. The Raiders taunted their opponents when they played lesser teams on Sundays: "You fucks'll never get on Monday night!"

"I'll never forget my first Monday-night game," Villapiano says. "I had a ton of tackles and Howard loved me. 'Phil *Vil*-a-pi-*anno* from *Bowling* Green Uni-*ver*-sity!' The way he said your name made you special. That's when I really saw the power of the *Monday Night* game. For weeks people came up to me, saying my name like Howard. '*Vil*-a-pi-*anno!*' La-Z-Boy was one of the sponsors, and they sent me a chair as Player of the Game. After we played a game on Sunday I'd stretch out on my La-Z-Boy and watch the *Monday Night* game, all achy and beat-up, with some provolone and salami and red wine, and say, 'Tell it like it is, Howard!'"

According to one *MNF* insider, "Our success was starting to create a monster." According to several insiders, Cosell began drinking during games. One night, suffering from a double dose of Smirnoff and the flu, he leaned over between plays and threw up on Meredith's boots. He'd expected the show's popularity to enhance his own, but an opinion poll asking Americans who they hated resulted in this top three: Richard Nixon, Howard Cosell, Satan. A stadium banner showed Cosell being flushed down a toilet. Another—quickly yanked by security guards—showed Howard with a giant penis in his mouth. When a letter writer threatened to kill Cosell with a bomb, Meredith scooted his booth chair away from Howard's.

According to Ohlmeyer, "The Ford Motor Company was our top sponsor, and they threatened to pull their ads unless Roone Arledge took Howard off the air. Roone told them, 'Go screw yourself. Nobody tells me who to put in the booth.'"

With irascible Cosell, good guys Meredith and Gifford, and the most immersive, expensive sportscast in history, *MNF* galvanized millions of football fans and created millions more. "It was such a gas," Lewin says. "We were new and different. When we came to town, local news crews chased Howard and Don through the airport. It was a time of rebellion, an antiestablishment time—the Vietnam War was still on—and the NFL wasn't corporate yet. Baseball was the establishment's pastime. Pro football was more rock 'n' roll, more appealing to young people, and it was becoming the national passion."

Each week's broadcast was "a circus," says former gofer Goodrich. "I covered two Olympics, and they were nothing compared to the crazy pressure of *Monday Night*. Roone Arledge ruled from on high. Chet Forte was a great director and a bit of a wild man. Chet and Don Ohlmeyer were always arguing about story lines, camera angles—everything. They'd point at the monitors in the production truck, yelling at each other."

Ohlmeyer says, "One night we were having one of our screaming matches in the truck. Chet's yelling, 'Jesus Christ, we gotta do better!' He wasn't pleased with my producing. In the midst of this chaos I tell him to put six cameras on Tom Jackson, the Broncos' linebacker. Who proceeds to intercept the next pass. I pointed at Chet and said, 'Okay, you fuck, now replay it!'"

The behind-the-scenes warring extended from the truck to the broadcast booth. Cosell, who saw sportscasting as beneath him, dreamed of crossing over to mainstream TV. He would get his chance with an Arledge-produced 1975 ABC variety hour, *Saturday Night Live with Howard Cosell*. But he left his edge in the *MNF* booth. In the show's debut, tennis champ Jimmy Connors warbled a tune written for the occasion, "Girl, You Turn Me On." Cosell pronounced it "a great magical moment in musical history." Tall, galumphing Howard pictured himself as the next Ed Sullivan but came across more like a six-foot-one sock puppet. His show, described by its own director as "one of the greatest disasters in television history," was canceled after four months. Its sole contribution to TV history was to keep a new late-night comedy program on NBC from using *Live* in its title. While Howard's program lasted, NBC and Lorne Michaels had to settle for calling *their* show *Saturday Night*. Michaels thumbed his nose at Cosell's resident comedy troupe, the Prime Time Players— featuring Bill Murray and Christopher Guest—by dubbing John

Belushi, Chevy Chase, and the rest of his cast the Not-Ready-for-Prime-Time Players.

Don Meredith was antsy, too. Earning $33,000 on a show that sold commercials for $100,000 a minute left Meredith feeling underpaid and unloved. No student of the game even in his playing days, he did little or no homework and wasn't always sure who was playing. After he credited a tackle to a player who was on the bench, Forte ripped into him on the feedback line only announcers and crew could hear: "You stupid son of a bitch! Don't talk till Howard asks you a question!" Meredith sulked.

Gifford, meanwhile, was blowing more lines than Belushi. He turned *fair catch* into "care fatch" and Detroit's *Lem* Barney into "Mel" Barney. Dreading his next stumble, Gifford studied rosters and practiced tongue twisters while Cosell and Meredith nudged each other and chuckled behind his back. He had particular trouble with the name of Falcons coach Leeman Bennett, whom he called Leeman "Beeman." Not always, but enough to make Gifford fidget during games involving the Falcons. As Cosell recalled, "The production assistants had a betting pool on which quarter Leeman Beeman would make his appearance."

One night, after vowing to get through a whole game without fluffing any lines, Gifford opened the broadcast by saying, "Hi, Frank, I'm everybody."

Cosell called him the Giffer or, sarcastically, Faultless Frank. He thought the ex-jocks were in league against him, and sometimes he was right. Before one 1973 game Gifford told Ohlmeyer, "We're not talking to Howard tonight."

The producer was startled. "On the air? What if he asks you a question?"

"We won't answer."

Ohlmeyer talked them out of it but couldn't defuse the tension in the booth. When Cosell gloated during a fumble-filled matchup between the Cowboys and the Giants, "Gentlemen, your respective teams are performing a comedy of errors," Meredith spoke for the jocks:

"Well, Howard, at least we have respective teams."

Arledge tolerated the tension, even cultivated it as part of the shtick that kept viewers watching when games got dull. After the first year he wasn't around much anyway, preferring to chair meetings in New York while his producer and director wrangled the divas in the booth. That suited Ohlmeyer, ABC Sports' twenty-eight-year-old wunderkind, and the cocky Forte, riding shotgun on the runaway stagecoach that was *Monday Night Football*. Forte had been "Chet the Jet" as an Ivy League star at Columbia, a five-foot-seven guard who averaged 28.9 points per game in 1956–57 to edge Kansas sophomore Wilt Chamberlain for the national scoring title. As a TV director he pioneered camera angles and screen graphics other sportscasts soon copied. Off camera, Forte was the '70s incarnate: a chain-smoking, skirt-chasing workaholic in tight designer jeans and a shirt unbuttoned to show the hair on his chest.

"Chet was a character. A hell of a director, and great company," says Ohlmeyer, who shared the perks of producing a top-rated show with his buddy Forte, including hotel suites, expense-account dinners, drinks and shoeshines, police escorts to stadiums, and the occasional *Monday Night* groupie. Cosell, a happily married fifty-five-year-old whose *MNF*-driven sex appeal shocked even him, sent groupies Forte's way by deceiving them. "Come to my hotel room, darling," he said, writing Chet's room number under his autograph. The horny, married director filled lulls in their telecasts with "honey shots" of cheerleaders and good-looking female fans. This was in keeping with Arledge's pre-*MNF* memo: *Very few men have ever switched channels when a nicely proportioned girl was leaping into the air or leading a band downfield.* But Forte took the honey shot to a more personal level, dispatching production assistants such as

Goodrich to ask selected honeys if they'd like to tour the *Monday Night Football* production truck, maybe even meet the director . . .

. . . until the night one of Forte's cameras focused on a honey who waved to 20 million viewers and chirped, "Hi, Chet!"

"Cut, cut!" Forte said. "My wife's watching this!"

Monday Night Football won its time slot in the 1973-74 season, finishing in the Nielsen ratings' top twenty and trailing only *Happy Days* and *The Six Million Dollar Man* among ABC programs. The network re-upped with the league for 1974–77 for $72 million, more than doubling the price of its first four-year deal. Rozelle's brainstorm was a national sensation.

In Week Two of '73, Ohlmeyer and Forte were entertaining a few shapely new friends in the production truck outside Texas Stadium. As far as they knew, their boss was fifteen hundred miles away. "Roone might phone the booth to make us think he was watching, but we didn't see him on the road," Ohlmeyer says. "Week after week, he stayed in New York."

Climbing out of a hired car outside the stadium, the president of ABC Sports was looking forward to his first location visit of the year. Expecting handshakes and backslaps from Ohlmeyer and Forte, he stepped into a production truck full of cigarette smoke, candy wrappers, pizza boxes, and pheromones. Peering through the smoke, seeing his producer and director sharing their chairs with two busty women in hot pants, Arledge turned around and left without a word.

Forte said, "Jesus, that was Roone!"

"We thought we were dead," Ohlmeyer recalls. "Roone went straight to the airport and flew back to New York. We heard nothing for days. We were going nuts thinking he'd fire us. But it never happened! When we went in to meet with him, he peered through his big aviator glasses at us and his message was clear—he was Roone and we were fuckups—but he let us keep our jobs. He wasn't going to screw with a winning formula."

A month later, in Buffalo, Cosell got a postcard: *Drop dead you Homo Fag Big Mouth. A Bomb in Rich Stadium will blow you up.* The FBI posted three guards in the booth that night. When a firecracker went off in the stands below, Cosell stood tall while Meredith dove for cover. Dandy Don made headlines by calling President Nixon "Tricky Dick" on the air that night. The next Monday at San Francisco's Candlestick Park, John Lennon stopped by the booth to shake hands with Howard. Lennon bumped into another celebrity guest, California governor Ronald Reagan. They made an odd couple, the long-haired Beatle with his granny glasses and the smiling, Brylcreemed Gipper. But they hit it off. Reagan spent a minute explaining American football to Lennon, who autographed an album for the man he called "guv'nor." Reagan waited his turn as the ex-Beatle chatted on-air with Cosell, peering out at the crowd, saying, "This makes rock concerts look like tea parties!" before departing with a cheery nod to Gifford. "Over to Giffer," he said. "Bye-bye."

A week later the defending Super Bowl champs hosted the banged-up Steelers. Cosell was right that the game needed "*ab-so-lutely* no buildup," but that didn't keep him from building it up as the culmination of the civil-rights movement, Gilliam's chance to prove that a black man could play the most important position in sports. Cosell's zeal rubbed off on Gifford, who described the quarterback trotting toward the Steeler huddle: "He's got a lot of poise, a lot of cool."

Gilliam's first pass of the night fell incomplete. His next was intercepted by safety Dick Anderson, who ran it back for a touchdown. Seven to nothing Miami. Yepremian kicked off, slamming the ball on a line past the goalpost, which was still set a yard deep in the end zone, a traffic hazard for receivers, defensive backs, and kickoffs.

The Steelers began their second possession at their own 20. Gilliam promptly threw another pick. Forte cut to two commercials—Joe Namath in a leisure suit, daubing Brut aftershave on his dimpled chin, saying, "Go all the way," followed by lumberjacks hoisting mugs of America's best-selling beer as if to prove the voice-over: "When you're out of Schlitz, you're out of beer." A competing beer called Miller Lite, test-marketed four months before, as novel as the World Trade Center and the brand-new Egg McMuffin, was about to go national.

In Miami, Gilliam pump-faked and fired—another interception, his third of the night. It was still the first quarter. With no completions and a single scramble for a 1-yard loss, his quarterback rating was zero, his historic night almost infinitely bad.

"Too bad!" Cosell said. "You don't like to see this happen to the young man. A lot of people have waited a long time to see this opportunity for Gilliam, for reasons that don't have to be amplified."

"True," Meredith said. "But he hasn't completed one to his side yet."

Griese found Jim Mandich alone for another Miami score, so alone that Cosell described his openness as "Blissful solitude—words written by Wordsworth."

"Ho ho," said Meredith. "Who'd he play for?"

It was 20–0. A red-faced Noll, embarrassed on national TV, yanked Gilliam and shoved the sore-winged Bradshaw toward the huddle, only to watch him throw *another* interception to Anderson, who now had four in the half, a record that wouldn't be matched until 2010. With the score 27–0, the *MNF* crew wondered aloud, were the Steelers out of their league?

"There are not words to describe this Miami team," Cosell said.

"Well, if there's words to describe them, you'll find 'em," Meredith said.

At halftime, Noll told his team that Miami "just showed us what championship intensity is." In the truck, Forte cued up Cosell's highlights of Sunday's action. "Even during blowouts, people kept watching to see Howard's halftime highlights," Ohlmeyer recalls. "But on nights like that, when it's thirty to three at the half, you could *feel* millions of people switching channels."

The millions who switched missed a preview of Super Bowls to come. In the second half, Noll's "Steel Curtain" defense (a term coined in a Pittsburgh radio contest) shut out Shula's Dolphins. Bradshaw engineered scoring drives of 53, 72, and 58 yards against a Miami defense that had allowed 101 points all season, an average of only 9 points per game. With two minutes left, Miami led 30–24. A three-and-out inside their own 10 left the Dolpins in danger. Punter Seiple was ready.

Dolphins safety Jake Scott had a better idea. Hustling up to Shula, he shouted, "Don't punt!"

Another fake punt by tricky Seiple? No—Scott's idea was more of a chess move.

With a nod to Scott, Shula left quarterback Griese in the game.

It was fourth down. Fourth down from their own 6-yard line, leading by 6 with the clock running out, and the Dolphins were going for it.

In the *Monday Night* booth, Meredith shrugged and sputtered, "What?"

Pittsburgh's front four lined up, licking their chops, Greene and Holmes and Greenwood and White firing out of their three-point stances, charging the quarterback . . .

. . . only to see the son of Sylverious Griese tuck the ball under his arm and run the other way.

Cosell was catching on. "Look at that!"

Griese ran backward through his own end zone for a safety.

"Brilliant!" Cosell said.

The safety made the score 30–26. It gave the Dolphins a free kick from their 20. Miami punter Seiple thumped a 75-yard rainbow that pinned Bradshaw and Harris inside their own 10, and the clock ran down to zeros. Miami's chess move worked; the Dolphins would glide to the playoffs with a 12-2 record while Pittsburgh slipped in as a wild-card team. The Steelers would need to win two playoff games on the road to reach their first Super Bowl, a road that started with another showdown against the Raiders. In Oakland this time—the Snake pit, where Ken "the Snake" Stabler and the Raiders were dying to avenge the Piece-of-Shit Reception.

"Bring 'em on," the Snake said.

5

THE RAIDER GODDAMN WAY

John Madden's Raiders were spoiling for a scrap. "We figured it was our time," recalls quarterback Ken Stabler, "and the Steelers kept getting in the way." The Steelers represented lunch-bucket Pittsburgh, while the loud, rowdy Raiders were football's version of their Bay Area boosters, the Hells Angels. This was a team that even NFL Films called "the most bizarre group of misfits in NFL history." Originally named the Oakland Señors in a 1960 newspaper contest—rigged, of course—the team commissioned a sombrero logo but soon ditched it in favor of a helmeted pirate that became the most hated and envied symbol in the league. The Raiders' logo would be among the first adopted by urban gangs, originally in the Bay Area, later in Los Angeles and elsewhere, and one of the league's leading merchandise brands. Among NFL players the team's logo and silver and black were loathed because the Oakland Raiders bent the rules, and envied because they had a hell of a good time doing it.

Their nicknames suggested that they were nobody's role models. Snake handed off to the Rooster. Oakland's secondary featured Dr. Death, the Assassin, and the Hit Man. The Raiders unofficially led the league in bar fights. "We used to say, 'Welcome to Oakland, home of the Hells Angels, Black Panthers, and Oakland Raiders," said longtime Raider Ben Davidson, "sometimes all three in the same person." Coach Madden threw hair-pulling tantrums at referees—"Whyn'cha call a penalty on the *other guys* sometime?" Owner Al Davis, who claimed the team's motto was Pride and Poise, could have added Paranoia. Davis, a Nixonian operator, suspected that planes flying over his practice field were spying on the Raiders. He was said to plant listening devices in the visitors' locker room at Oakland Coliseum. Davis and Madden were convinced that the refs curried favor with Rozelle by favoring the Raiders' opponents, the Immaculate Reception being only one example. Oakland fought back by making its own rules. A sign at the Raiders' training camp listed two team rules. Rule number one: CHEATING IS ENCOURAGED. Rule number two: SEE RULE NUMBER ONE.

The Raiders often smuggled underinflated footballs into home games. A mushy ball was less of a problem for soft-tosser Stabler than for enemy gunners such as Bradshaw. Oakland linemen wore white pads on their forearms during games against teams that wore white jerseys, and dark pads against teams with dark jerseys, to make it harder for the refs to see them holding. Oakland linebackers and defensive backs wore custom-made forearm pads that covered the wrist and the back of the hand. "We'd dip 'em in hot water and they'd harden like a plaster cast," says Phil Villapiano. "You cock that forearm and swing it against a guy's neck, he's gonna feel it." Cocking that forearm was known as cocking the bone. The Raiders were such experts at it that other teams "complained to the refs, and before every game the umpire would check us. No problem—we wouldn't wear those pads before the game! He'd check us during warm-ups and clear us to play, then we'd run off the field and strap on our hard pads. Now we're set for the national anthem." Against Buffalo, Villapiano knocked O. J. Simpson senseless with a forearm to the neck followed by a blow to the chin he called "the can opener" because it sometimes knocked the runner's helmet off. The Raiders often got fined for such hits, or for fighting between plays, but the fines were only $75 or $100, and they didn't pay them anyway. Defying league rules, the team paid the fines.

"Oakland was devastating on defense," recalls defensive end Cedric Hardman, then with the 49ers. "Devastating and dirty."

Oakland's home-field groundskeeper turned the Coliseum turf into a swamp to slow opposing runners such as Simpson. The Coliseum timekeeper ran the clock faster when the visitors had the ball. Other clubs employed the same tricks, but the Raiders added twists of their own. Nervous, spindly receiver Biletnikoff, the last NFL player to suit up without pads, smeared so much stickum on his hands and arms that in natural-turf games he'd be covered with grass by halftime. "Freddie looked like the Swamp Thing," says Stabler. Teammates sometimes applied Biletnikoff's stickum (brand name Kwik Grip Hold Tight Paste, made with wood resins, beeswax, lanolin, turpentine, amber, and petrolatum) directly to the ball. Stabler would call for a new football, but rookies weren't always so savvy. In his first-ever game in Oakland, Bradshaw faded back, fired . . . and felt the ball still clinging to his palm. He shook it like a man discovering mud on his hand and managed to fling it at his own foot.

The Raiders trained in Santa Rosa, a low-rise town an hour north of Oakland, where Stabler recalls "reading the game plan by the light of a jukebox." He sipped Johnnie Walker Red long after Madden's lightly enforced eleven o'clock curfew while teammates downed what they called Santa Rosa shot glasses (pitchers of beer) to warm up for a night of serious drinking. Some NFL players worried that the alcohol in their blood might stunt the effects of the steroids they took. So they took more steroids. The drugs were legal with a prescription—the NFL wouldn't ban steroids for another decade and wouldn't test for them until 1987, which was still seventeen years before major-league baseball began steroids testing.

Drug use was by no means exclusive to Oakland. According to Dr. Rob Huizenga, who joined the team later as the Raiders' team physician, "At some positions half the players in the league were taking steroids." The Cowboys' strength coach said at least a quarter of his players used them. One NFL player estimated that the eventual number was closer to half the league "and ninety-plus percent of defensive linemen." Several Steelers told sportswriter Bill Chastain that steroids were rampant in their locker room, with the offensive line consuming the most. Still the Raiders pushed the limits. Oakland's locker room featured tall jars of gray amphetamine pills that players called rat turds. Some ate them by the handful. Center Jim Otto says he could tell which defensive linemen on other teams were flying on uppers by the wide, dilated pupils in their eyes. Some players added a rudimentary strain of human growth hormone, culled from pooled cadaver brains, to their booze, amphetamines, and steroids. Several Raiders combined rat turds, steroids, and HGH with horse testosterone. "Our trainer also worked at the racetrack," one Raider says. "He fed us stuff that had a picture of a horse on the label. It made you feel like kicking some ass." The 220- and 230-pound footballers took the stuff full strength, in doses intended for 1,200-pound horses.

The Raiders were the only NFL team with no dress code for road trips. Madden spurred them to see themselves as renegades. "They want to fuck us—the officials, the league, everybody!" he said. Each week the coach passed out a mimeographed schedule that listed meetings, team meals, Sunday's bus departure, and game time. The line reserved for kickoff time showed four words: WE GO TO WAR. Yet it wasn't just attitude that made them a force to be feared. It wasn't just uppers, horse hormones, or even talent. It was their only-in-Oakland 100-proof team spirit.

"A rockin' group of bearded longhairs, that was us," says Stabler.

"Hearts and guts, that's what we had," recalls Villapiano, the hotheaded linebacker who was hospitalized after a run-in with several Hells Angels. Most of the bikers loved the team, but one night a dispute over a parking spot outside a bar led to a brawl. Villapiano took a hammer to the head, "and then it got ugly." After he wound up in the ER, teammates including Jack Tatum, Gene Upshaw, and Art Shell formed a war party. They were ready to find the bikers and fight it out until Madden stopped them, saying, "Save it for Sunday. Phil's gonna be okay."

"We put it all on the line every week. For John Madden. For each other," Villapiano says. "Were we crazy? Maybe. Maybe we knew there were risks, but we were in a fight. That was the Raider goddamn way."

Headstrong center Otto helped define the Raider way. "We prided ourselves on hitting harder than anybody, even after the whistle. We bent the rules we didn't break," recalls Otto, who wore number 00 (a pun on his name, *aught-oh*). "But we were pros. We worked hard at the game." For fifteen years Otto snapped the ball on every Oakland offensive play, including long snaps on field-goal attempts, which he perfected. As a young pro in the early '60s, he practiced until his long snaps traveled for precisely seven-tenths of a second, spinning so that the ball arrived with the laces facing forward and the more kickable "sweet side" toward the placekicker. This saved a split second. On other teams, the kicker had to wait an instant while the holder rotated the ball.

"Nobody loved the blood and guts more than Jim Otto," says Dave Newhouse, who covered the team for the *Oakland Tribune*. "A lot of the Raider attitude goes back to him. One time he tore five ligaments on one play. They flew him to LA for knee surgery. He sneaked out of the hospital, flew back to Oakland, drove his VW Bug to practice, and hobbled onto the field. 'I'm back,' he said. Madden threw a fit. 'Get out of here!' Otto's leg was *black*. He said, 'Let me practice. If I can't do the job, I'll leave.' He played the whole season and made the Pro Bowl."

As Otto puts it, "I'm not a complainer." From 1960 through 1974, he started a record 308 consecutive games, finished them all, and wasn't fully healthy in any. "I broke fingers and ribs, of course. Played with a broken jaw, kicked-in teeth, pneumonia. Broke my back twice. Broke my nose so many times I quit counting at twenty." After retiring in '74 he endured two metal-shoulder implants, twelve knee replacements, and so many follow-up knee operations that the nerves around his right knee died. You could light a match to that leg and Otto couldn't feel it. The leg could get gangrenous, he wouldn't notice. So he let his doctors saw it off in 2007 and replace the leg with a prosthesis stamped with the Raider logo.

"No regrets," Otto says today. "I just wish we'd beat Pittsburgh a few more times."

These were the Raiders coming out of the tunnel at Oakland Coliseum to face the Steelers in the 1973 playoffs. A team still angry about the Piece-of-Shit Reception the year before. A Raider fan waved a sign that read MURDER FRANCO. Out of the tunnel came Otto, clutching a football in one gnarled paw as if to squeeze the breath out of it. And Stabler, the left-handed gun. "Snake really set the tone," says Matt Millen, who learned about the Raider way when he joined the team several years later. "A big part of every team's character had to do with the quarterback's guts. In those days you had to practically maim the passer to get called for roughing, so the question was, how much beating could your QB take and still deliver? John Unitas had that toughness. Snake, too." At times, Stabler, out on his feet, ran huddles and completed passes while concussed and semiconscious. Those were called zombie plays. "You could knock the piss out of him, he'd shake it off and come right back." Stabler came out of the tunnel for the '73 playoffs along with his favorite target, the pallid

Biletnikoff, who emerged from the home locker room after a loud pregame bout of dry heaves. And here came the all-black "Soul Patrol" of defensive backs Willie Brown, George "Hit Man" Atkinson, Jack "Assassin" Tatum and Skip "Dr. Death" Thomas, leaving the corner of the locker room they called the Ghetto. And kicker George Blanda, forty-six, the former quarterback who'd been Sid Luckman's backup in his rookie year of 1949, bushy gray sideburns bracketing his stony face. And thirty-two other players showing various levels of Raider rage, plus Coach Madden, his face the color of Pepto-Bismol, reddened by eagerness and worry. Nearby stood owner Davis, looking over his shoulder for the "twenty-nine kinds of motherfucker" he liked to claim were out to screw him and his team.

The wild-card Steelers entered the game 10-4, a better record than the AFC West–champion Raiders, who'd gone 9-4-1, including a 17–9 loss to the Steelers. In that game Joe Greene leveled Stabler with a second-quarter hit, knocking him out of the game with a twisted knee. Trainer Anderson rigged up a brace he called the Knee-Stablerizer, and the Snake went on to complete 163 of 260 passes for the year, an NFL-best completion rate of 63 percent. A more modern quarterback than his predecessor, the bomb-throwing Daryle Lamonica, Stabler took a shorter drop and settled for what the league's evolving defenses allowed, dissecting them with 8- and 10- and 12-yard throws. The Raiders won their last four games to qualify for the playoffs.

"This playoff game was basically good versus evil," recalls Roy Blount, "sainted Art Rooney's team against scheming Al Davis and his gleaming silver-and-black mean machine. All my raunchy sportswriter friends were for Oakland." Not Blount. After a year on the road and at home with the Steelers, the *Sports Illustrated* writer liked most of them, loved a few. Watching Coliseum fans wave signs reading HURT BRADSHAW and JOE GREENE WEARS PANTY HOSE, hearing them chant, "P-U-S-S-Y," at the Pittsburgh bench, he felt an arm around his shoulder. It was Terry Bradshaw, who sang a few bars of a country song: "Hello, trouble, come on in . . ." Later, when Blount asked Steelers lineman Craig Hanneman how the Oakland crowd made him feel, Hanneman said, "Hotter than a freshly fucked fox in a forest fire," and proved it by flipping them off.

Raiders glared and yapped at the Steelers before and during the national anthem. Before the first play from scrimmage, Pittsburgh's Ray Mansfield reached down for a football the Raiders had scrawled with their usual Magic Marker message: *FUCK YOU.*

Center Mansfield surprised Bradshaw with a quick snap on the first play. Smart—he'd caught an Oakland lineman leaning offsides. The penalty made it first-and-5 on the Steelers' opening drive. Franco Harris ran for 8 yards and a quick first down, but that series was one of the visitors' few highlights. Soon it was 10–0 Raiders. With the crowd chanting curses, the Raiders and frustrated Steelers scuffled between plays. Pittsburgh linebacker Loren Toews traded punches with a couple of Raiders, and suddenly a spray of goo splashed off the back of Toews's neck. A sniper? No—an ice-cream cone hurled from the upper deck. Harris, the gentle superstar, brought Toews a towel.

Stabler spent most of the game flipping 6- and 7-yard passes. His left arm lacked the voltage of Bradshaw's right, but it was more precise, slinging humpbacked passes that split the 2 and the 5 on Biletnikoff's jersey. Stabler completed 14 of 17 passes while Oakland's front four—harder to block due to the Vaseline they illegally smeared on their jerseys—slipped through the line to pressure Bradshaw into a pair of interceptions. Still it was only 16–7 Oakland in the third quarter. While Pittsburgh coach Noll barked commands, Bradshaw rolled his eyes as if to say, *Yeah, bla bla.* "Chuck Noll was tougher than shit on me," Bradshaw recalls today. "I *so* wanted him to like me, but it never worked. I didn't study hard enough for him. I was never accurate enough. With him it was always 'I'll bench your ass!'"

With the Steelers advancing, Bradshaw looked for Preston Pearson on a sideline route. He failed to see the Soul Patrol's Willie Brown closing the gap. Brown had read the quarterback's eyes and drawn a bead on Pearson. Bradshaw almost strong-armed his way through his blunder, zipping the ball to a spot between Pearson's outstretched fingers and Brown's. Brown reached a few inches farther, tipping the pass, juggling it for a long, slow-motion instant before he clamped it to his chest and high-stepped 54 yards for an Oakland touchdown that avenged three straight losses to the Steelers.

After the game, Noll blamed Bradshaw for Pittsburgh's 33–14 loss. "It was a play-action pass," he said of the clinching interception. "Bradshaw was supposed to preread the coverage, and he didn't."

Madden saw the postgame stats differently. "We had twenty-four first downs, 361 yards total offense, no turnovers. Not a bad day's work!"

Bradshaw hung his head in the Steelers' locker room. He would skip the team flight back to Pittsburgh, fleeing home to Louisiana for Christmas. The rest of the Steelers shuffled through their postgame ablutions. The place was quiet except for the sound of tape and pads being stripped off, muttered curses, dropped helmets clonking the floor, the scratch of a couple of matches lighting postgame cigarettes, the drum of water in the showers. Four years into the '70s, the losing Steelers were nobody's idea of the Team of the Decade. They had won no Super Bowls. They had yet to survive an AFC Championship game. They had made the postseason twice in the team's forty-one-year history but were 1-2 in those appearances, their lone playoff victory an Immaculate Fluke.

"Forty-one years in the doldrums," Franco Harris says. "That was our history."

The locker room went from quiet to silent when Noll cleared his throat. After five years as Pittsburgh's head coach, he looked stricken. "We are too good a team . . . ," Noll began. He swallowed and began again. "We are too good to keep losing. We're going to take a long, concentrated look at the season, to find out where our mistakes came, and why." The Steelers knew what he meant by that. Some of them wouldn't be here next year. They would be weeded out.

Noll tried to smile. Raising his eyes to his bruised, beaten team, he said, "All I can tell you is, merry Christmas."

6

SEA OF HANDS

A week later, on the opening drive of the 1973–74 AFC Championship, the Dolphins came out of their huddle at midfield on the blue-green Poly-Turf at the Orange Bowl. The visiting Raiders had the defending Super Bowl–champion Dolphins where they wanted them: third-and-long. Running backs Larry Csonka and Mercury Morris flared into the flat, drawing coverage from two linebackers. The Raiders, fresh off their blowout of the Steelers, dropped into their nickel prevent, the defense they'd used fifty-three weeks before on the play that became the Immaculate Reception.

Bob Griese took the snap. The Dolphins quarterback waited a beat—a breath—giving the Raiders time to cover his receivers. Then ran the ball up the middle.

"We had the running backs covered, the Soul Patrol dropping deep," recalls Villapiano, "so Greise runs up the middle and there's nobody there. He's in his own zip code. We took off after him, thinking, 'This fucking coverage screwed us again!'"

Ex-altar-boy Griese, hurrying as if late for church, scampered for

27 yards. Csonka bulled 11 more on the following play for the first of five Miami scores in a 27–10 victory that sent the Dolphins to Super Bowl VIII. Coach Don Shula's four-yards-and-a-cloud-of-Poly-Turf attack amassed 266 rushing yards against the AFC's best defense, with Griese handing off 53 times and throwing only 6 times to set a record that still stands: fewest passes in a modern playoff game. The Raiders flew home to nurse their bruises and grudges while the Dolphins went to their third straight Super Bowl, with a chance to join the Packers as winners of two in a row.

The Dolphins' opponents in Super Bowl VIII were the Minnesota Vikings, who got a quick lesson in Super luxury, '70s style. The game would be played at Rice Stadium in Houston. The Vikings' practice facility was a threadbare high school field with a locker room that featured hooks instead of lockers, and leaky showers with intermittent hot water and floors furred with moss. "I don't think our players have seen anything like this since junior high," said Minnesota coach Bud Grant. After a week of workouts his Purple People Eaters, an aging '60s-style unit whose front four averaged just under 230 pounds, took on a Dolphins team that looked poised to dominate the decade.

To cover the story, *Rolling Stone* magazine sent the Wild Turkey- and-mescaline-fueled gonzo writer Hunter S. Thompson—a Raiders fan, naturally—who was by no means the only journalist in Houston with a buzz on. Several prominent journalists smoked joints before they went to work, and much of the press corps had an unquenchable thirst for the free booze at Super Bowl parties. What set Thompson apart was his view of the game as a cultural force. He was there for the big picture and regarded his all-expenses-paid presence among "hookers and drunken sportswriters jammed together in a seething mob" as a sign that Super Sunday was now a secular holiday. Covering the Super Bowl, he wrote, was "a crazed and futile effort to explain the extremely twisted nature of my relationship with God,

Nixon and the National Football League. The three had long since become inseparable in my mind, a sort of unholy trinity."

Readers who relished the vampire bats and drug dreams in Thompson's *Rolling Stone* dispatches may have missed his keen eye for the state of the game. "The NFL blew the sacred institution of baseball off its 'national pastime' pedestal in less than fifteen years," he wrote, correctly dating the league's rise to 1958, when Unitas thrilled a nationwide TV audience by throwing for 349 yards in the Colts' "Greatest Game" victory over Frank Gifford and the Giants. "If sporting historians ever look back on all this, there will be no avoiding the argument that pro football's meteoric success was directly attributable to its early marriage with network TV."

The bald, bug-eyed, six-two Thompson haunted both teams' practices that week before retiring to his bottle-strewn room at the Houston Hilton. Stoked by drugs at least as potent as anything the players were taking, he hammered away at his IBM Selectric typewriter, the world's most advanced writing device, a machine with the heft of a bowling ball and a leatherette carrying case to match. Years later, when the typewriter jammed, he shot it. In 2005 the aging Thompson, who never liked computers, would sit at his desk in Woody Creek, Colorado, rolling a clean page into a later-model Selectric, type a single word, *counselor*, on the page, then place his .45 revolver in his mouth and blow his head off. But in 1973, still spry enough to keep himself awake by doing jumping jacks in his room, the thirty-six-year-old Thompson saw the NFL more clearly through his druggy kaleidoscope than other writers saw through their bifocals. Cornering the Steelers' Tom Keating one day, Thompson dared him to deny the "drug rumors" he'd heard about football players. Keating smiled knowingly and changed the subject, denouncing the NFL as "the last bastion of fascism in America." That was something they could agree on. Thompson made the line part of his *Rolling Stone* cover story, "Fear and Loathing at the Super Bowl."

The magazine's cover, showing an ape in a football helmet peering hungrily at a dollar bill, wasn't what the league had in mind when it gave Thompson a press credential.

Miami and Minnesota were both 14-2 coming into Super Bowl VIII. The defending-champ Dolphins were 6-point favorites. Thompson, unimpressed by clean-cut Bob Griese, heaped praise on Miami wideout Paul Warfield, "a game-breaker who commands double coverage at all times because of his antelope running style, twin magnets for hands, and a weird kind of adrenaline instinct that feeds on tension." Warfield gave the grind-it-out Dolphins an extra dimension. They might run the ball nine times out of ten, but Warfield kept defenses honest. Faster than all but two or three defensive backs, he ran the league's tightest patterns. "You hear stories about Raymond Berry being precise," Miami's Dick Anderson said of Unitas's favorite receiver. "Well, Paul Warfield was Berry with speed." But Warfield had a balky hamstring that week—a bit of news that lifted Thompson's eyebrows. Thompson knew that Warfield's injury would tempt bettors to bet on the Vikings. Bookmakers would respond by reducing the point spread. Thompson also knew that Warfield, injured or not, was going to serve mainly as a decoy on Super Sunday. Here was a chance to make some Super money.

Shula and the Dolphins saw the forward pass as a gadget play. They won by running the ball down opponents' gullets, averaging a league-record 210 rushing yards per game with Csonka, Morris, and Jim Kiick running the ball. Miami's "No-Name Defense" contained the run while Dick Anderson, Jake Scott, and the other DBs played a flexible zone that prevented the bomb. The Dolphins were the early '70s incarnate, as conservative as Nixon, reliable as Maytag. Thompson had already put a couple thousand on Miami minus 6. He grabbed the phone, called his bookie, and doubled his bets when the line dropped to 5. If the Dolphins won by exactly 6 points, he'd win the new wagers and get a push—his money back—on his first round of bets. If they won by more than 6 he'd earn more from his bets than *Rolling Stone* was paying him.

Joe Namath limped into the TV booth for the pregame show. Broadway Joe had been hurt most of the year, missing the Dolphins' 31–3 downing of the Jets but not a TV date with Farrah Fawcett, who lathered him up in a popular shaving-cream commercial while trilling, "Let Noxema cream your face." Now, beaming at CBS's camera during pregame festivities, Namath said he expected the Dolphins to cream Minnesota. "If Miami gets the kickoff and scores on the opening drive, the game's over."

Miami won its third consecutive Super Bowl coin toss. Shula elected to receive the kickoff, and seven plays later the score was 7–0. As everyone from Shula to Namath to Hunter Thompson expected, Miami's offensive line had no trouble keeping the smaller Vikings on their heels. Anchored by catlike tackle Alan Page, Minnesota's Purple People Eaters defensive line led the league in get-offs, springing forward at the snap. Shula countered by having tackle Wayne Moore cross-block Page. If Page eluded Moore, he ran into pulling guard Bob Kuechenberg. Page spent the first half reaching vainly for Csonka, Morris, and Kiick as the Dolphins built a 17–0 lead. The Vikings kicked pads and Super Bowl programs around their Rice Stadium locker room at halftime while expressionless Coach Grant, who resembled the farmer in Grant Wood's *American Gothic*, fumed. Up in the press box, Hunter Thompson did a happy two-step as the University of Texas marching band played patriotic tunes with Miss Texas on fiddle.

A fourth-quarter touchdown by aging scrambler Fran Tarkenton prevented the first Super Bowl shutout, but the game's 24–7 final had nobody singing the NFC fight song. Who could doubt that the Dolphins were the team of the '70s, or that the AFC was better than the establishment conference? Since the 1970 merger, the AFC was

4-1 in Super Bowls, with three straight blowouts that had pundits grousing that the ultimate game had turned "superdull." As in the conference championship, Griese set a record for fewest pass attempts. He threw only 7 times, still a Super Bowl low, while handing off 53 times. This was hardly the crowd-pleasing aerial circus the Competition Committee imagined when it moved the hash marks. The NFL seemed to be slipping back toward the grind-it-out '60s of Lombardi's Packers, when six yards between the tackles was a big play and pride mattered more than television money.

Like Joe Gilliam's passes that year, the 1970s were one-third complete. So far they belonged to back-to-back champion Miami, the only franchise with three straight Super Bowl appearances, the only team with a perfect season to its credit. The Dolphins swept into the 1974 season with a chance to make the decade theirs, but the tide was starting to turn. At its annual off-season confab, the Competition Committee, featuring power brokers including Paul Brown, Al Davis, and Cowboys president Tex Schramm, made its boldest moves yet. Effective in '74, the league moved kickoffs from the 40-yard line back to the 35. It banned blocking receivers by cutting them off at the knee. The committee helped pass-blockers by trimming holding penalties from fifteen yards to ten. It introduced sudden-death overtime, and moved the goalposts from just behind the goal line, where they were often in play, to the back of the end zone. Shifting the goalposts removed a traffic hazard: sly receivers had used the posts to set end-zone picks on defenders; clumsy DBs sometimes plowed into the posts, coldcocked by the goal itself. But the committee's objective wasn't to cut down on collisions. It was to cut down on field goals, which had risen to three per game, an unplanned result of narrowing the hash marks. Like a panel of Frankensteins, the committee was hacking the game's DNA by trial and error, creating something new and untested.

Another rule further hamstrung the kicking game: from now on, field goals missed from outside the 20 would be spotted at the line of scrimmage, not the 20. "Narrowing the hash marks had made chip-shot field goals easier. Moving the goalposts added ten yards to every field goal, and spotting the ball at the line of scrimmage made long ones riskier," says Brian Billick, whose Ravens would win Super Bowl XXXV. "They were consciously shifting scoring away from field goals to touchdown passes. But the biggest change was limiting defenders to one chuck. Up until then you could chuck, bump, jam—basically mug a receiver—until the ball was in the air. Now, once a receiver was three yards off the line of scrimmage you got one and only one hit." Coaches were left with a riddle: how much luck could a one-chuck chucker have while covering his man? Bud Carson, the Steelers' defensive coordinator, had an answer.

The Competition Committee expected the one-chuck rule to boost the passing game. It did, but the rule also led to a crucial shift in pass defense. Before 1974 most NFL defenses employed either a "man-free" coverage, with one defender on each receiver and a free safety roaming deep, or a three-deep zone, in which cornerbacks cover outside routes and the free safety covers the deep middle. Carson had a better idea. In his Cover Two, the cornerbacks moved up to the line while the safeties dropped deeper than normal. (Each of the two safeties was responsible for a zone half the width of the field, giving the coverage its name.) At the snap, the corners chucked the receivers, disrupting their routes. This called for big, punishing cornerbacks, and Pittsburgh's Mel Blount and J. T. Thomas fit the bill. At six-three and 205, Blount was the ideal Cover Two corner; Thomas was almost as big. Sheer speed was less vital because once they'd bashed a receiver, messing with his route, they let him go. At that point he was a linebacker's responsibility. The outside line-backers each covered an intermediate zone from the hash mark on his side of the field to the sideline. That left the middle linebacker dropping twenty to thirty yards deep in the heart of the field, with the safeties manning their deep zones.

There were seams in the Cover Two. To make it work, a team needed a ferocious front four rushing the quarterback, to keep him from finding the seams. The Steelers' Joe Greene, Ernie Holmes, Dwight White, and L. C. Greenwood were more than a match for any team's offensive line. A Cover-Two club also needed a fast middle linebacker, fast enough to cover tight ends on his own. The Steelers' Henry Davis wasn't as quick as Coach Noll and coordinator Carson would have liked, but he'd do for now.

The rules changes of 1974 favored the oncoming Steelers more than Shula's Dolphins. Miami had tried a version of the Cover Two before Carson arrived in Pittsburgh, but the Dolphins played mostly man-to-man while the Steelers set about perfecting the Cover Two, with an assist from the best draft any team ever had.

Twenty teams chose before the Steelers in the 1974 NFL draft. Dallas chose six-nine pass rusher Ed "Too Tall" Jones, who'd followed Gilliam out of Tennessee State, first overall. Next, San Diego took Colorado running back Bo Matthews. The New York Giants selected an Ohio State guard, John Hicks. Eighteen picks later, Pittsburgh chose USC receiver Lynn Swann, who slipped to twenty-first overall because he'd been a tick slow in predraft workouts. Scouts also doubted Swann's toughness. He was known to have taken ballet lessons.

In the second round, Pittsburgh selected Kent State's Jack Lambert. A skinny six-four, 220, with a gap-toothed snarl he owed to an old basketball injury, Lambert wore a four-tooth denture off the field but ditched it when he suited up. He looked unstoppable the day personnel director Art Rooney Jr., the Chief's son, scouted him. The Kent State Golden Flashes were practicing on a gravel parking lot not far from the spot where National Guardsmen shot and killed four Vietnam War protesters during Lambert's freshman year.

Rooney watched Lambert fly all over the lot making tackles, picking gravel from gouges in his bare legs between plays. Rooney raved about the kid to Noll, who oversaw the team's draft. Pittsburgh took Lambert with the forty-sixth pick. He would soon make a strong impression on his pro teammates. At training camp, when a veteran ordered him to sing the Kent State fight song, the rookie said, "Kiss my ass. I'm not singing."

The fourth round brought Alabama A&M receiver John Stallworth, thanks to some chicanery by Steelers scout Bill Nunn. In those days, four teams saved on scouting expenses by combining forces in BLESTO, which stood for Bears-Lions-Eagles-Steelers Training Organization. When Stallworth ran a sluggish 40-yard dash on a muddy field for BLESTO scouts, Nunn saw something the others missed. A former newspaperman who had helped the team find such players as Blount, Holmes, Greenwood, and Gilliam at small, traditionally black colleges, he faked the flu and spent another day in Huntsville. The next morning Nunn timed Stallworth at full speed. Weeks later the Alabama A&M coaching staff sent BLESTO a highlight reel of Stallworth making circus catches in an A&M game. The film mysteriously disappeared in Pittsburgh. The Steelers used the eighty-second choice of the '74 draft on Stallworth, then completed their grand slam by tabbing Wisconsin center Mike Webster in the fifth round, 125th overall. All four of their selections—Swann, Lambert, Stallworth, and Webster—were thought to be small, slow, or otherwise suspect. All four would go to the Hall of Fame. As Rooney Jr. put it, "We got out on the right side of the bed that year. The stars lined up." In fact it was Noll the old messenger guard and Nunn the clever scout, looking for overachievers like themselves, who lined the stars up.

In a 1974 preseason game, linebacker Henry Davis took a savage blow to his head and neck. Davis, thirty-one, never played again. Noll and defensive coordinator Carson turned to rookie Jack Lambert.

Lambert's jack-o'-lantern grimace and feral preplay posture—arms and legs quivering as he awaited the snap—made him look and sound like a rookie werewolf. His speed and wingspan made him the ideal Cover Two middle linebacker. On opening day 1974, Lambert stepped into the starting lineup. The Steel Curtain was in place.

Nixon chose resignation over impeachment that year and choppered into the sky over Washington, replaced by former Michigan Wolverines center Gerald Ford. Chicago's new $150 million Sears Tower topped New York's World Trade Center Towers as the world's tallest building, gas hit fifty cents a gallon, and an Ohio supermarket cashier rang up sixty-seven cents for Juicy Fruit gum, the first-ever sale on a bar-code scanner. *Monday Night Football* won its time slot, but Howard and Frank couldn't match the ratings of *All in the Family*, featuring crotchety bigot Archie Bunker, who hunkered in his favorite armchair, grumbling about gays, women's libbers, politics ("Don't talk that way about Ford—he's doin' good for a guy that got hit in the head playing football"), and the "spooks" and "jungle bunnies" he saw running the ball on *Monday Night Football*. Dandy Don Meredith left *Monday Night* for NBC, signing a $200,000 deal stipulating that no one would call him "Dandy Don" or "Danderoo" on the air. To replace him, *MNF* boss Arledge considered ex-Packers Paul Hornung and Bart Starr as well as former college football players Burt Reynolds and Bill Cosby. Just about anyone would have been a better choice than the man Arledge tabbed, Chiefs cornerback turned actor Fred "the Hammer" Williamson, star of *Black Caesar* and *Hell Up in Harlem*. "I'll bring some color to the booth," Williamson joked. It turned out to be his best line; Arledge canned the wooden Williamson after three weeks.

Howard Cosell hoped his best football friend would join the *Monday Night* team. According to Cosell, "O. J. Simpson is a kind man, a thoughtful man, and a sensitive man. As a sportscaster, he has exactly the right combination of humor, insight, knowledge, and irreverence." But sports' biggest star wasn't about to retire from the Bills at age twenty-seven, coming off a season in which he ran for a record 2,003 yards. Howard would have to wait nine years for O.J. to join *MNF*. Arledge turned instead to ex-Lion Alex Karras, best known for getting suspended in 1963 for betting on NFL games and for punching a horse in *Blazing Saddles* earlier in '74. Karras matched Williamson by getting off a single memorable line in his first season, quipping that the Raiders' shave-headed Otis Sistrunk was from "the University of Mars."

In September the man whose records Simpson was breaking made a statement of his own. Jim Brown, thirty-eight, doffed his dashiki to pose fully frontal in *Playgirl*, as if to say, "Top this, O.J." Pro football players were now all but officially the sexiest jocks alive. Fans swooned when they rolled through Holiday Inn lobbies with their suede pants, muttonchop sideburns, and bushy mustaches, gold chains snaking through their chest hair. Two NFL roomies sharing a $25-a-night room at the Holiday Inn was the height of luxury compared to the road trips of the '50s and '60s, with bugs in fleabag-hotel bathtubs and snowy breezes coming through cracks in the walls. In the mid-'70s pro football players began earning enough to quit selling cars or insurance in the off-season. In 1973 the average NFL salary was $29,000. In '74 it topped $30,000 for the first time, on its way to $60,000 by the end of the decade. Thirty grand was no pittance—equal to about $90,000 in 2012 dollars. Still the owners had the upper hand. The league was selling Super Bowl commercials for $200,000 a minute, which meant that a single Schlitz or Right Guard ad was worth more than the combined salaries of the Dolphins' Super Bowl backfield. The age of the multimillion-dollar athlete was years ahead, the stars of the '70s earning a fraction of the wealth banked by players such as Bears lineman Julius Peppers, who earned $20 million in 2010, or $2.8 million per sack. The gap is so great, in fact, that even adjusting for inflation Peppers made more in 2010 than the 1973 Super Bowl–champion Dolphins—more than the '73 Dolphins' entire forty-man roster, as well as all their coaches, trainers, and front-office staff.

With free agency twenty years off, NFL players had two options. They could suit up for the teams that owned their rights, or they could quit. Jim Brown retired at age twenty-nine and took his talents to Hollywood. For more than thirteen hundred other men who sweated and bled on Sundays and Mondays, wealth was a pot of gold beyond the end zone. The real money was more years away than they had left in the league.

John Mackey wanted to change that. The Baltimore Colts' tight end had followed Brown from Syracuse to the NFL. Mackey joined the Colts in 1963, when a tight end was still considered a sixth offensive lineman, a blocker. Mackey was big for his time, six-two and 224, and faster than any other tight end had ever been. When the Colts asked him to return punts and kickoffs, he averaged 30 yards per return. Along with Raymond Berry he became one of the great Unitas's favorite targets, a Hall of Famer, but his greatest contribution to league history was serving as the postmerger president of the National Football League Players Association. Soon after the 1970 merger, Mackey met with Cowboys president Tex Schramm and several other owners' reps. He never forgot how the suit-and-tie-wearing white men around the conference room treated him. "They said, 'Young man, before we talk we want you to sign this paper, to show your good faith,'" he recalled. "And my lawyer agreed, saying, 'It's boilerplate. Sign it.' I thought, 'Wow, my lawyer's with them, too.'" Mackey asked Schramm and company to leave the room while he thought about their offer. After they left he studied the contract he was supposed to sign, a proposal stacked in the owners' favor. "Then I tore that paper into little pieces." When the meeting

reconvened, Mackey won a pair of concessions. Management grudgingly agreed to raise the minimum salary to $12,500 and to allow
NFL players to hire agents. But Schramm couldn't resist a dig about
the clothes he'd seen Mackey and some other black players wearing.

"Those velvet jumpsuits," Schramm said, shaking his head with
distaste.

"Well," Mackey said, "some of us may not like you wearing white
socks with a suit."

Four years later, NFL players went on strike. The first picket line
in sports history formed outside the Chargers' training camp in July
1974. Striking players wore T-shirts showing a clenched fist and
the slogan NO FREEDOM, NO FOOTBALL. Mel Renfro, the Cowboys'
erudite cornerback, waved a placard reading UP THE OLIGOPSONY,
which sent even Roy Blount to his dictionary (*oligopsony: a market in
which a few buyers determine prices*). The thirty-two-year-old Mackey
was gone by then, discarded by his former team along with nineteen
other union officers and player reps. He supported the players' cause
with an op-ed in the *New York Times*: "Some say that freedom for
athletes will destroy the NFL. I say nonsense. But I also say this: If
freedom will destroy the NFL, then the NFL should be destroyed."
Mackey's successors demanded the end of the so-called Rozelle Rule,
which allowed the commissioner to penalize clubs that signed free
agents. The union would eventually beat the Rozelle Rule in federal
court, but in 1974 Rozelle's oligopsony was working even better than
baseball's reserve clause. The average NFL player earned $3,000 less
than the average major league baseball player and was doing still
worse compared to his counterparts in hockey and basketball. The
typical NFL player made about half the NHL average and less than a
third of the $92,500 NBA average.

Hunter Thompson saw the future coming. The *Rolling Stone* gonzo
predicted "mandatory urinalysis of professional athletes" and a
premature end to the Dolphins' dynasty. With the fledgling World

Football League throwing money at players, Thompson forecast "brutal raids on NFL teams . . . among the Dolphin contracts coming up this year are those of Larry Csonka, Jake Scott, Paul Warfield, Dick Anderson and Mercury Morris, all established stars earning between $30,000 and $55,000 a year."

As if on cue, Miami's Csonka, Warfield, and Jim Kiick signed with the World Football League's Toronto Northmen. They announced that they would honor their NFL contracts through 1974, helping Shula and Griese lead Miami's run for a third straight Super Bowl title. Then they would join the Northmen in '75. Csonka, who freely admitted he was "selling out," would get an 834 percent raise, from $50,000 a year to $467,000. *Time* magazine called the Dolphins' defection "the deal that astonished sports."

Rookies weren't yet members of the players' union. They flocked to 1974 training camps that summer, hoping to beat striking players out of their jobs. A few veterans joined them. The scabs included ambitious third-stringers, special-teams guys hoping coaches would learn their names, thirty-five-year-old geezers hungry for a last pay-check—and Joe Gilliam, who saw the players' strike as his chance to beat out Terry Bradshaw. "I have to cross the picket line. This is my shot," Gilliam said.

When the strike ended after eight weeks, Chuck Noll made an announcement: "Joe Gilliam's our quarterback." Many Steelers were shocked. It wasn't just that Noll was rewarding a strikebreaker; he was undermining the incumbent. Bradshaw had thrown for 1,183 yards and 10 touchdowns the year before. Still only twenty-five, the country boy had hit on 49 percent of his throws, and while his 10 touchdown passes were offset by 15 interceptions, the team went 8-1 in the nine games he started. Bradshaw could still whistle 60-yard bullets that left bruises on receivers, but privately he felt like a weakling, a flop. He knew Coach Noll didn't trust him to execute or even comprehend a game plan, and his off-field life was unraveling.

In a *Playboy* interview, Bradshaw admitted his marriage to Missy Babish, a former Miss Teenage America, had been a bad idea. "I was very lonely. Didn't love her," he said. "I tried to break the wedding up two days before, but she was crying and bellyaching." In '74 they divorced, "and I felt a lot of guilt over the divorce. I didn't become an alcoholic or a whoremonger, but I was moody and depressed, and I drank and hustled women in bars." In the mornings, shaking off his hangovers, Bradshaw worked out on his own while Gilliam auditioned for Noll.

Once Noll made up his mind, no force on earth would change it. If Joe Greene and the other Steelers didn't like his decision, they were welcome to lump it. Coach Noll wasn't looking for input. For all his Me Decade methods, he was starting to seem as rigid as Paul Brown, an approach that could only perpetuate what Franco Harris called the Steelers' forty-year doldrums.

It had been twenty years since another stubborn Steelers coach, Walt Kiesling, opened every game by sending fullback Fran Rogel into the line. Kiesling kept calling the play even after fans began chanting, "Hi diddle diddle, Rogel up the middle!" Finally owner Art Rooney demanded a pass to start the next game. Quarterback Jim Finks lofted a long one for a touchdown, but the play was called back. The Steelers were offside. Only later did the Chief learn that Kiesling had ordered a lineman to jump offside. "If that pass works," Kiesling told the lineman, "the owner's gonna be sending us plays every week."

In 1955 Kiesling's depth chart had Finks, a future NFL general manager, and future Colts and Ravens coach Ted Marchibroda at quarterback ahead of a rookie. In Kiesling's opinion the rookie, Pittsburgh native Johnny Unitas, was too dumb to play quarterback in the pros. Kiesling cut him. Two years later the Steelers passed on Jim Brown in the '57 draft. Rather than entering the '60s with Unitas handing off to Brown, Pittsburgh endured eight more losing seasons in the next dozen years. Unitas took a job running a pile driver at a Pittsburgh steel mill, playing semipro ball for $6 a game on the site of the old Allegheny Arsenal, where the dirt and grass were flecked with rusty musket balls left over from the Civil War. A year later the Colts signed him for $7,000. Forty thousand yards, 287 touchdown passes, and three Most Valuable Player awards after that, tight end Mackey compared him to "God in the huddle." By 1973 Unitas was playing out the string in a baby-blue San Diego Chargers uniform, tutoring rookie quarterback Dan Fouts. Like others of his football generation, the great Johnny U was broken down at forty, barely able to reach up and drag a pocket comb through his crew cut, much less skip out of the pocket to dodge a blitz. Waiting for the rush, he said, felt like "Okay, Buick, run me down."

The Steelers' 1974 depth chart had Gilliam, Bradshaw, and Hanratty at quarterback. If never quite friends, they were friendly enough. Bradshaw had welcomed Jefferson Street Joe to the team by challenging him to a beer-drinking contest at the 19th Hole, a dive bar near training camp in Latrobe. Neither was much of a drinker. Gilliam chugged Rolling Rock. Bradshaw matched him. After a few more Rolling Rocks, Gilliam, looking woozy, threw up in Bradshaw's lap. A second later the nauseated Bradshaw puked right back on Gilliam.

Mean Joe Greene wasn't the only one who disagreed with the way Noll ranked his quarterbacks. A *Pittsburgh Post-Gazette* poll asking who should play quarterback resulted in a landslide for Bradshaw. Howard Cosell and others blamed racist voters, but most of the Steelers agreed with the poll. Gilliam had an overweening sense of his own talent, a growing taste for drugs that would eventually ruin him, and a bit of a persecution complex. He saw racism behind every criticism. He told Roy Blount he felt surrounded by "people who seem sincere, and all the time they're planning to fuck your mama and blow you up, too." Calling his own plays, Gilliam called his own number again and again. After shutting out the Colts 30–0 in their '74 opener—middle linebacker Lambert's pro debut—the Steelers flew to Denver in Week Two. Gilliam rained a franchise-record 50 passes on the Broncos, but the result was a 35–35 tie. The following week he went 8 for 31 with 2 interceptions in a loss to the hated Raiders. Noll was reluctant to yank him—that would be admitting he'd chosen the wrong quarterback. But if Bradshaw was dumb, what do you call a guy who won't hand the ball to Franco Harris on third-and-3?

In October the Oilers picked off two more of Gilliam's throws. The Steelers won anyway, and won their next two as well to go 4-1-1 despite Gilliam, who was now 35 for 86 with a touchdown and 3 interceptions over three games. At the next team meeting, Noll tried to sound casual as he switched quarterbacks. "Brad, you're up this week," he said.

Gilliam was "totally shocked," he said. *This is racial*, he thought, and some of his black teammates agreed. The team was in first place, wasn't it? *Sports Illustrated* had put "Pittsburgh's Black Quarterback" on its cover. Why fix what ain't broke?

Noll might have had a mutiny to deal with if not for Joe Greene. When asked to speak up on the race question, Greene shrugged. His silence effectively ended the debate. Greene's wordless support of Terry Bradshaw meant that Bradshaw, for all his faults and dumb-ass country ways, was going to be the Pittsburgh Steelers' quarterback for better or worse, till death or the Raiders got in their way.

With Bradshaw calling signals, handing off to Harris 28 times, Pittsburgh edged Atlanta to go 5-1-1. Harris had a career-best 141 yards while halfback Rocky Bleier carried 15 times for 78 yards.

Rocky Bleier was another unlikely character. Called Boulder for his chiseled physique, Bleier was one of only two NFL players injured in combat in Vietnam. (Bills tackle Bob Kalsu, killed in action in 1970, was the other.) In 1969, in a rice paddy near Chu Lai, he took a bullet through his left thigh. Specialist Bleier hobbled toward his platoon only to see a Vietcong grenade bouncing toward him. He dived side-ways, a move that probably saved his life, but shrapnel peppered his right foot. Recuperating in Tokyo, he heard doctors tell him he would never play football again. Bleier received a Purple Heart, a Bronze Star, and a postcard from owner Art Rooney: *Rock, the team's not doing well. We need you.* After a grueling year of rehab, he reported to training camp in Latrobe. Noll, who had no use for a running back slowed by grenade shards in his foot, cut him. But owner Rooney insisted on keeping Bleier on the taxi squad. Rocky hammered his way through gym and track workouts, slashed his time in the 40 from 4.9 to 4.6—a mere tick behind Lynn Swann—and made the team two years later. Joining Bradshaw and Harris in the backfield, blocking for both, he averaged 4.2 yards per occasional carry in 1974.

Guards Gerry Mullins and Jim Clack mowed paths for Bleier and Harris that year, pulling so hard ahead of the 230-pound Franco that by the end of the year they weighed less than he did. Rookie receivers Swann and Stallworth gave Bradshaw two new targets. Rookie linebacker Lambert filled the middle of defensive coordina-tor Carson's Cover Two. The Steelers even got help from equipment manager Tony Parisi's mother-in-law, who took in the linemen's jerseys and sewed strips of double-sided tape inside the shoulders to keep the jerseys tight around their pads. A little Vaseline on those tight jerseys—a trick they'd picked up from the Raiders—made the linemen slick as seals in the trenches.

Pittsburgh clinched the AFC Central with a 21–17 victory at New England, Harris rushing for 136 yards and rookie Swann, who gained most of his yardage that season as a kick-return special-ist, making a tumbling snag for a 7-yard touchdown. The Steelers were becoming as tight-knit as their jerseys, with stars and scrubs alike gathering at Franco's house for poker on Tuesday nights. They smoked cigars, ate fried chicken, and drank Iron City beer while Joe Greene, the poker expert, explained the ins and outs of Texas Hold

'Em. Greene played smart, while Harris, Swann, and Frenchy Fuqua bet wildly. Fuqua was so sure of his luck he'd raise without looking at his hole cards.

The Steelers downed Paul Brown's Bengals 27–3 to close the regular season 10-3-1, with 6 wins and 2 losses in Bradshaw's starts. They hosted the Buffalo Bills in the first round of the playoffs. "We knew we'd have to stop the run," Greene recalled, thinking of O. J. Simpson. Get past the Bills and Pittsburgh would face either Miami or Oakland in the next round. The defending-champion Dolphins had always beaten the Steelers when it mattered, while the Raiders had steamrolled them in the '73 playoffs.

A new term made its debut that fall: a bunch of scientists using modems to link their computers called their network the Internet. A maddening gift called Rubik's Cube topped 1974 Christmas lists. The top innovation in Pittsburgh was the Stunt 4-3, a bit of defensive geometry devised by Greene along with Noll, defensive coordinator Carson, and defensive line coach George Perles. The Stunt 4-3 had Greene lining up at a forty-five-degree angle to the center, rather than head-up on the right guard. From this "tilted-nose" alignment Greene pounced when the ball was snapped. "It started out as a pass technique," Noll explained, "but we found it screws up run block-ing, too, because our front four isn't reading the offense. Instead, they're the ones making things happen." The alignment gave Greene so much leverage on the center he wondered why nobody had tried it before. If the center and guard double-teamed Mean Joe, then Lambert or Ernie Holmes charged into the backfield. If not, Greene shot the gap himself.

Using the Stunt 4-3 for the first time, the Steelers held O. J. Simp-son to 49 yards in their first playoff game. For the Steelers, Bradshaw scrambled for 48 yards and threw for 203, including a touchdown strike to the balletic Swann, who had babysat Simpson's children in his USC days. Swann had caught only 11 passes all year as he worked his way into the offense. His diving touchdown catch in Pittsburgh's 32–14 victory foreshadowed postseason highlights to come.

Now the Steelers were one step from their first Super Bowl. All they had to do was beat the winner of that weekend's other AFC divisional playoff between the Dolphins and the Raiders, a game newspapers were calling Super Bowl VIII½.

Over the past three years, Miami's two-time Super Bowl champs had won 43 games and lost 5. They had won 8 of 9 coming into the 1974 playoffs. The Raiders, AFC West champions for the fourth time in five years, had run up a league-high 355 points while allowing only 228. On a brisk forty-nine-degree Saturday, a rowdy-as-usual Oakland Coliseum crowd waved Raider-black towels at Shula's white-clad Dolphins. A banner read DOLPHINS BELONG IN A FISH- BOWL NOT SUPERBOWL. The crowd's roar rose as Miami's Nat Moore gathered in Blanda's kickoff, but the fans went quiet as Moore cut left to the sideline and sprinted 89 yards to the end zone. Now you could hear a beer cup splat on Coliseum concrete. Twenty seconds into the game, it was 7–0 Miami.

Oakland coach Madden, standing next to quarterback Stabler, said, "This could be a long day."

Stabler spat. He said, "Yeah. For them."

Trailing 10–7 in the second half, Stabler took a snap at the Dolphins' 15. He looked left to bluff the defense, then threw to Biletnikoff on the right sideline. The pass arrived at the intersection of end zone, receiver, and cornerback Tim Foley, who got a hand up. The ball popped free. Biletnikoff and Foley tumbled, legs tangled, Foley pinning the receiver's right arm to his side. The right-handed Biletnikoff had only his left arm free, the ball floating in the air as both men fell away from it. At the last instant he got his left hand around the ball and clutched it to his chest while remembering to drag his feet in bounds. Stabler would call it the best catch anybody ever saw. Blanda's point-after gave Oakland a 14–10 lead.

A Griese-to-Warfield touchdown and Yepremian's 46-yard field goal put the Dolphins up 19–14. Minutes later Stabler underthrew Cliff Branch, who fell and skidded catching the ball. Untouched by the Dolphins all around him, Branch bounced up and ran 27 more yards for a score that put Oakland ahead, 21–19.

Two minutes left. Griese, cool as a refrigerator pipe, directed a 68-yard drive that had Madden kicking air on the sideline. Now it was 26–21 Miami. That would be the final, barring yet another last-gasp surprise.

Throwing under the safeties in the Dolphins' prevent defense, Stabler led the Raiders to Miami's 14. There were still forty seconds left. The season came down to this: third down and a yard to go, the Dolphins stacking the line, expecting a run. Stabler drifted back seven steps, looking downfield. Miami's six-six, 250-pound Vern Den Herder closed in on him, the clock ticking to 00:35, Stabler skipping forward while Den Herder, blocked, falling, clutched at Stabler's ankles, pulling his feet out from under him. Stabler, falling forward like a bowling pin, heaved a wounded-duck pass toward second-string running back Clarence Davis. There would be irony in this if it had been anything but a wild guess. Davis was a backup who'd scored two touchdowns all year. Teammates called him Cement Hands and ribbed him for treating passes as if he were fending them off. Now, with the game and the season on the line, with three defenders all over him, Davis went up for Stabler's desperation pass. He came down with the ball, but so did two Dolphins whose four arms wrestled him for the pass until Davis pulled it free and the referee's arms flew skyward.

The rest was anticlimax. Villapiano intercepted Griese's desperation pass and raced the ball to Madden on the sideline. "I handed John the game ball and you should see him, all sweaty and happy." And pink, with a wide grin that radio announcer Bill King said made Madden's face look "like a split watermelon."

Al Davis shook his fist in the Raiders' delirious locker room. "Yeahh!" Clarence Davis, looking surprised to see reporters around his locker, recounted and re-recounted the play Oakland writers would call the Sea of Hands. Two-pack-a-day smoker Biletnikoff lit a cigarette off the ember of another. Otto sat in a folding chair grinning, trying to straighten his leg. Stabler gave a rebel yell. After going 20 for 30 for 293 yards and 4 touchdowns, he said the game-winner "was a dumb play. I shoulda thrown the ball away. But sometimes you get away with a dumb play."

And Madden, flush with victory, mobbed by reporters with cameras, mics, and notebooks, said the one thing he should never have said. Relieved and elated, he was eager to praise the beaten Dolphins. "We beat the best team in football today," Madden said.

The Steelers were listening.

7

MEN OF STEEL

I t had to happen: us and Oakland," says Pittsburgh's Andy Russell. "We hated them and they hated us. There was respect, too, but that week we pretty much stuck to the hate."

The Raiders had barked and gloated during a 17–0 face-rub in Pittsburgh earlier that season, when Joe Gilliam was still the Steelers' quarterback. The Steelers were irked to hear that Raiders coach Madden gave each member of Oakland's defensive unit $100 for the shutout. (Bonuses for shutouts and big plays were a tradition later perverted by the injury bounties New Orleans Saints coaches paid during the "Bountygate" years of 2009–11.) Raiders owner Al Davis annoyed the Steelers, too. Knowing that plenty of rival players wished they could join the fun-loving, hard-drinking, AFC West–winning Raiders, Davis liked to sidle up to a key opponent or two during warm-ups and say, "We like you. We might trade for you." It didn't have to be true to plant a seed of hesitation in their heads, to make them think twice about hitting too hard or too dirty. But when Davis tried it on Greene—"Joe, we like you . . ."—Greene shut him up with a fierce look.

What the Steelers hated most during the week of the 1974 AFC

Championship was being an afterthought. In the ruckus that followed Oakland's Sea of Hands miracle in Miami, the Raiders were the press and oddsmakers' clear favorites to advance to Super Bowl IX. Media coverage looked back toward the Dolphins-Raiders epic rather than ahead to the AFC Championship. Madden, still burbling about his team's last-gasp victory over the Dolphins, said, "When the two best teams in football get together, anything can happen."

Chuck Noll underlined that quote in the *Post-Gazette.*

Compared to the blustering, bearlike Madden, Noll was an odd duck. Noll, forty-two, with the first traces of gray in the sandy hair under his headset, guest-conducted the Pittsburgh Symphony, grew geraniums in a backyard greenhouse, and donned an apron to cook gourmet dinners for his wife. No less intense than Madden, Noll had the stone-cold confidence to buy a Cessna before he took his first flying lesson. Later, when the plane's engine died with his wife and children aboard, he made an emergency landing without breaking a sweat.

The Steelers didn't know what to expect when Noll held up the *Post-Gazette.* "The coach of the Raiders," he began, unwilling to utter Madden's name, "said the two best teams in football played in Miami. Well, the Super Bowl is three weeks from now, and the best team in football is sitting right here in this room."

"I levitated right out of my seat when I heard that," Greene remembered, "because it was very unlike him. That's why it had so much power."

Despite being 6-point underdogs in Oakland, the Steelers felt invincible. Not long before the kickoff, defensive end L. C. Greenwood sat outside their dressing room, watching the Vikings-Rams NFC Championship on a TV in the hallway. "I want to see who we'll play in the Super Bowl," said Greenwood. Minutes later Joe Greene went up to Pittsburgh owner Art Rooney to offer a handshake. "We're gonna get 'em," Greene said.

Hostilities began before the first play from scrimmage. Otto, the

Raiders' creaky bulldog of a center, was approaching the football as it lay on the Coliseum grass. Before he could take his stance, the Steelers' Ernie "Fats" Holmes stepped over the ball. Holmes pointed at All-Pro guard Gene Upshaw, the Raiders' offensive captain, and bellowed. "Upshaw! I'm going to kick your ass!"

The Raiders' initial play was a handoff to Sea of Hands hero Clarence Davis, who followed Upshaw into the Steelers' line. Davis churned forward for 4 yards before Holmes wrestled him down. Holmes bounced up and spat in Upshaw's face. With an arrow-shaped Mohawk on his shaved scalp, Fats Holmes would spearhead the Pittsburgh front four. Two plays later, with Joe Greene lined up in the tilted Stunt 4-3, Holmes looped around Greene to take on guard George Buehler, which left Otto to block Greene one-on-one. Greene dunked the thirty-six-year-old center to the turf with one hand, shot past him, and sacked Ken Stabler.

The first half was all defense. Pittsburgh stuffed the run and chased Stabler while Oakland stopped Bradshaw and his running backs. Following a Steelers punt, Stabler spent a series dodging six-six left end Greenwood, who sported gold-painted, size-14 cleats; left tackle Greene, stunting past Otto and Buehler; 260-pound right tackle Holmes, his arrow-shaped Mohawk pointing the way to the Oakland backfield; and six-four, 255-pound right end Dwight "Mad Dog" White, whose Pittsburgh fans called themselves Dwight's Whites. Like Oakland's Soul Patrol, the Steel Curtain front four were all black, but Greene, Greenwood, Holmes, and White didn't segregate themselves from the rest of the team. They led it. They were out to avenge two losses to Oakland, the 17–0 regular-season shutout and the playoff game the year before—eight quarters in which the Raiders had shredded the Steel Curtain for 50 points and 409 yards on the ground.

Blanda's 40-yard field goal and a boot by Gerela made it 3–3 at halftime. With six minutes to play in the third quarter, Stabler looked for Cliff Branch. "Cliff was our rocket," the quarterback says.

"He could outrun the cars on the interstate." In his third pro season, Branch had led the league with 13 touchdown catches. He'd spent much of this afternoon blowing past cornerback Mel Blount like a Porsche passing a mailbox, but the outside linebackers and safeties in the Steelers' Cover Two had contained him. Now Stabler hit Branch for a 38-yard touchdown that put Oakland ahead 10–3. Still the Steelers believed they were the better team. On one play Greene sacked Stabler less than a second after the snap, so quickly he was flagged for jumping offside. The film shows he wasn't offside, just impossibly fast. "Quick and dirty," according to Otto. "Joe Greene cussed me out and then kicked me in the crotch when I was lying on the ground."

Jim Tunney's officiating crew blew yet another call when the Steelers' John Stallworth made a one-handed catch with his toes barely in bounds. No catch, the refs ruled. Not even Madden could accuse them of screwing the Raiders today. But Greene wasn't fazed. *We'll give you that. You have no chance,* he thought. Late in the third quarter, with Oakland still up 10–3, Greene dunked Otto again on his way to another sack. In Roy Blount's words, Mean Joe went through the future Hall of Famer "like a 275-pound chill through a man with no coat." In the fourth quarter, Bradshaw took the Steelers 61 yards in eight plays, handing off to Franco Harris for 8 yards that tied the score, 10–10. On Oakland's next posession, Stabler ducked and weaved. He faked handoffs, but everyone from Noll to the peanut vendors knew he had to throw. With the Raiders' running game stagnant, the front four could chase the Snake while linebackers Russell, Lambert, and Ham roamed the seams of their zones.

The Steelers charged. Middle linebacker Lambert, twitching as he bounced from heel to toe, saw Stabler's eyes flick toward safety-valve running back Charlie Smith. Stabler didn't see Lambert until a split second after he let the ball go. Forty years later, looking back

A relaxed Joe Namath guaranteed a Jets victory in Super Bowl III. *(Walter Iooss Jr./ Getty Images)*

Commissioner Pete Rozelle (*right*) with AFL founder Lamar Hunt (*left*) and Chiefs coach Hank Stram in 1970. *(Rod Hanna—US Presswire)*

Owner as iconoclast: Oakland's Al Davis was Rozelle's longtime nemesis. *(Malcolm Emmons—US Presswire)*

Coach Don Shula (*left*) and bespectacled, mild-mannered quarterback Bob Griese led the Dolphins to a 14-0 record in 1972. *(Al Messerschmidt Archive/Getty Images)*

An instant after Franco Harris's Immaculate Reception, the Raiders' Phil Villapiano (41) took off after Harris. *(Dick Raphael/Getty Images)*

A stunned-looking Harris shook hands with a fan after his Reception gave Pittsburgh a miracle win in the 1972 playoffs. *(Malcolm Emmons— US Presswire)*

The Bills' dangerous O. J. Simpson won four rushing titles and set a record with 2,003 yards in 1973. *(Malcolm Emmons—US Presswire)*

The top choice in the 1970 draft, quarterback Terry Bradshaw (*left*) looked for approval from Steelers coach Chuck Noll. *(Malcolm Emmons— US Presswire)*

Things got hairy for Oakland's Ken "the Snake" Stabler (*left*) and Coach John Madden when they took on the Steelers. (*Malcolm Emmons—US Presswire*)

Center Jim "Pops" Otto chose number "aught-oh" and shrugged off injuries that would have ended other players' careers. (*Malcolm Emmons—US Presswire*)

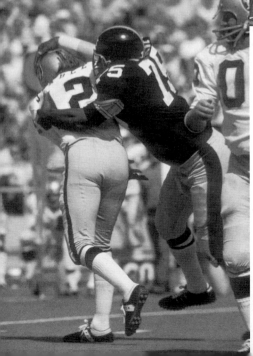

With Don Meredith (*left*), Howard Cosell (*center*), and Frank Gifford in the booth, *Monday Night Football* became a pop-culture phenomenon. (*ABC Photo Archives/Getty Images*)

Joe Greene blew past Otto to sack Stabler in one of the Steelers and Raiders' bruising battles. (*Malcolm Emmons—US Presswire*)

Versatile middle linebacker Jack Lambert helped Greene anchor the Steelers' defense in four Super Bowls. *(Tony Tomsic/Getty Images)*

Scrambling Roger Staubach served a five-year hitch in the Navy before joining the Cowboys as a twenty-seven-year-old rookie. *(Dick Raphael—US Presswire)*

Cowboys coach Tom Landry and assistant Mike Ditka (*right*) told Staubach, "We're going to experiment with a shotgun formation." *(Malcolm Emmons— US Presswire)*

Free safety Jack Tatum, aka the Assassin, helped make Oakland's hard-hitting secondary the most feared in the league. *(Malcolm Emmons—US Presswire)*

The towering Tooz, defensive end John Matuszak (*left*), and safety George Atkinson locked horns with the Vikings in Super Bowl XI. *(Malcolm Emmons—US Presswire)*

Lynn Swann's circus catch in Super Bowl X followed an AFC Championship Game in which the Raiders put Swann in the hospital. *(Heinz Kluetmeier/Getty Images)*

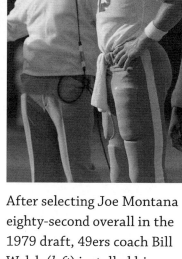

After selecting Joe Montana eighty-second overall in the 1979 draft, 49ers coach Bill Walsh (*left*) installed his so-called West Coast Offense. *(Malcolm Emmons—US Presswire)*

A four-time Pro Bowl choice, linebacker Phil Villapiano partied almost as hard as he tackled. *(James Flores/Getty Images)*

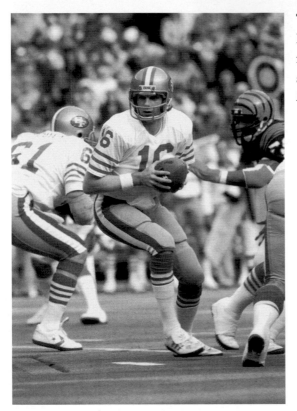

The nimble, quick-thinking Montana seemed born to run San Francisco's carefully scripted attack. *(Malcolm Emmons—US Presswire)*

Dwight Clark beat the Cowboys' Everson Walls and clawed The Catch from the sky in the 1982 NFC Championship Game. *(Walter Iooss Jr./Getty Images)*

on more than 4,000 passes he threw as a pro, Stabler would call that flip to Smith the one he most wished he could take back.

Lambert intercepted and raced the ball to the Raiders' 9-yard line. A minute later Lynn Swann faked outside before cutting to the back of the end zone. Bradshaw hit him for a touchdown that gave Pittsburgh its first lead, 17–10.

The Snake struck back, conducting a 78-yard drive. Sixty of those yards were completions to Branch, who was still turning cornerback Blount inside out. "I remember telling Snake, 'Fling it hard as you can. Cliff will run under it,'" recalls Tom Flores, a Raiders assistant coach that year. "Snake never had a cannon like Bradshaw, but what a competitor he was! He threw so hard he spun around like a discus thrower." Branch snagged the pass and streaked toward pay dirt, a touchdown that would tie the game. The Raiders' home crowd stood and screamed—here was the game-changer that would help give Oakland a third straight victory over the Steelers.

Lambert closed the gap on Branch. On one of the decade's key plays, the skinny rookie linebacker caught up with the Raiders' rocket. Lambert brought Branch down after a 42-yard gain. Three plays later the Steelers blitzed yet again, forcing Stabler to throw the ball away. The Raiders settled for a Blanda field goal and trailed 17–13.

They got the ball back with 1:48 to play. Plenty of time for a team that had beaten the two-time champion Dolphins with seconds to spare. Stabler hit Branch for 18 yards. Moments later he took Otto's snap, dropped back, and saw Russell blitzing. "I was inches from getting him," says Russell. Stabler, hustling to avoid a sack, heaved the ball downfield. Pittsburgh cornerback J. T. Thomas intercepted his desperation pass and returned it to the Raiders' 24.

The clock read 00:47. Second down, 7 to go. Bradshaw handed off to Franco Harris, who chugged 21 yards to a touchdown that sealed it: Pittsburgh 24, Oakland 13. Harris would call the Steelers' pivotal '74 AFC Championship "the biggest game of the '70s," a game that turned what could have become the Raiders' decade into something else entirely.

According to the *New York Times*, "The Pittsburgh Steelers, who in their time fielded some of the most inept teams in the history of the National Football League, had one made of tempered steel today." After allowing those 409 rushing yards in two previous games against Oakland, Greene, Holmes, Lambert, and the rest of the defense had allowed 29. Clarence Davis's 4-yard run on the game's first play turned out to be the Raiders' longest of the day.

Madden's eyes were puffy, moist. "Defeat," he said, "is a bitch."

The Steelers' plane landed in Pittsburgh in the predawn hours of Monday, December 30, 1974. More than a dozen of them carpooled directly to Franco Harris's three-story brick house on the north side, where they played poker and feasted on steak and eggs washed down with champagne. "Boy, that was fun," Harris says today. "Before the game I'd told a friend of mine, 'Buy some steak, eggs, and champagne. We're going to win, and then we'll have a party.' And that day when we beat the Raiders in Oakland—that's when we knew we were the best team in football. On the plane home we're yelling, 'We're goin' to the Super Bowl!' Then we piled off the plane and went to my house." Some Steelers crashed on Franco's couch or on the floor after the party, waking just in time to greet the last day of the first half of the '70s.

The Reverend Norman Vincent Peale, pop philosopher, welcomed 1975 by announcing the advent of a secular holiday. "If Jesus Christ were alive today," said Peale, "he'd be at the Super Bowl." The Messiah wouldn't have needed a miracle to get a ticket to the game. Due to construction delays, the New Orleans Superdome wasn't finished in time to host the game it was named after, so the Steelers and NFC champion Vikings would play at rain-soaked Tulane Stadium, where, for the last time, there would be hundreds of empty seats at the Super Bowl. Scalpers unloaded $20 tickets for $5.

Throughout the season and the playoffs, Pittsburgh fans had applauded and backslapped the Steelers on sidewalks, at grocery stores and gas stations, in bars and in church. Virginia-born Dwight "Mad Dog" White said of Steelers fans, "They're out of Appalachia, dirty-faced coal miners and smutty-faced steelworkers. This ain't Fort Lauderdale. The water's brown and the sky's brown." But the future was looking black and gold. "Self-esteem," he said, "is a hell of a thing." Super Bowl fever proved medicinal for Mad Dog, offsetting the pleurisy and pneumonia that put him in a New Orleans hospital the week of the game. After losing eighteen pounds, White rose from his hospital bed on game day, telling his doctors that if he was going to spend Super Sunday on his back, the Vikings would have to put him there.

While Minnesota's dour Bud Grant kept his Vikings in their hotel rooms except for practices and team meetings, Noll urged the Steelers to explore New Orleans. He told them to "get the partying out of your systems" and broke his own road-trip rule by allowing players' wives to stay with them in the team hotel. "Noll didn't buy the old no-sex idea," recalls Russell, who announced to the team that Noll had an ulterior motive: "He wants to see our wives in their nighties!" The flinty coach blushed.

On the brink of a Super Bowl that could vindicate his tenure as head coach and end forty years of football futility in Pittsburgh, Noll seemed be enjoying himself for once. "He was smart enough to realize that this was what we all shot for, *lived* for. Enjoy it while it's going on," Russell says. "Plus he knew we were gonna win."

After practice one day, Russell recited from a locker-room copy of the *New Orleans Times-Picayune*. "Sociologically speaking," he read, "the Super Bowl is a propaganda vehicle which strengthens the

American social structure." Noll laughed when Joe Greene snatched the paper, saying, "I can't *stand* that shit," and tore it up.

Russell and Mansfield rented a car one night and went barhopping in the French Quarter. Hours later, Russell leaned forward on his barstool, pushing an empty glass toward Mansfield, and said, "Ray, it's two in the morning. I'm going to bed."

"Okay, but leave me the car."

Russell stumbled back to the team hotel. In the morning, seeing Mansfield in the lobby, he asked, "Where's the car?"

Mansfield said, "What car?"

On the night before the Super Bowl, the television in Mad Dog White's hospital room showed the top-rated *Mary Tyler Moore Show*. In an episode filmed the week before, Mary's boss, Lou Grant, was instructing anchor-buffoon Ted Baxter in football betting. Lou and Ted gave the points. They bet their bankroll on the Steelers—and lost. As the credits rolled, Mary read a disclaimer: "If the Pittsburgh Steelers win the actual Super Bowl tomorrow, we want to apologize to the Pittsburgh team and their fans."

The sitcom's writers had good reasons for their prediction. *The Mary Tyler Moore Show* was set in Minneapolis, home of the Vikings, and while the Steelers were 3-point favorites, plenty of smart money fell on the other side of the line. Minnesota was in the midst of a six-year streak of NFC Central titles. Led by slippery quarterback Fran Tarkenton and the Purple People Eaters front four of Alan Page, Carl Eller, Jim Marshall, and Gary Larsen, the 1974 Vikings had scored 310 points and allowed only 195. They had routed a good Oilers team coached by Sid Gillman by a score of 51–10 and outslugged the Rams 14–10 in the NFC Championship. Vikings coach Bud Grant was beloved by cultural conservatives who saw his strictness as an antidote to the sex-drugs-and-disco tide of the times. A gaunt beanpole with a steel-gray buzz cut, the six-three Grant had played forward for basketball's Minneapolis Lakers, feeding the ball to George Mikan as the Lakers won the 1950 NBA title. After a six-year pro football career he went into coaching, in which he emphasized discipline above all. Grant was no strategist. "I don't know that Bud could diagram five plays," said Tarkenton. The Minnesota coach believed in old-fashioned toughness. A nonsmoking teetotaler, he banned booze and cigarettes on team trips—a shocking move at the time. He banned heaters on the Vikings bench even in subzero temperatures, letting his players shiver while opponents kept warm. Grant even made his team practice lining up for the national anthem, hands over hearts, looking grimly respectful. The Raiders used to point at them and laugh.

But the Raiders weren't going to Super Bowl IX. Bud Grant's Vikings were, and Mary Tyler Moore's writers were among millions who expected them to win.

The Vikings and the Steelers lined up like overgrown schoolboys in a Tulane Stadium tunnel, standing in parallel single-file lines, waiting to be introduced to 80,997 ticket-holders and a TV audience of 80 million. Like gladiators about to enter the original Colosseum, they heard trumpets and a roaring crowd as they stood in the tunnel's half-light. Finally Glen Edwards, the Steelers' free safety, broke ranks to greet Vikings lineman Charles Goodrum, a college teammate at Florida A&M. "Goodrum! How you doing?"

Goodrum said nothing. He shook his head. Bud Grant had ordered his Vikings not to speak to the Steelers.

Edwards asked again, "How you doing, man?" He looked at the other Vikings. "What's wrong with you guys?" Finally he shrugged. "Well, you better buckle up!"

The Steelers stood a little taller than the Vikings thanks to equipment manager Tony Parisi. Parisi, fretting about recent rain on Tulane's slippery natural-grass field, had ordered new shoes with extralong cleats. L. C. Greenwood's, as always, were painted gold.

New Orleans police guarded the path from the tunnel to the field. Bradshaw followed his teammates through the corridor of cops, fighting his jumpy nerves. He'd gotten desperate enough to try hypnosis during the season, and it helped. "The fans were hating me, everything bothered me," he recalls. A Pittsburgh hypnotist calmed his nerves with three words: *Relax. Confidence. Concentrate.* Now, looking at the Super Bowl fans jostling behind the cops, reaching toward the players, he mumbled his mantra. *Relax. Confidence. Concentrate.* One of the fans was stout and red-faced, shirtless, wearing a Vikings helmet. While Bradhsaw watched, the man in the Vikings helmet collapsed, dead of a heart attack. "And it didn't stop the program for a second," Bradshaw would remember. "That's when I realized the Super Bowl wasn't a life-and-death situation—it was more important than that. Seconds later I ran onto the field."

Pittsburgh's defense had allowed a league-low 189 points over sixteen games. The Vikings' People Eaters had led the NFC, allowing 195. Minnesota quarterback Tarkenton was known as a scrambler but had thrown for a league-best 7.4 yards per pass attempt, double the Steelers' average of 3.7. Still the Steelers shut him down early. With no deep threat like the Raiders' Cliff Branch to fillet Pittsburgh's Cover Two, the Vikings spent the first quarter trying and failing to cross their own 40. In the second quarter, pinned to his own goal line, Tarkenton tossed a pitchout to halfback Dave Osborn, who fumbled. The ball caromed off one of Greenwood's golden shoes into the end zone. Tarkenton averted a Pittsburgh touchdown by falling on it as woozy Dwight White, who had gone from the hospital to the stadium, defying pneumonia, eluded silent tackle Goodrum and fell on Tarkenton for a safety. That was the lone score of the first half, which ended 2–0. Anyone who doubted that defense was still ascendant, or that the Steelers were its prime engine, had only to check the combined halftime scores of their last two postseason games: Pittsburgh 5, Opponents 3. What Howard Cosell called a "deleterious dearth of offense" was an ongoing problem for the Competition Committee, but Noll and the Steelers weren't complaining.

During a terse halftime speech, Noll focused on the second-half kickoff. "Let's start with a good deep kick." Kicker Roy Gerela took the coach's words to heart. Gerela opened the second half of Super Bowl IX by swinging his leg so hard that he slipped and nearly whiffed, topping an accidental onside kick that boinged off the wet turf. The Steelers recovered the bouncing ball at the Vikings' 30. Franco Harris's off-tackle run gained 24. Harris lost 3 yards on the next play, but he was not to be denied. On second-and-goal he swept left for 9 yards and the game's first touchdown. Gerela's point-after made it 9–0 Pittsburgh. The comedy continued when Greenwood batted a Tarkenton pass back to the Vikings' quarterback, who grabbed it, Yepremian-style, and with a far better arm than Garo Yepremian fired downfield for a 40-yard gain. A flurry of flags reminded him that the rules allow only one pass per play.

Lambert went down with a leg injury. Then Russell limped off with a torn hamstring. ("I leg-whipped a guy and my leg went numb.") Still the Vikings got nowhere. With the clock running down, Greene taunted them: "Run, you fucking faggots!" While Harris, Bleier, and a scrambling Bradshaw racked up 249 rushing yards on the day, Minnesota would average 29 inches per carry. Pittsburgh's Steel Curtain held the Vikings to 9 first downs, 17 yards rushing, and 119 total yards—Super Bowl records that still stand. Bradshaw, itching to throw, was a Griese-like 9 for 14 for 96 passing yards while Super Bowl MVP Harris ran for 158 yards, which was 39 more than the Vikings' total offense.

When it was over, Noll yanked off his headset. There were no Gatorade showers yet—that was ten years in the future, and the Steelers wouldn't dream of dousing Chuck Noll any more than the Packers in their heyday would have rubbed shaving-cream pies in Lombardi's face. Noll stood alone on the sideline for a long, slow-motion moment. If he cracked a smile, the game film didn't catch it. His wife, Marianne, ran up to him and Noll shook her hand, saying, "Well, we did it."

Ray Mansfield didn't want to leave the field. Bruised and turf-burned, the Steelers' center stood near midfield, soaking up post-game music, teammates' hugs, shouting, and cheers. Then he saw the football sitting on the turf. "Players were running right past it. Fans, too. We'd been fighting for it so long," Mansfield recalled, "and now it's just lying there." He scooped the ball up and gave it to his buddy Russell.

Minutes later the winners were whooping it up in Tulane's locker room, spraying each other with beer and champagne, waiting for Commissioner Rozelle to bring them the Lombardi Trophy. As captain of the defense, Russell would present a game ball to the Steelers' top defender, as he did after every game. "I was going to give the ball to Joe Greene, who had a hell of game," Russell recalls. "Then I looked over and saw the Chief."

Steelers owner Art Rooney, seventy-three, a bespectacled, respectable gent half a century removed from the Steeltown brawler who'd tackled Jim Thorpe and risked $2,500 to bring an NFL franchise to Pittsburgh, stood in a corner of the locker room. Russell, gimpy on his leg-whipping leg, took a step toward Rooney and said, "Chief, come up here. This is your ball." The white-haired owner stepped through cheering players as Russell yelled, "This one's for the Chief!" Rooney always said he loved that ball more than the Super Bowl trophy.

8

HAIL MARYS

I looked off the safety, Paul Krause," says Roger Staubach. "Then I flung it and hoped. They used to call that an alley-oop." It took three and a half seconds for Staubach's 55-yard rainbow to descend. The clock showed twenty-eight seconds as Cowboys receiver Drew Pearson, stride for stride with Vikings cornerback Nate Wright, bumped Wright and stutter-stepped around him. The ball came in, arcing to a point about a yard behind the two men.

"It didn't look good," Staubach remembers. He and the Cowboys were trailing the Vikings 14–10 in the 1975 NFC playoffs. The clock drained to 00:26 as Staubach's alley-oop slipped through Pearson's hands. Game over; Vikings win. Except that after it slipped through his hands, Pearson somehow pinned the ball between his elbow and his right hip and two-stepped into the end zone. Game over; Cowboys win. Just then something orange streaked past Pearson's feet. A flag? Offensive pass interference? No, it was an orange. Vikings fans feeling further screwed, endlessly screwed by their postseason history, were throwing fruit at the field. They thought Pearson had pushed off, and TV commentators agreed. The play spurred debate about using replays to review crucial plays. Instant-replay advocates said the new technology could help referees. Purists said it would take the human element out of the game. In any event the play stood. Staubach's bomb to Pearson won the game. Three years after the Immaculate Reception, the secular religion had another miracle, and the Vikings were losers again. Fans of the star-crossed Buffalo Bills, losers of four straight Super Bowls in the '90s, winners of none, might feel a kinship with Minnesotans, who saw their team make four Super Bowls from 1970 to '77 and lose by at least 10 points each time. The Vikings of the '70s lost with Alan Page, the first defensive player to win the MVP award, and 1975 MVP Fran Tarkenton. They lost Super Bowls with Page, Tarkenton, Carl Eller, Paul Krause, Ron Yary, and coach Bud Grant, all future Hall of Famers, a near-winning tradition that Minnesota teams of the '80s, '90s, '00s, and '10s have failed to live up to. Since 1970 the Vikings have made the playoffs twenty-four times, trailing only the Cowboys and the Steelers in that department, but they haven't reached the Super Bowl since 1977.

Staubach was giddy after the Cowboys' win in '75. Remembering the seconds when his heave to Pearson was in the air, he said, "I closed my eyes and said a Hail Mary." Desperation passes weren't new, but the name was. Quote-hungry reporters wrote the term in their spiral notebooks. Since then every last-second prayer has been a Hail Mary.

At the same time, Staubach's prayer answered one of Pete Rozelle's. The commissioner was eager to counter a growing view of pro football as a sport played by muscle-bound, drugged-up thugs cheered on by mean drunks. Too many NFL games were marred by drunken fights in the cheap seats. Fans seemed inspired by the hit movie *Network* and its mad newsman yelling, "I'm mad as hell and I'm not going to take it anymore!" At Minnesota's Metropolitan Stadium, seconds after the Hail Mary pass, a whiskey bottle followed the orange whizzing out of the stands. The bottle beaned field judge Armen Terzian, who dropped as if he'd been shot. Rozelle worried that he might have a ref's assassination on his hands, but Terzian suffered only a cut and a headache. The next day a relieved Rozelle opened his *New York Times* to the headline "Bloody Sunday for the Violent Game." He needed a hero to represent the modern NFL.

Roger Staubach was a smiling, curly-haired straight arrow out of the Naval Academy, class of 1964. After winning the Heisman Trophy, he skipped half a decade of NFL paychecks to serve a five-year hitch in the Navy. Tex Schramm and the Cowboys spent a tenth-round pick on him in the '64 draft, waited five years, and welcomed him to training camp in '69 as a twenty-seven-year-old rookie. A scrambling gambler with a knack for the game-breaking play, Staubach played with a white towel hanging from his belt that made him look like a hustling waiter. Six years older than Terry Bradshaw, a year older than Joe Namath, he played younger. Five years of military duty were easier on the knees and skull than NFL combat. At thirty-three, Staubach could scramble and strike like Bradshaw, if without so much arm, or loop an alley-oop like a right-handed Stabler without the hangover. While Namath and Bradshaw fought physical and personal demons, Staubach couldn't have been more comfortable in his skin. And despite his late start, he entered his prime with something Bradshaw couldn't match and Namath couldn't beat: a Super Bowl title. Staubach had started the 1971–72 season as a part-timer. Dallas coach Tom Landry had reduced him and Craig Morton to messenger quarterbacks, sending Morton into the game with a play, then replacing him with Staubach on the next play. Staubach eventually won the job, led the Cowboys to victory over Miami in Super Bowl VI, and was named the game's Most Valuable Player. Still he was Dallas coach Tom Landry's pawn. Unlike Namath, Bradshaw, Stabler, and almost every other pro quarterback, Staubach wasn't allowed to call his own plays. The Dallas offense was too complex for that, Landry said, and good-soldier Staubach followed orders. Usually. "My favorite play was the busted play," he says. Any play that allowed him to wing it. The former altar boy from Ohio was actually the perfect Texan, a churchgoing member of the Fellowship of Christian Athletes who liked to raise a little hell on the field, defying Landry's orders if he saw a man open. All Staubach wanted to do was win or lose on his own merits, his own arm and brains and heart and guts.

He was funny, too. Asked about Dallas's demanding fans, he said, "Cowboys fans love you, win or tie." And despite his monogamous, churchgoing habits, Roger Staubach was no prude. Asked about Namath's rep as a ladies' man, he said, "I like sex as much as Joe Namath does. I just have it with one woman."

After Hail Marying the hapless Vikings, Staubach and the Cowboys pounded the Rams 37–7 to advance to the tenth Super Bowl. That same day, two thousand miles away at Three Rivers Stadium, the Steelers and the Raiders faced off for the right to do the same.

"By then we really hated those Pittsburgh motherfuckers," says Oakland's Villapiano. "Year after year, it was them or us."

By then the World Football League's Birmingham Americans had won the upstart WFL's championship, the World Bowl. It was also the last WFL championship. A creditor seized the champions' uniforms in hopes that they might have some worth as souvenirs, but the Americans' jerseys proved less valuable than the McDonald's coupons the team used as meal vouchers.

The WFL struggled from the start. After the Philadelphia Bell announced ticket sales of 64,719 for a home game, reporters revealed the real paid attendance: 6,200. The WFL's Charlotte Hornets contrived to miss the playoffs after *making* the playoffs: the Hornets qualified for a first-round game but couldn't afford the road trip, so they forfeited. The Jacksonville Sharks' owner borrowed

$27,000 from the team's coach, then fired him. The Toronto North-
men of ex-Dolphins Larry Csonka, Paul Warfield, and Jim Kiick got
kicked out of Canada by Prime Minister Pierre Trudeau to protect
the Canadian Football League from US competition. The Northmen
became the Memphis Southmen. At their home opener, Southmen
fan Elvis Presley listened to Charlie Rich's national anthem, then
said to Rich, "Tough song, ain't it?" Soon WFL officials were trotting out star-spangled uniforms: they wanted receivers to wear
orange pants, with green pants for running backs and white pants
festooned with stars for quarterbacks. "I won't wear 'em," Kiick said.
"I'd look like a lime . . . or some kind of fruit." Csonka said he'd put
on lime-green pants "when the coaches wear pink suits with high
heels." When the WFL folded in 1975, Csonka joined the New York
Giants. Reflecting on what jumping leagues had taught him, he said,
"You can make a lot of money in sports."

In the end the WFL's prime function beyond enriching Csonka
and a few others was to woo the Dolphins' stars away from Miami,
hastening the end of the Dolphins' dominance, leaving the rest of
the decade open to anyone who could claim it.

In Pittsburgh, Noll corrected his one glaring blunder by install-
ing Bradshaw at quarterback once and for all. "We won the Super
Bowl and that established me as number one," Bradshaw told
Playboy. "I didn't do anything great except hand off to Franco, but
I was out there calling my own plays. I felt the vote of confidence
from Chuck Noll, which is really what I'd needed. All I needed was
that handshake: 'Hey, Terry, you played a great game and you're my
quarterback.'" Asked if that was a direct quote from Noll, Bradshaw
admitted, "Well, he never said it. I just pretended he did."

Linebacker Lambert was set to be the twitching heart of the Cover
Two for the near future.

Lambert's 1974 Rookie of the Year award, following Joe Greene's
1969 award and Franco Harris's in '72, proved that Noll and his

scouts were the game's best judges of talent. Pittsburgh's roster featured three of the last six rookies of the year, plus '74 draftees Swann and Stallworth. Favored to repeat in the AFC Central in 1975, the Steelers went 12-2 in the regular season, losing only to the Bills—O. J. Simpson breaking loose for 227 yards on 28 carries—and NFC West–champion Rams. The twenty-five-year-old Harris rushed for 1,246 yards, second only to Simpson in the NFL. No longer hitching rides to practice and taking the bus home, Super Bowl MVP Harris was a civic icon who seemed born for the Steeltown melting pot. His fans in the second deck at Three Rivers waved Italian flags and signs reading RUN PAISANO RUN, while Franco's Italian Army was an equal-opportunity outfit, with an Israeli unit and an Irish one that called him Frank O'Harris. When the waiters in the stadium's Allegheny Club cheered Harris, shouting, "Soul brother, *get it on*," Rocky the security guard said, "He may be a soul brother, but his legs are Italian."

Franco was the son of Cad Harris, an army supply sergeant who saw action in Europe in World War II, and his Italian war bride, Gina. Growing up in Mount Holly, New Jersey, just across the Pennsylvania line from Philadelphia, Franco considered himself black like his dad because the Italian kids chased him if he stepped into their neighborhood. When people asked what race he was, he said he was an individual. He had his own running style, too. Rather than slam into the line like Csonka or slip contact like Mercury Morris, Harris approached the line as if testing a force field, sometimes drifting sideways or backward a step while choosing his path. He loved the Steelers' reliable 13 Trap up the middle. On trap plays, a blocker "traps" his opponent by letting him go where he wants. When the pass-rusher makes his move, the offensive lineman blocks him farther in that direction, opening a hole where the pass-rusher started. The runner must read the block, waiting to let the hole develop before making his own move. Harris, six-two and

230 pounds with the feet of a hummingbird, had a gift for that sort of perusal. "He'd stop in the middle of a hole, then dart outside or inside," says linebacker Andy Russell. "Or put his head down and bowl you over. There were runners who made you miss, like O.J. and Floyd Little, and runners who'd go through you, like Csonka and John Riggins. Franco did both."

Harris wasn't eager to face the Raiders again. "They took cheap shots," he recalls. The black-clad rivals hadn't met in the regular season. While the Steelers claimed their fourth consecutive AFC Central title, John Madden's Raiders won their fourth straight AFC West crown with Madden throwing fits all the way, waving his fists as his face turned bright pink. The Raiders called him Pinky behind his back and at least once to his face. He was chewing out Biletnikoff when Freddie said, "I'm tired of this shit, Pinky." Madden burst out laughing. No dictator, he was just excitable. After a line judge flagged Jack Tatum for a cheap shot in Denver that year, Madden charged the official.

"You blind bastard!" he yelled.

"Who you calling a blind bastard?" the man asked.

"You look like the only blind bastard here!" said Madden as the ref threw another flag—15 yards for unsportsmanlike coaching.

The Raiders flew east for the 1975 AFC Championship. That was the year the league dispensed with alternating home fields in the playoffs, giving home field to the team with the better regular-season record. Thus the 12-2 Steelers hosted the 11-3 Raiders at Three Rivers Stadium, where the windchill at game time was twelve below zero. A tarp protecting the field had torn overnight, leaving the turf near the sidelines frozen and skating-rink slick. The visiting Raiders doubted the torn tarp was an accident. The field's icy periphery would give the home team an advantage over the Raiders, who ran more sideline routes, and the Steelers looked suspiciously well equipped for the cold, sporting special rubber cleats that equipment man Tony Parisi had ordered from Canada, warming their hands in fleece-lined pockets Parisi's wife had sewn to their jerseys. The first half played out as a trench battle, with Oakland stacking the line, daring Bradshaw to throw. The Raiders held Franco Harris to 34 yards in 17 bruising carries, the only points of the first half coming on a Roy Gerela field goal. After the third quarter the scoreboard stood frozen at 3–0 Steelers.

Harris took a fourth-quarter handoff and stepped to his left. He glided toward center Ray Mansfield's left heel, "but there was nothing there," Harris recalled, "so I kept sprinting outside. John Stallworth made a hell of a block." The second-year wideout toppled the Raiders' Jack Tatum and Monte Johnson with a single dive. Harris brushed off a tackle and cruised down the left sideline for a touchdown, retracing his Immaculate Reception steps on the same sideline three years earlier.

The Raiders charged back in the final minute. After the forty-eight-year-old Blanda's 41-yard field goal, his longest of the year, cut Pittsburgh's lead to 6 points with seventeen seconds left, the normally sure-handed Stallworth fumbled an onside kick. Oakland recovered. Stabler had time for one more play. He flung deep to Branch, who made the catch and set out for the icy sideline, hoping to stop the clock. Mel Blount corralled him, keeping Branch in bounds, as the clock ran down to 00:00. "We were shocked," recalls Oakland defensive end Ted Hendricks. Stabler had thrown for 246 yards, but for the seventh time in nine years, the Raiders had fallen in the playoffs to a team that went on to the Super Bowl. "One more play was all we needed," Stabler said. "How come time always runs out on us?"

Madden stood slump-shouldered in the visitors' locker room, mournfully answering questions. "What about turnovers, Al?" a reporter asked, confusing the coach with Oakland owner Al Davis. "My name's John, not Al," Madden said, "and John thinks it's all over.

This was going to be our year, the year we finally won everything after years of frustration, and now it's over. That's what John thinks."

Nobody outside Oakland felt much sympathy for John's team. Lynn Swann felt none. The Steelers' balletic receiver spent the night under observation at Allegheny General Hospital, watching the slow-motion replay that shocked viewers nationwide. On a third-quarter play that stirred the teams' bad blood, Oakland safety George "Hit Man" Atkinson had hooked a forearm around Swann's neck and hammered him to the rock-salted turf. Swann lay motionless. "I drilled his ass," Atkinson would tell Raiders chronicler Peter Richmond. "I hit him and drove his ass to the ground." Replay viewers missed the hit's immediate aftermath: Joe Greene bolted from the sideline and lifted his unconscious teammate. The image was a football pietà: Swann hanging limp, draped over Greene's brawny arms. Swann would be diagnosed with a severe concussion. Doctors said he might never play again. Atkinson said Swann was "soft." Pittsburgh and Oakland had just begun to fight, but the Steelers had won another round, earning the right to face the team they hated second-most.

Super Bowl X gave the Steelers a chance to join Lombardi's Packers and Shula's Dolphins as two-time Super Bowl champs. Aside from the trophy and the glory, they had visions of bonus checks dancing in their helmets. NFL players were starting to make more money, but Super Sunday's $15,000 winners' shares still represented a third of the average salary. While the Dallas Cowboys didn't make the Steelers see red the way the cheap-shot Raiders did, they were all that stood between the Steelers and the sport's biggest payday. And with the league's most complex offense, Dallas presented special challenges. Rather than plow forward for steady gains, the Cowboys danced around, employing multiple offensive sets and shifts, sending men in motion before the snap. "I really hate Dallas," said Steeler safety Glen Edwards. "They try to fool folks instead of outphysical-ing them, the way football should be played."

The Cowboys were the only pro team using the shotgun formation. "Starting that year, we made the shotgun central to our offense," Staubach says. "Tom Landry and Mike Ditka, one of Landry's assis-tants, told me, 'Roger, we're going to experiment with a shotgun on third down.' Hardly anyone had used it since the old single-wing days, but we could run draws and screens out of it, and it gave me more time to throw. I loved it!"

Landry's team had risen from the depths since its birth as an expansion club in 1960, the year coach Red Hickey's San Francisco 49ers introduced the shotgun to the NFL. The Cowboys went 0-11-1 in their inaugural season. When cowboy-movie hero Roy Rogers rode his horse, Trigger, onto the field for a halftime show, frustrated Dallas fans pelted them with paper cups and ice cubes. The franchise didn't get its first victory until the following season: a 27–24 squeaker over the equally lousy Pittsburgh Steelers. But Dallas got modern in that 1961 season, when Cowboys executive Tex Schramm began tinkering with a mainframe computer IBM had used to crunch data at the 1960 Winter Olympics. Schramm designed a questionnaire on which the team's scouts rated players rated from 1 to 9 on fifteen variables, from strength to speed to attitude. To analyze the results, the Cowboys paid for time on one of the company's latest computers. A machine the size and breadth of a bank-vault door, the IBM 7090-7094 was the most sophisticated computer ever built, with about one ten-thousandth the computing power of a modern laptop. The machine turned the scouts' ratings into columns of numbers on perforated printouts. As Schramm's system evolved, he and his statisticians tweaked and retweaked their formula. After judging speed to be 14.64 percent of a tight end's value in 1961, they reduced speed to 11 percent in 1962, boosting competitiveness from 7 to 10.5 percent. The result was quality control. While the Steelers beat the bushes for unnoticed talent, the Cowboys reduced the human element in scouting, anticipating by twenty years the approach that baseball geeks would call sabermetrics. During the '60s the Cowboys' ascent matched that of the NASA space program down the road in Houston. The gleamingly modern Cowboys pioneered luxury boxes in Texas Stadium, where the roof was open to the sky "so God can watch his favorite team." They anointed themselves America's Team. (When Don Shula asked Schramm who decided that Dallas was America's Team, Schramm said, "I did.") With grim efficiency, the Cowboys went from winless to winners. When someone asked Dallas fullback Walt Garrison if he'd ever seen Landry smile, Garrison said, "No, but I've only been here nine years."

Landry's Cowboys missed the playoffs only once in a nineteen-year stretch from 1966 to 1984. Sportswriter Leigh Montville called them "a team of efficiency and controversy and rhinestone glitter." A team with a choirboy passer and trick formations that made the lunch-bucket Steelers want to throw up. After Dallas thumped the Rams to advance to Super Bowl X against the Steelers, Jack Lambert toured sunny Miami the week before the game. Few men ever looked more out of place on a beach than the Steelers' pale, lumbering, gap-toothed linebacker. Asked his opinion of Cowboys quarterback Staubach, Lambert said, "I hope a shark bites his arms off."

Staubach still laughs about that line. "Lambert was a mean son of a gun," he says. "No front teeth, foaming at the mouth—he intimidated some of our players."

Pittsburgh was a 7-point Super Bowl favorite on the strength of a defense that had allowed only 12 points per game. The Steel Curtain defense would send eight of its eleven starters to the Pro Bowl. One of them, Texas native Fats Holmes, no more of a beachcomber than Lambert, said, "I feel like eating palm trees. I don't like this place. It's for people with arthritis who come here to play golf and die."

The Cowboys rode into Miami with nicknames of their own—scrambling "Roger Dodger" Staubach, also called Captain Comeback; hard-hitting safety Cliff Harris, aka Captain Crash; flashy linebacker Thomas "Hollywood" Henderson; and a Doomsday Defense anchored by defensive end Ed "Too Tall" Jones. The Big D defense had allowed 19 points per game. Its shutdown reputation was due mostly to Landry, a former All-Pro cornerback who now paced the sideline in his trademark checked suit and fedora, arms crossed, lips pursed like a schoolmarm's. Trained as an industrial engineer at the University of Texas, Landry was called "the man with the slide-rule mind." He had invented the standard 4-3 defense as the New York Giants' defensive coordinator in the '50s. (The Giants' offensive coordinator was Vince Lombardi.) Before the 4-3, NFL teams used five defensive linemen. Landry moved one of them back off the line. In Landry's scheme, the one in the middle stood up from his primordial crouch and moved back two yards. Presto: the middle linebacker. The Giants' Sam Huff was the original, a defensive signal-caller who could *blitz* (the German word for lightning), tackle Jim Brown, or cover Raymond Berry, all while serving as an assistant coach on the field. The middle linebacker position demanded versatility above all. It still does, which explains why middle linebackers haven't ballooned in size as the decades have passed. In the half century between Huff and today, a period starring six-three, 245-pound Hall of Famer Dick Butkus as well as six-four, 220-pound Hall of Famer Jack Lambert, middle linebackers stayed recognizably man-shaped while other players morphed into 300- and 350-pound mammoths. Fifty years ago, Sam Huff stood six-one and weighed 235. Today Ray Lewis stands six-one and weighs 245.

Landry refined the 4-3 defensive set with a wrinkle called the Flex. The Flex defense pulled two of the Cowboys' down linemen a yard back from the line of scrimmage. (As with the 4-3, being modern on defense meant stepping back from the trenches to a spot where a man could see what the offense was doing, and react.) Which linemen? That was the flexible question that gave the scheme its name. The answer depended on Dallas's computer-driven study of opponents' habits.

The Cowboys figured to see plenty of Franco Harris in Super Bowl X. Landry expected his Flex defense to hold Harris under 100 yards. With Dallas defenders reading holes from their side of the line while Franco did the same from his, the Flex could counter Pittsburgh's traps. In their NFC Championship blowout of LA, the Doomsday D had held Rams star Lawrence McCutcheon to 10 yards on 11 carries; the Rams had gained 22 yards on the ground to the Cowboys' 195.

"We were ready," Staubach says. "We were the only NFC team that could stay with those great AFC teams of the '70s—Pittsburgh, Miami, and Oakland. And I'll tell you something: going into that Super Bowl with the Steelers, we were the better team."

On January 18, 1976, both teams wore red, white, and blue patches honoring the nation's bicentennial. The tenth Super Bowl was part of a national celebration that included Bicentennial Minutes on TV, with celebrities narrating bits of US history, and a Super Bowl halftime featuring the polyester-clad pop group Up with People, serenading the nation with a tune called "Two Hundred Years and Just a Baby." With their Pepsodent smiles and peppy lyrics hailing people as "the best kinda folks we know," Up with People danced as stiffly as the Dallas backfield while thousands of red, white, and blue balloons climbed toward the Goodyear Blimp. The blimp, looming large on 30 million TV screens, would soon do the same in the disaster movie *Black Sunday*, which was filming in the Orange Bowl that day, actor Robert Shaw racing to keep terrorists from blowing up the Super Bowl. As the Steelers and the Cowboys took the field, CBS ran Ford and Hamm's beer commercials that cost the sponsors $220,000 a minute, triple the rate for the first Super Bowl. Ray

Mansfield, the Steelers' veteran center, stood on the Orange Bowl's blue-green AstroTurf taking in the pageantry—blimp, TV cameras, eighty thousand fans. He heard someone call, "Hi, Mr. Mansfield!" It was Cowboys tight end Ron Howard, who'd been a high schooler when Mansfield worked as a student teacher.

A few yards away, Steelers kicker Roy Gerela warmed up his leg, booting balls through the end zone. Oddly enough there were no nets behind the end zones. "Roy kicked about seven balls into the stands," Mansfield recalled, "and the fans kept 'em." Gerela climbed into the seats to retrieve a practice ball only to get bumped and shoved by rowdy spectators. He hustled back to the field. He and Mansfield sneaked to the Dallas bench and stole one of the Cowboys' balls for Gerela to kick.

Bradshaw lobbed a pregame pass to Swann, who dropped it. The willowy receiver hadn't been expected to suit up. After his mugging by George Atkinson in the AFC Championship and two nights in the hospital, Swann's timing was off, his concentration fuzzy. Doctors said another hit like Atkinson's could disable him for life. Would he sit out the Super Bowl? Noll left the choice to Swann, who was dying to start if only to prove he wasn't soft. Due to his girlish name and boyhood ballet training, opponents never tired of challenging Swann's manhood. "Girl," they called him between plays. "You pussy. Get up, girl." Even thirty-seven years later, Oakland's Jim Otto sniffs, "Lynn Swann was a crybaby." Now Atkinson, Otto, and the Raiders were out of the picture, but the Cowboys picked up the story line. "I'm not going to hurt anyone intentionally," Dallas safety Cliff Harris announced before Super Bowl X. "But getting hit again while he's running a pass route must be in the back of Swann's mind." Headhunter Harris was speaking in code. He might deny malice in public, but head-hunting was accepted, even applauded, ten years into the Super Bowl era. Helmet-to-helmet hits made Howard Cosell's *Monday Night* highlights. They earned cheers and pats on the back in team film sessions. Enforcers such as Cliff Harris and the Raiders' Soul Patrol didn't care if they won by intimidation or injury as long as they won. Even the Steelers were coached to injure opponents. One of Noll's assistant coaches told linemen, "If you get a chance to break a leg, do it."

Swann announced that he would play. "I read what Cliff Harris said. He was trying to intimidate me. He said I'd be afraid. He doesn't know Lynn Swann."

The Cowboys opened their box of tricks on the game's opening kickoff. Preston Pearson fielded the kick and handed off on a reverse to Hollywood Henderson, who saw only kicker Gerela between him and the end zone. After Henderson high-stepped for 48 yards, Gerela saved a touchdown with a clumsy, stumbling tackle but bruised his ribs on the play, a bruise that would affect the final score.

The game's next surprise was a botched punt. Pittsburgh punter Bobby Walden bobbled a low snap and fell on the ball. Dallas took over at the Pittsburgh 29. After a play fake, Staubach hit Drew Pearson for a touchdown—the only first-quarter touchdown the Steelers allowed all season. Dallas 7, Pittsburgh 0.

During the break between quarters, 58 million TV viewers feasted their eyes on the high-kicking Dallas Cowboys Cheerleaders. Founded in 1972, the half-dressed cheer squad became a poster- and calendar-selling phenomenon thanks largely to close-ups during Super Bowl X. CBS producer Chuck Milton said he focused on the Cowboys Cheerleaders "to give the fans a little sex with their violence."

Dallas safety Harris focused on the latter. When Swann came over the middle on a first-quarter pass route, Harris just missed decking him. "You got lucky," Harris said.

"What?"

"Lucky!" They yelled to hear each other over the crowd noise. "I'm coming after you!"

Swann said, "Come ahead. If anyone gets hurt, it's gonna be you."

Tough talk from a professional target, but barking at Harris calmed the butterflies in Swann's stomach. After days of bleary practices, he'd worried that he wouldn't be ready for the Super Bowl. Minutes after his shouting match with Cliff Harris he made a leaping 32-yard catch—his first catch since Atkinson put him in the hospital. *There,* Swann thought. *That's better.* He felt sharp and sticky-fingered. The Steelers drove to a third-and-1 at the Dallas 7-yard line. Bradshaw knew the Cowboys expected a handoff to Franco Harris. Noll did, too. Noll's game plan emphasized a grind-it-out running game. So Bradshaw called a pass. "Three thirty-three," he shouted in the huddle. A three-tight-end formation. The Cowboys recognized it—they knew the Steelers always ran from this formation. And Bradshaw knew they knew.

Tight end Randy Grossman faked a block. Grossman peeled toward the end zone; Bradshaw hit him with a bullet. Touchdown. Sore-chested Gerela's point-after tied the score at 7. If Bradshaw expected a hug or handshake from Coach Noll, he didn't get it. Noll nodded his way, that was all.

After a field goal put Dallas ahead 10–7, the Steelers faced third-and-6 from their own 10. Bradshaw called signals. Thinking *relax, confidence, concentrate,* he dropped back to his goal line. He let fly a 53-yarder that came down an inch out of Swann's reach. Or not quite an inch—Swann dived, stretching flat-out horizontal, cornerback Mark Washington falling away as Swann reeled in the pass, floating for an instant until gravity took hold again and he came down with the ball. Thirty-six years later, Swann's grab is still the best in Super Bowl history. It's still discussed as one of the sport's peerless moments: great throw, near-perfect coverage, perfect concentration, perfect catch. But it wasn't a touchdown, and Pittsburgh's drive stalled at the Cowboys' 19.

With twenty-two seconds left in the half, Gerela lined up a 36-yard field goal. This one fluttered wide left. Dallas took a 3-point lead into the locker room despite gaining only 98 first-half yards to the Steelers' 194. Steelers placekicker Gerela iced his bruised ribs. The news got worse for Pittsburgh: Joe Greene was done for the day, hobbled by a groin pull. Linebackers Russell and Lambert would have to play meaner.

The Steelers made the first big play of the second half, a third-quarter interception by cornerback J. T. Thomas. He ran it back to the Dallas 25. Franco Harris carried three times—left, then right, then left—for a first down. But Bradshaw overthrew Swann in the end zone, and the Steelers stalled. Gerela, wincing, pulled a 33-yard field goal. Another miss. Cliff Harris *loved* that. The Cowboys' Captain Crash jogged to Gerela, patted him on the helmet, and said. "Nice going, that really helps us."

Lambert wasn't about to let the Cowboys insult a teammate. He plowed into Harris and hurled him to the turf. Players from both teams came running, ready to fight.

Referee Norm Schachter pointed at Lambert. "You're out of this game!"

"What? This is the Super Bowl," Lambert said. "You can't throw me out."

Russell chased Lambert and said, "Jack, calm down. Don't be insane." Russell hated Harris, too, but they were already missing Greene. "We can't afford for you to get thrown out."

Referee Schachter, still pointing at Lambert, said, "Get in the huddle and shut up."

Lambert said, "Yes, sir."

Soon Lambert downed Preston Pearson for one of his 14 tackles on the day. Then he kicked Pearson. "That set me off," Staubach recalls. "I hollered at Lambert, saying things I'd go to confession for. Oh, I was hot. One of the officials said, 'Roger, I didn't think you talked like that!' I got up in Lambert's face, but then I realized I didn't really want to take him on. I kept hoping one of our linemen would come over and smack him."

Dallas still led 10–7. With eleven minutes remaining Mitch Hoopes, the Cowboys' rookie punter, took a long snap with his back to the goal line. Pittsburgh sent a ten-man rush. Rusher Reggie Harrison sidestepped a blocker, launched himself at Hoopes, and blocked the punt. The ball rebounded through the end zone for a safety that cut the Cowboys' lead to 10–9. After the ensuing free kick, the Steelers stalled again in Dallas territory. Gerela, gritting his teeth, punched a 36-yard field goal that tumbled over the crossbar. Pittsburgh 12, Dallas 10.

On the next series, the Steelers' front four took their stances, itching to go after Staubach. Lambert stood behind them, shivering with eagerness. They charged, Staubach threw—a pass that safety Mike Wagner intercepted and carried to the Dallas 7. Again the Flex defense stiffened. Franco Harris hit the line and lost the ball, but recovered his own fumble. In Roy Blount's sideline account, Harris "fumbled up into the air, looked up at the ball as an unusually collected man might look up at his arm just blown away, and snatched it back." Again Gerela gutted out a field goal, this one an 18-yarder to cap a four-series, 8-point run by Pittsburgh.

After an L. C. Greenwood sack and a Hoopes punt, the Steelers got the ball back. With three and a half minutes left, the Steelers led 15–10. Bradshaw clapped his clammy hands in the Pittsburgh huddle. He'd always suspected that men such as Franco and Greene and Lambert and Noll had an easier row to hoe than he. They were more sure of themselves. Not now. Expecting a blitz that would leave Swann in single coverage, Bradshaw called 68 Basic. A deep ball.

Dallas blitzed. Linebacker D. D. Lewis had a bead on Bradshaw but the quarterback ducked sideways, slipping a step to his left. He threw toward Swann just as tackle Larry Cole flattened Bradshaw with a haymaker to the chin. He went down like a sandbag. "I was out cold before I hit the ground," he recalled. Sixty-five yards downfield, Swann pulled the ball in and glided to the end zone. Cornerback Washington fell again, his hand clawing down the middle of the 88 on Swann's back. The achy Gerela flubbed the point-after, but the Steelers looked safe, up 21–10 with 3:02 to play.

Staubach drove the Cowboys 80 yards on 4 passes. Suddenly the score was 21–17. Landry called for an onside kick. Pittsburgh recovered. Three runs and three Dallas time-outs later, the Steelers faced fourth-and-9 at the Cowboys' 41. The Cowboys had no time-outs left; a decent punt would pin them inside their 20. At this point, roughly a hundred out of a hundred other coaches would send in the punting unit.

Noll went for the first down.

Andy Russell's jaw dropped. Was his coach as nuts as Lambert?

Dallas coach Landry thought, *Thank you.*

Noll had his reasons. His punter, Walden, had already bobbled a snap and nearly had two punts blocked. Noll believed above all in his defense. Still his second-guessable decision left defensive captain Russell shaking his head as Rocky Bleier picked up 2 yards on the fourth-and-9. "I wasn't going to second-guess Chuck Noll, but I couldn't figure it," Russell says. "We had a four-point lead and a chance to push them back. Instead we give Staubach the ball with field position."

Staubach led the Cowboys' offensive unit onto the field. Staubach ran for 11 yards to the red, white, and blue NFL symbol at midfield. He hit Preston Pearson for 12 yards, Pearson turning inside when he should have gotten out of bounds. Staubach fired incomplete to stop the clock, but Pearson's misstep had burned twenty seconds. With twelve seconds left, Staubach launched a Hail Mary—deflected, incomplete. There was time for one more Hail Mary on Staubach's last-minute rosary. From the shotgun, he took the final snap with three seconds to play. He pump-faked and threw deep. His pass was in midflight as the clock ticked to 00:00.

Tipped in the end zone, the ball was still alive. Steelers safety Edwards picked it out of the air and was still running as his teammates poured onto the field. Game over, Noll's risky call vindicated, the Steelers' Super Bowl title defended. Bradshaw had literally stepped up, ducking a Dallas rush that tested his skill and his skull. Lambert had added a touchdown-saving deflection to his 14 tackles and momentum-turning throwdown of Cliff Harris. Swann won the MVP award for his Super Bowl–record 161 yards on only 4 catches.

Moments later, Noll faced reporters firing questions about the last series. Wasn't he worried Staubach would beat him with a Hail Mary, the way he beat Minnesota?

"No."

"Why not?"

"We're not Minnesota."

"What about Lambert?" somebody asked. "Why'd he go after Cliff Harris?"

"Jack Lambert," said Noll, "is the defender of all that is right."

9

"KNOCK THEIR DICKS OFF"

That winter, in *Mackey vs. NFL*, the players' union beat the Rozelle Rule in court. That meant the commissioner could no longer order compensation—usually high-round draft picks—for teams that lost free agents. The Rozelle Rule had effectively tied players to the teams that drafted them. With its demise, NFL players were free to sell their services to the highest bidder—a right the NFL Players Association promptly gave up in the next round of bargaining with owners. In March 1977, in exchange for what amounted to a pocketful of beads ($13.65 million over ten years), the union accepted a new version of the Rozelle Rule. Thirteen million seemed like a fortune at the time, but turned out to be a pittance compared to what NFL players might have earned as true free agents. The players would beat NFL owners in court again in 1987, only to settle for modified free agency and a salary cap.

Though the NFLPA proved weaker in the long run than its baseball and basketball counterparts, its members felt fatter and happier as the '70s progressed. Steelers captain Andy Russell's pay went from $12,000 his rookie year to $100,000 in 1976, worth about $400,000 in 2012 dollars. Jack Lambert held out and won a $200,000 contract. Franco Harris was also at $200,000, plus a white Thunderbird he got for endorsing a Pittsburgh Ford dealership. Terry Bradshaw was at $400,000. In the bicentennial year a growing NFL made room for eighty-six new players by adding two expansion teams, the Seattle Seahawks and the Tampa Bay Buccaneers. The Seahawks would go 2-12 in their first season while Tampa Bay proved itself the anti-Miami by going 0-14. The league's new television package was worth $107 million, a 70 percent boost in only two seasons. To put that number in perspective, it was 328 times the value of the NFL's original TV contract signed in 1962, a huge sum but a pocketful of dimes compared to the growth that lay ahead. The $107 million that delighted NFL owners in '76 was less than one-half of one percent the size of the roughly $40 billion TV deal the league would sign in 2011, when the NFL's televised rights surpassed the GDP of Lebanon and Kenya, outstripping the market capitalization of the vast majority of the S&P 500. With rising TV ratings, expansion, ever-bigger and faster players, and new rules that favored offense, the league was taking on its modern form.

In the spring of '76 the Competition Committee banned spearing ballcarriers who fall or slip and make no move to get up. The "Ben Davidson Rule" was named for the Oakland defender who'd famously speared Chiefs quarterback Len Dawson in an apparent attempt to cut Dawson in half. "I was honored," recalls Davidson. "Getting an illegal move named after you—that's pretty Raider, huh?"

Stabler was Oakland's best-paid player at $200,000 a year (up from $37,500 in 1974). It stood to reason that Pittsburgh's stars earned more—the Steelers were back-to-back champions and the Raiders were . . . what? The class of the AFC West? No NFL team had a better record since 1968, when the Raiders lost the only Super Bowl they got into. They had reached six conference championships since then only to go 0-6 in those games, losing each time to the eventual Super

Bowl champion. Oakland's frustrations ate at Al Davis, who believed every year was going to belong to his silver-and-black. At one league meeting, the Oakland owner was sitting with Commissioner Rozelle and the Cowboys' Tex Schramm. "When we win a Super Bowl, I'm taking some time off," Davis said. "I'll climb Mt. Kilimanjaro, forget football for a while."

"Gee, Al," said Schramm, "do you think Mt. Kilimanjaro will still be there then?"

In 1976 "Madden gave a speech on the first day of training camp," Villapiano recalls. "He was sweating—really fired up. He was so pissed we kept losing to Pittsburgh." Madden said the Raiders were switching to a 3-4 that year, the Orange Defense, to make better use of their linebackers. The 3-4 represented a further step in the evolution of defense, with yet another down lineman turning into a linebacker. A three-man front with four linebackers suited Oakland's personnel and freewheeling style. Otis Sistrunk, nose tackle Dave Rowe, and newly signed John Matuszak would bull the line while Villapiano, Hendricks, and two other linebackers blitzed or filled holes or dropped into coverage. As for pass coverage, Madden said, "We'll play a Cover Three," a zone rotating toward the weak side, "and a Cover One." The Cover One was man-to-man with a free safety deep. "On offense, we're gonna trap block and run the ball down their throats."

Madden paused. The players expected to hear more specifics. Instead he clapped his hands. "This is our year, so let's not get fancy. Let's just kick ass."

During camp the team bunked at the El Rancho Tropicana, a shabby motel where the ambience was boot camp meets *Animal House*. "We practiced hard and partied the same way," recalls Stabler, who led by example. Moments before bedcheck at eleven, Stabler's black Corvette would zip into the parking lot, skidding backward into a space near his suite—the better to make a fast getaway later.

The fully dressed Snake would slip into bed before the assistant coaches came around, "but they'd usually skip his room anyway," Otto says, "because if Stabler wasn't there, they didn't want to know. They'd whisper, 'Don't tell Madden—he'll blow his top!'"

Stabler shared Suite 147 with Biletnikoff and three others. The suite was party central for the pigeon-toed passer and his buddies, the walls festooned with bras and panties, the medicine cabinet stocked with A-200 Pyrinate, an ointment for fighting crab lice. Three wheezing old refrigerators held beer, pies, and candy bars. Stabler and friends lounged around drinking, playing records, and watching TV, sending rookies out to scout the local bars. "A Raider has to be resourceful, determined, and quick-witted at all times, and this is one of them times," Stabler told the rookies in his adenoidal drawl. "Raiders are also expected to sweet-talk women."

On forays to the Hilltopper and Melendy's Lounge, their favorite dive bars, Raiders enjoyed Pass-the-Pitcher Nights that bled happily into pass-the-flask mornings. "We were a team of individualists," recalls Hendricks. A six-seven, 235-pound physics major from the University of Miami, he'd been a star with the Colts and Packers but found a band of kindred spirits when he joined the Raiders in '75. "Ted was one of us right off," Stabler says. "He came to his first Raider practice *on horseback*. I'll never know where he got the horse, but we look up and here's this huge, gangly guy riding onto the field with a German army helmet on his head, waving a traffic cone like a lance. He rode up to Madden and said, 'Coach, I'm ready to play some football.' Hendricks's nickname used to be Mad Stork, but we called him Kick 'Em, short for Kick 'Em in the Head Ted. One time Kick 'Em smashed his head into a locker and caved it in. The locker, not his head."

"My big contribution to training camp was the weight-lifting bench," says Hendricks. "The coaches prescribed a major weight-lifting regimen that year, so I designed a bench. We dragged it onto the practice field, and we strung barbed wire on it. The final touch was a five-hundred-pound barbell. The barbell was fake—it weighed about thirty pounds. We'd run out to the bench and pump that five hundred like it was nothing, showing the coaches how strong we were."

Hendricks shared his new team's quirky take on what he called "the weird world of pro football." Madden walked the sideline urging the Raiders to hit opponents hard enough to "knock their dicks off." His favorite motivational saying was "Don't worry about the blind mule, just load the wagon." Nobody knew what that was supposed to mean. One afternoon guard George Buehler, the team's mad scientist, strapped firecrackers to a radio-controlled tank and sent it into the coaches' office, where it exploded. When Madden hustled out, pink and sooty, Buehler sent the charred tank in hot pursuit of the coach. Another time, someone hired a girl to streak the practice field. "We saw this naked woman, running hard," Tom Flores says. "But she didn't realize how long a football field is. Around midfield she started running out of gas, like a lineman running back a fumble. She slowed down and staggered away. But she got a nice round of applause."

The veterans were missing Jim Otto. Double-zero had retired after fifteen years in the league, leaving Oakland vets to tell rookies how "Pops" had talked his way into one of Madden's practices with that torn-up, blackened leg of his and went on to make All-Pro, and how he once made bed check by lifting a car. "He was in a bar that just had one door," Stabler said. "Now, some guys felt Pops was a little too much of a good citizen. They figured he ought to miss curfew at least once. So they moved his VW Bug to where it *plugged* the door. Nobody was goin' through that door. Well, Pops squeezes himself out the bathroom window. Goes around to his car, squats down, hauls up on his front bumper. Moves the car an inch. Goes to the back, another inch. He kept that up till he could drive away, and he made bed check."

By 1975 the mangled, thirty-seven-year-old Otto had known it was time to call it quits. He asked Madden to give him one more play, and Madden used him in a preseason game. "This was the guy who snapped the ball on the franchise's very first play back in 1960, when *I* was the quarterback," Flores recalls, "and every single Raider play after that, for fifteen years. On his very last play, Pops snaps the ball and just *labels* the guy across the line—drives the label on his helmet right through him. Then he limps off the field with a smile on his face. One last hit."

Dave Dalby replaced Otto at center in '76. Davis and Madden retooled the defensive line with one of the sport's leading head cases, John Matuszak. At six-eight and 280, "the Tooz" had biceps like the cables on the Golden Gate Bridge. While squandering his potential as the first overall pick in the 1973 draft, he may have led the league in substance abuse. As former Raiders team physician Rob Huizenga put it, "Some guys took low levels of amphetamines before games. They were called crop dusters. Others indulged more heavily. They were 747s. The Tooz was called John Glenn." Matuszak had already flopped with two other teams. In Kansas City he fought with his wife, who tried to run him over with their car while he fled to a cemetery and hid behind a gravestone. They made up by having sex in the Chiefs' locker room. Later Matuszak was popping pills and guzzling Chivas Regal when he keeled over. He wasn't breathing. Chiefs coach Paul Wiggin pounded on Matuszak's chest until he came around. Kansas City traded him to the Redskins, who released him. Skins coach George Allen said he couldn't use a player whose diet consisted of "vodka and Valium, breakfast of champions."

In fact the Tooz breakfasted on bagels slathered with Cheez Whiz, chased with high-test drugs. This was not out of character for a Raider except for the bagels. According to former team physician Huizenga, who joined the franchise in 1983, "The Tooz was hardly the only player looking for an edge in the '70s. It was the ape-human stage of sports medicine in football. Horse testosterone—why not? As for dosage, they figured that if one was good, three was better. And you have to ask yourself: if you were an NFL lineman in 1976, would you have played clean? Your performance may suffer. You could cost yourself thousands of dollars, or your career. And you'd no longer be part of the group. Your teammates would look down on you. I don't blame the players as much as I blame team doctors who were out of their minds, thinking of Super Bowl rings."

Linebackers Hendricks and Villapiano had pestered Madden and Davis about Oakland's need for a dominator on the defensive line. They told the owner, "Al, we can't play a three-four without help. Get us a defensive end." Finally Madden asked Hendricks if he thought free-agent Matuszak might fill the bill. Or was the Tooz too much of a wing nut?

"Look around you, John," Hendricks said. "What's one more going to hurt?"

The next day, Davis stopped Villapiano and said, "Phil, I got you your fucking defensive end. Now you can help look after him."

Bay Area bartenders learned what to pour when the Raiders rolled in after practice: Left Sides were triple Scotches for left-side defenders Villapiano and Matuszak; Right Sides were triple Crown Royals for right-side defenders Hendricks and Otis Sistrunk. They'd often drink with fans who happened by, but few fans could keep up. "We'd each have three or four Left Sides or Right Sides," says Villapiano, "to warm up for a night out." And while Matuszak didn't reform—he chain-smoked joints and added cocaine, quaaludes, steroids, speed, and HGH—he was dead set on making the most of his chance with a team he already loved. For his first meeting with owner Davis, Matuszak dressed up in a black suit and silver shirt. Says Villapiano, "Tooz was so glad to be a Raider he wanted to spill blood for us."

Davis liked to wander the weight room, making sure he was getting full effort from his employees. He smiled watching Matuszak bench four hundred pounds, nothing much compared to today's strongest linemen, who bench five hundred with ease, but enough to make him the strongest 1976 Raider as well as the tallest. Still Matuszak was a second-stringer when the Raiders broke camp at the end of August. That night, per team tradition, the rookies lined up in the order in which they'd been drafted. Howling like coyotes, they piled into veterans' cars for the annual Rookie Parade, a crooked procession through Santa Rosa. Some stood in the back of a flatbed truck, tossing candy to puzzled bystanders. Upon reaching the highway, the convoy peeled out, slowing only when the lead vehicle was pulled over by the California Highway Patrol. Luckily for the players, the patrolmen were Raiders fans. They gave the caravan a police escort to Melendy's Lounge, then returned to the party after they got off duty. The festivities culminated with an air-hockey tournament. "There are two rules," party commissioner Villapiano announced. "Rule number one, you gotta be drunk. And rule number two, you gotta cheat."

Enforcing the first rule was simple. One of the off-duty cops let the Raiders use his Breathalyzer. As for rule number two, tournament favorites Stabler and Biletnikoff brought a secret weapon.

Honorary Air-Hockey Queen Carol Doda jounced through the door in a silver-and-black outfit that made no attempt to hide her 44-25-35 figure. The star attraction at San Francisco's Condor Club, a strip joint that billed itself as "home of the world's first topless and bottomless entertainment," the thirty-eight-year-old Doda was among the first silicone-enhanced exotic dancers. "I loved the Oakland Raiders. Everybody did," she recalls today. "Fred Biletnikoff and Ken Stabler used to come see my show at the Condor. Fred liked to have a quiet sort of good time. Ken was more animated, a leader who rode high in the saddle like John Wayne. I agreed to help them with their air-hockey tournament, and I was well received."

"Everybody was hollering their heads off," Villapiano recalls. "Carol Doda pulls out an enormous breast, leans over the air-hockey table, and blocks the goal with it. There was no way the other guys could score! It was the ultimate Raider defense."

The Steelers, whose pranksters tended more toward water cups on doorsills and Heet ointment in jockstraps, opened 1976 with the champions' traditional exhibition against the top graduating seniors from college teams. Once a premier event, the Chicago College All-Star Game had featured future president Gerald Ford and Texas Christian's Sammy Baugh for the collegians, who defeated the pros nine times, including a 20–17 victory over Lombardi's 1963 Packers. By the '70s, however, the fireworks had fizzled. Collegians could no longer keep up with pros, even with the NFL coaches pulling their starters early. In the forty-third and last College All-Star Game, the Steelers faced a college lineup starring Archie Griffin, Lee Roy Selmon, Chuck Muncie, and Mike Haynes. Pittsburgh went ahead 24–0 without breaking a sweat. When a downpour stopped the action in the fourth quarter, hundreds of soggy, beery fans stormed the field and tore down the goalposts. The teams surrendered Soldier Field to the mob with 1:22 on the clock, making the last College All-Star Game officially endless. Pete Rozelle crossed the game off the NFL calendar.

With TV ratings in mind, Rozelle's scheduling committee sent the Steelers to Oakland to start the regular season. The first half was marred by shoving, spitting, and taunting on both sides, with Jack Tatum and George Atkinson threatening Swann, who got thumped on every pattern. In the second quarter, Bradshaw slipped the Raider rush and found Franco Harris open. Fifteen yards away, Hit Man Atkinson delivered a forearm shiver to the base of Swann's neck. It was an evil, cheap shot, Atkinson's malice signaled by the fact that he'd ignored Harris running past him with the ball.

Swann collapsed with another concussion. Today such an attack like that would get the defender a hefty fine and suspension. That day no official threw a flag. With Swann out, Oakland beat the Steelers 31–28, a loss that left Noll as angry as he'd ever been. "You have a criminal element in all aspects of society," he told reporters. "Apparently we have it in the NFL, too." No one doubted that he meant Madden's team. Atkinson, Noll said, "should be kicked out of the league."

A decade earlier, tempers might have cooled. But Howard Cosell's halftime highlights and football's booming popularity had spawned expanded local and national sports segments that ran and reran the week's big plays, a public relations boon for the NFL that became an embarrassment as fans watched replays of Atkinson mugging Swann. Rozelle, fearing for the game's image if not its future, fined Atkinson $1,500 for what the commissioner called a "flagrant" cheap shot. He fined Noll $1,000 for his "criminal element" comment, a necessary move under a league bylaw barring public criticism of other teams and players. Finally the commissioner sent the two coaches a letter:

> *Dear John and Chuck: A review of your September 12 game indicates that your "intense rivalry" of recent years could be on the verge of erupting into something approaching pure violence.*

Reggie Williams was a Bengals rookie in '76. "It was like stepping into the Wild Wild West," says Williams. "As a rookie out of Dartmouth I was instantly abused: 'You Ivy League wimp!' And that was my teammates talking. They said I'd better hammer somebody senseless right off." The new Bengal earned his stripes by clubbing receivers with a padded forearm. A linebacker with a knack for recovering fumbles, Williams had quick hands and a strong sense of self-preservation. "It was hell in pileups. You'd grab the ball, but with both hands on the ball you can't protect your eyes, so somebody's gouging your eyes. The Raiders had pileups down to a science. They'd knee you in the nuts to get the ball. And that's when all your biceps curls and leg curls pay off. You go into a fetal position—'head and ass in the grass,' it's called—and wrap both arms around the ball. You move the ball down through all those arms in the pileup, down under your nuts where nobody can get it."

Williams was dazzled to be in the pros. "The NFL! It was like being in a movie. The best teams had personalities set by their top guys. The QB and the coach, usually, and a defensive dominator. Bradshaw, Noll, and Mean Joe Greene. Staubach, Landry, and Too Tall Jones. Quarterbacks were still tough—Bradshaw would lower a shoulder and give you a lick. Coaches weren't CEOs yet. The fans got involved—the Steelers' Terrible Towel was invented in the '70s. The wave, too. Billy 'White Shoes' Johnson was down in Houston inventing the touchdown dance—*I'm partying right in your face.* Walter Payton ran a thousand yards for the first time in my rookie year. I loved Walter." In a preseason game, Williams had a clean shot at Payton but let him run out of bounds. A coach grabbed his face mask. "Hit him!" On Payton's next carry, the rookie delivered "a kidney shot. Legal, but I knew it hurt." Next the six-one, 228-pound Williams encountered the five-ten Payton setting a block. "I load up and hit him with my best forearm shiver, and Walter *disappears*. I'm thinking, 'Where's Walter?'" Payton had been knocked flying. He picked himself off the turf and gave Williams a hug. He said it was a hell of a hit.

The rookie got another thrill in Week Six, when the Bengals went to Pittsburgh. The two-time champions were dinged up. Swann's ears were still ringing from his latest date with the Raiders, Bradshaw was sidelined: on an ugly play the week before, the Cleveland Browns' Joe "Turkey" Jones had wrapped Bradshaw up after the whistle, lifted the 215-pound quarterback, and speared him downward like a javelin, a move that could have broken his neck. The Browns won 18–16 and Pittsburgh looked finished. After their season-opening mugging in Oakland and losses to the Patriots, Vikings, and Browns, their record stood at 1-4, the worst start ever by a Super Bowl champion. Hosting Cincinnati in Week Six, Pittsburgh needed to run the table to have any chance to reach the playoffs. They needed nine victories in a row, starting with the 4-1 Bengals.

In the home locker room, Joe Greene called for his teammates' attention. "If we have to be in this position," he said, "all I can tell you is I'd rather be in it with this team, with these people, and particularly the man running this team." Nodding to Noll, Greene led the Steelers up the tunnel to the field.

Lining up with the visitors, Williams felt wobbly. "Three Rivers Stadium felt like the Roman Colosseum, this amazing cathedral with flags flapping in the wind," he recalls. "There's Joe Greene looking like a giant. Jack Lambert with no front teeth, with his neck in a brace, ready to play. And Jack Ham. My defensive coordinator had a Ham fetish—loved the guy. There's Franco and Bradshaw and Swann, Super Bowl heroes. And Rocky Bleier—I admired him for his service in Vietnam. I was singing my heart out on the national anthem, almost wishing I didn't have to give Bleier my forearm."

With Bradshaw nursing his Turkey'ed neck and Joe Gilliam out of the league, a cocaine and heroin casualty at age twenty-five, backup quarterback Mike Kruczek led the Steelers out of the huddle. Kruczek spent most of the day handing off to Franco Harris, who carried a league-record 41 times for 143 yards. Lambert and Glen Edwards each picked off Cincinnati's Ken Anderson in a 23–6 win that lifted the champions' record to 2-4. They were still alive.

The following evening a brassy, new *Monday Night Football* theme led into what Cosell termed a "critical confrontation" between the Patriots and the Jets. Frank Gifford credited quarterback Steve Grogan and receiver Darryl Stingley for pacing New England's 3-2 start, Alex Karras sang a peppy tune to the 1-4 visitors (*"And the Je-ets are rollin' along"*), and a 41–7 blowout by the Patriots devolved into a skirmish between drunken fans and Boston police. One brawler broke a cop's jaw. Another smashed a liquor bottle over a woman's head. Another stole a wheelchair out from under a disabled man. The harried police handcuffed unruly fans to a fence outside Schaefer Stadium and hustled back inside. In the fourth quarter, with the sloshed crowd spilling onto the field, a spectator collapsed with a heart attack. A paramedic kneeling to deliver mouth-to-mouth felt something warm on his back. A fan was peeing on him.

If anyone could restore order to a chaotic season, it was the Steelers. After humbling the Bengals they mounted a display of defensive prowess to match anything the league had seen. The front four blew through offensive lines. Linebackers Lambert, Ham, and Andy Russell shut off passing lanes and abused ballcarriers. Defensive backs Edwards, J. T. Thomas, and Mel Blount punished receivers. The linebacker-strong Blount would hook wideouts and lift them off the ground; sometimes the receiver's feet kept whirling like a cartoon character's. Pittsburgh shut out the Giants 27–0 in Week Seven, holding Larry Csonka to 44 yards. The following Sunday, twenty-one days after getting upside-downed by Turkey Jones, Bradshaw returned to throw for one touchdown and run for another as Pittsburgh blanked the Chargers, 23–0. A week later at Arrowhead Stadium, the Chiefs ran the ball 22 times for a total of 34 yards in the Steelers' third consecutive shutout: Pittsburgh 45, Kansas City 0. Over three weeks the left-for-dead champions had outscored opponents 95 to 0. Five more victories ran their streak to nine and carried 10-4 Pittsburgh to the playoffs. In winning nine straight must games, the Steelers allowed 2 touchdowns while scoring 234 points.

"We were the best team in the league and the best defense ever," Russell says. "We knew it, other teams knew it. We could see it in their eyes. They hoped they'd get beat by a touchdown or two and not get hurt."

In Oakland, Matuszak bulled his way into the lineup by leading a goal-line stand in a 14–13 victory over the Oilers. Al Davis rented a house for Stabler and the Tooz to share during the season. One evening Stabler was watching *Monday Night Football* when the phone rang. A Highway Patrol officer told him they'd arrested Matuszak for driving drunk and blasting away at stop signs with his .357 Magnum. Stabler brought him home from the police station, Matuszak apologizing all the way. Before long they were partying again, setting a team record by entertaining seven women in their hot tub. "Hey, Snake," the Tooz asked, "if I put two more girls on my shoulders, will that count as nine?"

Villapiano and a teammate dropped by chez Tooz one day. Finding nobody home, they redecorated. "We put his bed in the kitchen and the kitchen appliances in the bathroom. We took his record albums and lined the front yard with them—gave him a record-album fence. A week later the records were back in the den, but Tooz's bed was still in the kitchen. He liked it there. It was easier to reach the beer."

In October, on the Sunday when Turkey Jones speared Bradshaw in Cleveland, the 3-0 Raiders were in New England, getting trounced by Grogan, Stingley, and fullback Sam "Bam" Cunningham, who bowled through Oakland's Orange Defense for 101 yards. Yet even in a 48–17 defeat, their most lopsided loss since 1963, the Raiders moved the chains. They had 25 first downs to the Patriots' 27. Stabler completed 20 of 35 passes including a dozen to tight end Dave Casper. A six-four, 240-pound Notre Dame All-American, Casper had taken three years to crack the starting lineup, but his cutlass-edge routes had made him Stabler's most reliable target. The Raiders called him Ghost, and not only for the name he shared with the comics' Friendly

Ghost. The pale, blond Casper was "the whitest human being in history," Matuszak said, "like a pillowcase with eyes."

Moping in the visitors' locker room after the loss to New England, the Tooz fixed his eyes on a Boston reporter. He lifted the man like a barbell, shook him at the ceiling, and told him to stop hurting his teammates' feelings with "mean questions."

Oakland got back on track in San Diego, outlasting a 3-1 Chargers team with a backfield featuring Dan Fouts and Mercury Morris. Quarterback Fouts, twenty-five, was approaching stardom with help from a cerebral, prematurely white-haired offensive coordinator, Bill Walsh. Gimpy running back Morris, twenty-nine, a shell of his old Dolphin self, slowed by a bum knee, ran 7 times for 21 yards. The Chargers led by 3 until Stabler hit Branch for 41 yards to put Oakland ahead. The Snake had a near-perfect day—20 of 26 for 339 yards and 3 touchdowns, including a seeing-eye lob to Casper—as Oakland reclaimed its rightful spot atop the AFC West.

A month later the surging Steelers walloped Kansas City, 45–0, while the Bears knocked Stabler silly with a helmet-cracking sack. He sat out a few series, trying to shake the sand out of his head. When that didn't work, he went back in. Stabler's teammates half-expected one of his semiconscious zombie TD passes, and they got one. Stabler's fourth-quarter heave toward Cliff Branch should have been intercepted, but Branch reached back over cornerback Virgil Livers, tapped the ball with both hands like a volleyball setter, and corralled it for a touchdown that put Oakland ahead by a point. When Bears kicker Bob Thomas's last-second field-goal try bopped off the right upright, Oakland had its eighth victory against a single loss. Easy wins over the Chiefs, Eagles, and expansion Bucs got the Raiders to 11-1 going into a *Monday Night* rematch with the AFC Central–leading Bengals.

The Oakland-Cincinnati game had a plot—division leaders collide—and a better subplot. If the Raiders lost, Cincinnati would

clinch the AFC Central and Pittsburgh, despite its nine-game winning streak, would be out of the playoffs. Eliminating the Steelers
would be a sweet sort of backdoor revenge for Oakland, and Madden
had a semihonorable way to do it. All he had to do was rest his stars.
Oakland had already clinched its playoff spot. Giving Stabler and
other starters a week off or even the second half off after a bruising
season made sense. But Madden never considered it. "We're gonna
do this the right way," Madden told his players, "because it's not just
getting what you want that counts. It's how you get it."

No Raider disagreed. "We were all with John," says Villapiano. "I
mean, the idea of the Raiders laying down—it's not happening. John
told us to destroy 'em." As Atkinson put it, "It was us telling Pittsburgh,
'We're going to do you a favor first. Then we're going to fuck you up.'"

Cincinnati's troubles began before the whistle. "Here came the
Raiders with those clubs on their arms," the Bengals' Reggie Williams recalls. "Their DBs were trash-talking, telling us what they
were going to do to us." Oakland picked off the Bengals' Ken Anderson three times while Stabler—"the in-*im*-itable *Kenneth* Stabler,"
according to Cosell—threw 20 passes and completed 16, including
two touchdowns to Branch and one each to Biletnikoff and Casper.
Madden called his team's 35–20 triumph "the most proud game I
ever coached."

Back in Pittsburgh, the Steelers—relieved, but in no mood to
thank the Oakland Raiders for their help—practiced for the playoffs.

Stabler completed two-thirds of his passes that season, the
second-best percentage in NFL history. Protected by the league's
strongest, quickest offensive line—Art Shell, Gene Upshaw, Dave
Dalby, George Buehler, and John Vella—he threw short to Casper,
deep to Branch and Biletnikoff, and set a modern mark in what may
be the most important stat: the Snake averaged a record 9.4 yards per
pass attempt. In a sport that was more and more about the forward
pass, it wasn't total yards or completion percentage that mattered

most; it was how many yards each throw was worth. In 1976 Stabler gained almost ten yards ppa—not per completion, per pass *attempt*.

The Raiders opened the '76 playoffs by hosting New England, the only team to beat them all year. Villapiano and Hit-Man Atkinson delivered an instant message to Russ Francis, the Patriots' six-six, 240-pound tight end—a two-man can-opener that separated Francis from his helmet and broke his nose. Francis left the field with blood running down his chin onto his jersey. Oakland nursed a 10–7 lead into the third quarter, when Francis trotted back into the Patriots' huddle, his nose held in place with a bloodstained bandage. Villapiano told Atkinson, "We're in a war now."

Francis cut between them for a 26-yard score that put New England up by 4. Another Patriots touchdown made it 21–10. The Raiders looked beaten. Then, bizarrely, the Patriots got cute. They ran a tight-end reverse. The idea was for Francis to wreak revenge with a game-breaking gain. Instead, with Otis Sistrunk charging him, Francis pulled a Yepremian: the busted-nosed six-six tight end looped a wobbly pass that Skip Thomas intercepted. That play changed NFL history. A New England touchdown would have put the game away. Instead the Raiders scored. New England 21, Oakland 17. The Raiders were on life support, but still alive. On third-and-18 with 1:24 to play, Stabler threw incomplete, but for once the zebras saved the bad guys: nose tackle Ray "Sugar Bear" Hamilton, who had barely brushed Stabler, was flagged for roughing him. With new life, Stabler scrambled to the end zone for a 24–21 victory.

Losing to football's dirtiest team was a bitter pill for the Patriots. New England's Darryl Stingley had a warning for the Raiders: "They better clean up their act."

A day later the East-champion Colts hosted the AFC's other divisional playoff. The 11-3 Colts had led the NFL in scoring with 29.8 points a game. The previous week they'd clobbered the Bills, 58–20.

Still the visiting Steelers won 40–14, rolling up 526 total yards to the Colts' 170. Pittsburgh looked primed to defend its back-to-back Super Bowl titles. Still, there were omens: Harris and Bleier were banged up, doubtful for the conference championship, and in the moments after their first-round win in Baltimore, a plane crashed into the just-emptied upper deck at Memorial Stadium. No one was hurt, not even the deranged pilot, who climbed from the wreckage, but some Steelers felt weirded-out by their postseason trajectory. Looking up at the Piper Cub mashed nose-first into the cheap seats, Pittsburgh center Mansfield cracked, "I thought it was a kamikaze from Oakland."

For sheer hate and hype, no NFL rivalry has matched Steelers-Raiders in the '70s. Atkinson, Oakland's kamikaze safety, had already filed a $3 million defamation lawsuit against Noll for his "criminal element" comments. Commissioner Rozelle suspected—correctly—that Oakland owner Davis was paying Atkinson's lawyers. The "intense rivalry" that Rozelle fretted about had metastasized. It wasn't just Oakland against Pittsburgh anymore, it was Oakland against Rozelle, the league office, other owners, and the referees, and probably Oakland against Up with People, too. It was Oakland against the world, just the way Al Davis liked it.

The 1976 AFC Championship would be Oakland's fifth consecutive postseason battle with Pittsburgh, dating back to the Immaculate Reception. The Raiders had beaten the Steelers once, lost three times, and reached zero Super Bowls. "Don't let no one tell you the Pittsburgh-Oakland rivalry is press hype," Stabler said. "We hate them, they hate us, and we *owe* them." The Raiders weren't scared of Pittsburgh, he said, "but we still got that piano on our backs till we win the big 'un."

As Madden put it, "Now, dammit, this is a hurdle we've got to get over."

Harris (bruised ribs) and Bleier (bum toe) wouldn't play, leaving the running to backups Frenchy Fuqua and Reggie Harrison. Fuqua, thirty, bopped around the 'Burgh in his platform shoes less nimbly now, having lost a step since serving as middleman on the Immaculate Reception. "We knew we could stop Frenchy," says Villapiano. Early in the AFC title game, Fuqua took a Bradshaw handoff and ran into Oakland left-siders Matuszak and Villapiano, who lifted him off his feet and drove him back two yards. Villapiano and Tooz celebrated by punching each other, smacking each other's chest and pads so hard you could hear it on TV.

Three Oakland scoring drives made it 17–7 at the half. In the third quarter, the Raiders advanced from their 37 to the Steelers' 4-yard line. Stabler flipped a 5-yard floater to Pete Banaszak to put Oakland ahead 24–7. With Harris and Bleier watching from the bench, Pittsburgh rushed for only 72 yards on the day while Swann and Stallworth totaled 4 catches, 76 yards, no touchdowns. The Steelers' Super Bowl run was over. The Oakland Raiders, still seeking their first Super Bowl title, owner Al Davis's Kilimanjaro, cruised to a Super Bowl date with—who else?—the Minnesota Vikings.

It was the Vikings' fourth Super Bowl in eight years. Oh for three so far, the 13-2-1 Vikings were the only NFL team whose history matched the Raiders' for brilliance and futility. Their Purple People Eaters defense had allowed 12.6 points per game, second only to the Steelers. On offense, Chuck Foreman had rushed for 1,155 yards, while quarterback Fran Tarkenton, thirty-six, was already the league's all-time leader in completions, passing yards, and touchdowns. In 1976 he'd hit Foreman and wideouts Ahmad Rashad and Sammy White for 2,144 yards and 14 touchdowns.

The Raiders were favored by four in Super Bowl XI. They looked like a lock to Hunter Thompson, who expected Oakland's offensive line to blow the relatively puny People Eaters off the line; and George Carlin, who rooted for his Raiders to "dip the ball in shit and shove it down the throats of all the wholesome heartland teams that pray together and don't deliver late hits"; and *Los Angeles Times* columnist Jim Murray. "The Vikings play football like a guy laying carpet," Murray wrote. "The Raiders play like a guy jumping through a skylight with a machine gun."

The Raiders cut their last practice short. "It was Super Bowl week," Tom Flores recalls. "Snake was dropping back and throwing, dropping back and throwing, and the ball never hit the ground. That's how sharp we were. *Dozens* of passes, and not one hit the ground. It was eerie. Finally John claps his hands and says, 'Okay, that's enough.' We were ready."

10

TRIAL AND ERROR

The deep thump of disco music pounded from a hotel ballroom in Newport Beach, California, an hour south of Pasadena. Broad-shouldered men and big-haired women boogied to Wild Cherry's "Play That Funky Music" and the Bee Gees' "You Should Be Dancing." John Matuszak flung a football at a chandelier. The music spilled from the ballroom into hallways strewn with champagne flutes, beer bottles, silver-and-black napkins, and confetti. The Raiders were celebrating.

A pair of TVs showed grainy highlights of Super Bowl XI:

The Vikings' offensive line surging forward on second-and-goal in a scoreless game, Villapiano spearing through the line, dislodging the ball with his helmet . . .

Stabler hitting Biletnikoff deep and throwing short to Casper, who shucked a tackler and headed downfield . . .

Matuszak stuffing Chuck Foreman, driving the ball into Foreman's gut . . .

Tatum hitting Minnesota's Sammy White so hard that White's chinstrap snapped and his helmet flew out of the frame, Tatum staring down as if he couldn't believe White's head was still attached . . .

Cornerback Willie Brown picking off a Fran Tarkenton pass, Brown's eyes widening as he goes 75 yards to put Oakland up 32–7, and it's all over but the party.

Eight hours after the final whistle, Stabler, waving a bottle of Johnnie Walker Red, crossed the ballroom and hugged Biletnikoff. They were a flammable pair, the quarterback spilling Scotch and the receiver holding a cigarette. "MVP!" Stabler hollered over the music. Biletnikoff looked as if he were going to bawl. He'd wept a few seconds after the two-minute warning, when the stadium announcer told a Rose Bowl crowd of 103,438 and 80 million TV viewers that Fred Biletnikoff had been named the game's Most Valuable Player. And he'd teared up after the game, too, sucking a cigarette as he told reporters, "To accomplish this with a group of guys you love, well, it feels like someone stuck a needle in my arm and pumped me full of warm blood. It hits your heart."

Stabler had hit him in the Minnesota secondary. Catching a fourth-quarter pass at the Vikings' 35, Biletnikoff weaved between tacklers on his way to the end zone, losing steam all the way. Dragged down at the 2-yard line, chain-smoker Freddie had been as winded as the training-camp streaker they'd watched five months before. Stabler razzed him when he returned to the huddle. "Puss! You shoulda scored!"

"I was looking for a gas station on the way," Biletnikoff said. Not that it mattered. Pete Banaszak promptly punched past the Purple People Eaters for 2 of Oakland's Super Bowl–record 429 yards of total offense.

In the ballroom, hugging his players and their women, John Madden looked pink as ever, flushed for once with joy rather than worry. Before the game he'd said, "Guys, this will be the biggest event of your lives," and paused before adding, "as long as you win." The coach had been a wreck in the first quarter as the Raiders racked up yardage but scored only 3 points. Stabler recalls seeing him "running his hands through his hair, bitching and moaning. I said, 'John, don't worry. There's more points comin'.'" Oakland's line had been blowing the People Eaters backward. Center Dave Dalby, who weighed 255, was the lightest of the Raiders' offensive linemen, while 250-pound tackle Doug Sutherland was the heaviest member of the Vikings' front four. In that way Super Bowl XI resembled a match between a 1970 NFL club and a 1980 team. The more modern Raiders had 265-pound Gene Upshaw blocking 235-pound Alan Page, and 290-pound Art Shell bowling over 225-pound Jim Marshall. They were small compared to offensive linemen of the next century—such as the Ravens' Michael Oher, hero of the book and the movie *The Blind Side*, a cat-quick 313 pounds, or college power Alabama's 2009 line, weighing in at 348, 310, 315, 320, and 318—but Oakland's quick-footed hulks were too much for the undersized Vikings. "They totally dominated us," Tarkenton said after the game.

Al Davis wrote a message on the blackboard in the winners' locker room: AN ORGANIZATION NEVER DESERVED IT MORE. After the game Davis, forty-seven, had made it to the mountaintop at last. Kiliman-jaro still stood, and his Raiders were Super Bowl champs. "Maybe it's good we didn't win before. You worry about reaching the pinnacle of life too early," he told reporters, standing with his arms crossed, eyes flat and dark, fingernails ragged. He'd been chewing his nails. Asked why he'd kept a low profile that week, he cracked, "If I came around, I'd say something controversial, and the commissioner wouldn't get the headlines." During the trophy presentation, Davis stepped forward to take the Lombardi Trophy from the manicured hands of Pete Rozelle, the enemies making nice for TV. Upshaw called out, "We made you shake hands with the commissioner!" Viewers listening closely heard George Atkinson in the background, cursing Rozelle.

That night at the party, Atkinson spread his arms as if to hug the whole world. Biletnikoff lit another smoke. Madden settled into a chair a couple of sizes too small for him, looking spent. Some day this had been, from pregame flop sweat to first-quarter frustration to elation. He'd even had an up-and-down departure from the field. Immediately after the game several Raiders including Hendricks lifted Madden onto their shoulders, but due to his three-hundred-pound bulk and a photographer who got in the way, they dropped him. It was the best bruise he ever got.

As the party wound down, assistant coach Flores watched the last Raider on the dance floor. "For a huge man, Matuszak had great rhythm," Flores remembers. "When everyone else got tired, the Tooz was still out there, jitterbugging all by himself."

In the spring of 1977, NFL owners voted on a new contract and a raise for Commissioner Rozelle. Given the league's growth, the result was never in doubt. The measure passed, 27–1. Al Davis cast the no vote.

Next came the clack of a gavel in Courtroom 3 of San Francisco's Federal Building. With labor-management peace established at little cost to the league—another of Rozelle's victories—Davis and his Super Bowl champions resumed their war against the rest of the league. *Atkinson v. Noll* was ostensibly about Steelers coach Chuck Noll's ripping Raider safety George "Hit Man" Atkinson as part of "a criminal element in the league." In a larger sense, the trial pitted Atkinson, Davis, and the Raiders against Noll, Pittsburgh owner Art Rooney, Rozelle, and the league's establishment. Many NFL players were delighted—they saw the Raiders and the Steelers as the league's dirtiest teams. Atkinson's lawyers argued that Noll had slandered their client. The Oakland side's lead attorney was future San Francisco mayor Willie Brown. As sharp as the suits, silk ties, and pocket squares he wore, Brown planned to put the NFL on trial. The case was "pro football's Watergate," he said. He assured the jury—four women and two white-haired men, none of whom knew a forearm shiver from a Seahawk—that his client was no criminal. If there was a "criminal element" in pro football, he said, it was Noll, and not poor George Atkinson, who was its ringleader. "The Pittsburgh Steelers are the leading cheap-shot artists in the NFL," Brown declared. With that he summoned Noll to the witness stand, where the coach shifted stiffly while Brown showed the judge and the jury film clips of illegal hits dispensed by Steelers defenders.

Al Davis, sitting near the jury box in an undertaker suit and silver tie, winced and said, "Oh! *Oww*," with each crackback block, can-opener, or forearm shiver. At that point Steelers president Dan Rooney, the Chief's son, may have been rethinking his legal strategy. Rooney's attorneys had urged him to settle the $3 million lawsuit for $50,000, but Rooney refused. "We've got to go to court to save the game," he told them. Now Willie Brown was showing Coach Noll and the jury a blackboard headed NOLL'S NFL CRIMINALS. A single name was on the list: GEORGE ATKINSON. Brown made a sensible point: if Noll was right about a "criminal element" in the NFL, there must be more than one player in it.

"Who else belongs on this list?" Brown asked.

Noll may have wished he were crash-landing a plane or walking on hot coals, anything but sitting in the witness box, clearing his throat while Brown repeated, *"Who else?"*

Finally Noll said, "Jack Tatum." Brown wrote JACK TATUM on the blackboard under Atkinson's name. Now there were two members of Oakland's Soul Patrol secondary up there, the Hit Man and the Assassin. But they couldn't be the only dirty players, could they? Two criminals do not an element make.

Noll was trapped. His fury at Atkinson for head-hunting Lynn Swann was well placed; Oakland's Hit Man was one of the league's most notorious rule-breakers. But so was Pittsburgh's Mel Blount. The Steelers may not have dispensed illegal hits with as much gusto as the Raiders, but they broke rules, too. In a game that celebrated violent contact, a game built on hard hitting, Oakland and Pittsburgh were the league's most violent winners. To suggest that only the Raiders were thuggish was hypocrisy, and Noll was guilty of it. Under Willie Brown's withering questioning, the coach named others known around the league for taking cheap shots. "Mel Blount," he said. "Ernie Holmes . . . Joe Greene." His own guys! Blount would file a slander suit of his own against Noll, vowing he'd never play for the Steelers again.

Next Al Davis took the stand. Davis needed little prompting to go on the attack, accusing the league of promoting violence and then demonizing one of its own—a Raider, of course—for winning by intimidation. Davis was followed by the calm, perma-tanned commissioner, who supported Noll and the Steelers by calling George Atkinson an outlaw. "His conduct is clearly outside the rules and calculated either to disable opposing players or to intimidate them," Rozelle said.

Noll's lead attorney, James Martin MacInnis, who was paid by the Steelers, made a peculiar closing statement. Noting that Coliseum fans had cheered Atkinson's mugging of Swann, he called NFL violence "a sad commentary on the motives of our generation . . . sadistic. This secret love of violence, the spectacle of liking to see others hurt, happiness at pain, the love of blood—that's the America of George Atkinson." And not just Atkinson. MacInnis was describing the favorite sport of millions of Americans, a sport inseparable from the violence that helped make it thrilling to watch.

Willie Brown's summation was louder. In soaring tones he compared the National Football League to "a nation unto itself . . . second only to the United States in terms of power, scope, and potential," a claim that was a least a little bit premature.

The jury ruled for Noll. The league was vindicated. Noll and the Rooneys embraced; Atkinson and Al Davis went home empty-handed. But far from ending the feud between the Raiders and the rest of the NFL, *Atkinson v. Noll* brought them closer to war. At that year's league meetings, Rozelle angered Davis by removing him from the powerful Competition Committee. Now the renegade owner would have little if anything to say about future rules changes. The commissioner chose the right time to hit back at Davis—at the same meetings, Rozelle announced the grand terms of another TV deal he'd negotiated with the networks. Owners were hoping for a boost from the previous contract's total of $2.2 million per team, maybe up to $3 million. There were gasps when Rozelle revealed the new terms: $5.2 million per team. Twenty-seven of the twenty-eight owners applauded him. The NFL sweetened the deal for Roone Arledge and his fellow network execs by agreeing to add two games to the schedule, going to a sixteen-game season starting in 1978, and adding a round to the playoffs. More games would necessarily add to the risks players ran, but at the time no owners, executives, coaches, players, or trainers saw weekly NFL combat as a serious threat to players' health. Now, for the first time ever, owners would earn more from TV rights than from selling tickets to their games.

Also on the docket at the 1977 league meetings was the $17 million purchase of the Bay Area's lesser franchise by the pint-size son of an Ohio shopping-mall magnate. Edward DeBartolo Jr., thirty, would run a troubled 49ers team further into the ground before making a hire that turned the team around. At the same meetings the Davis-free Competition Committee banned the head slap, a tactic practically trademarked by Deacon Jones. Jones, the Rams' recently retired defensive end, would slam his padded forearm to the earhole of a lineman's helmet at the snap, ringing the guy's bell. By the mid-'70s the move was Joe Greene's choice for stunning linemen on his way to the quarterback. Opponents such as Conrad Dobler, the Cardinals' notorious offensive lineman, saw that a head slap left the slapper's ribs vulnerable. Dobler would retaliate with a punch to the solar plexus. Still he was sometimes called for holding. "He earholed me!" Dobler would growl to the referee. "Anyway I wasn't holding. I was punching."

Banning head slaps might protect linemen's brains and extend their careers, but that wasn't why the NFL amended the rules. "The league's whole philosophy was to open up the game and let the stars shine," recalls Don Shula, who joined the Competition Committee in 1975. Rules that slowed defenders would "give the quarterback time to throw the football. Before, big defensive linemen would be in the quarterback's face, creating the possibility of knocking a star player out of the game." According to Shula, the committee wanted "more big plays, to make the sport more exciting. That was our mandate from the owners."

The league's attempts to turn 13–7 slogs into high-scoring shoot-outs seemed to backfire at first. Touchdowns fell to 4.2 per game in 1977, the lowest average since the World War II days of the stumbling Steagles. Scoring dipped to 34.4 points per game, a 12-point tumble in less than a decade. The run/pass gap reached historic proportions that November, when Chicago Bears quarterback Bob Avellini threw 6 times for 33 yards in a grinding 10–7 victory over Bud Grant's Vikings, while Walter Payton ran 40 times for a league-record 275 yards.

Rozelle, scanning marketing reports in his Park Avenue office, understood that football fans couldn't care less about blocking schemes and the relative merits of the Cover One and Cover Two. Fans wanted touchdowns. Better yet, touchdown passes. And so, in 1978, the Competition Committee tweaked the balance of power between offense and defense once more. Starting in '78, offensive linemen were allowed to extend their arms and open their hands when pass-blocking. In effect, the rule legalized holding on pass plays. The committee went further. Since 1974, defenders had been limited to a single hit on receivers after they were three or more yards downfield. Now they could *only* deliver that hit within five yards of the line of scrimmage. After that they couldn't lay a finger on a receiver until the ball arrived. The Mel Blount Rule, as it was called in honor of the Steelers' wideout-bashing cornerback, "was huge," says former Ravens coach Brian Billick. "Now the bump-and-run of the early '70s was totally outlawed. Defenses could go to more zones, but if you were an offensive coordinator, you knew your guys could now run patterns unobstructed and reach a certain spot on the field at a certain time. Suddenly timing patterns made a lot more sense." Under the Blount Rule, many more of the newly unbumpable wideouts would need to be double-teamed, leaving single coverage for tight ends and running backs coming out of the backfield, under the zones.

"I loved it," says Roger Staubach. "If you look at tape before 1978, you'll see guys getting pounded downfield on every play. Just *erased*. The league wanted offense, so they passed a rule to help the passing game. They'd tried before; this time it worked."

Within three seasons, passes would jump from 38 percent of offensive plays to almost half. Scoring would rise from 34.4 to 41 points per game. TV ratings climbed the same rising curve. Seventy-nine million viewers watched Staubach and the Cowboys crush the Denver Broncos in Super Bowl XII, a second straight Super blowout, thoroughly forgettable except for the first play: After winning the coin flip at New Orleans' finally finished Superdome, Dallas coach Landry rolled the dice on the first play from scrimmage—a double reverse. Fumble! Butch Johnson saved him by recovering the ball. Staubach went on to complete 17 of 25 passes for 183 yards, while his ex-rival Craig Morton, now leading the Broncos, connected on 4 of 15 and had 4 more picked off by the Cowboys' Doomsday Defense. Dallas coasted to a 27–10 victory that had culture critics dismissing the Super Bowl as an overblown bore.

Staubach wasn't bored. "Now we'd won two Super Bowls, same as the Steelers," he says. Same as the Dolphins and Packers, for that matter, with everybody else at least one behind. "If we beat Pittsburgh to three Super Bowls, we'd be the best of our time."

In Pittsburgh, the Steelers adapted. Rather than fight the Mel Blount Rule, Coach Noll supported the Rooneys, who supported Rozelle, who wanted more offense. Mel Blount backpedaled off and on the field, dropping his slander suit against Noll and giving receivers a yard's cushion before leveling them the split second the ball arrived. And Noll, picturing the 1978 season in light of the new rules and his evolving roster, liked what he saw. The Steel Curtain years had risen on a defense-first team well suited to its time, but the near future would favor the deep ball.

A maturing Bradshaw turned thirty that year, his neck healed, his arm as strong as ever, his receivers the best in the game. "This rule is to stop people laying all over receivers' backs," he told the *Pittsburgh Press.* "That could help me, because a lot of what has held us up is receivers jammed by a cornerback all over him." Translation: the Blount Rule would make Lynn Swann and John Stallworth practically uncoverable. Looking back today, Bradshaw calls the rule a gift to the Steelers. "I thought, 'No more bump-and-run? You're gonna let Swann and Stallworth run free?' I was licking my chops."

Staubach was just as eager to look downfield for Tony Hill, Drew Pearson, and second-year running back Tony Dorsett. Stabler and the Raiders pictured Cliff Branch going deep while Dave Casper found seams underneath. But first, the Raider Way would ruin a young man's life.

August 12, 1978, was a breezy Saturday at Oakland Coliseum. A preseason game between the Raiders and the New England Patriots meant nothing in the standings and not much to most of the players. NFL players earned $99 a week in the preseason. But even exhibition games had meaning to the Soul Patrol: Each one was a chance to send receivers a message they'd remember when the games counted. Late in the first half, Raiders up by 3, New England's Darryl Stingley lined up on the strong side—the side of a formation where the tight end lines up. Stingley, twenty-six, an All-America wideout from Purdue, was feeling fine that day. A few plays earlier he'd broken loose on an end-around. "I gained twenty-four yards but must have run fifty, cutting up, cutting in, cutting back, dodging hits from Tatum and all those other cats swinging their heavily padded arms," he recalled in his book, *Happy to Be Alive*. Like most receivers, Stingley detested the Oakland defenders. Even in exhibition games, free safety Jack Tatum would deck him and spit, "Get up, fag." Safety Atkinson, padded, taped, and snarling, would hook receivers with a forearm to the chin and say, "It's gonna be like that all day, fucker." But they wouldn't rattle Stingley today. He'd just agreed to a guaranteed contract that would make him one of the best-paid receivers in football. His agent, Jack Sands, was going to finalize the deal when Stingley and the Pats got back to Boston after the game. Before the team flight to Oakland, Sands had joked, "Just don't break your ankle out there."

Late in the first half, Patriots quarterback Steve Grogan called 94 Slant, a crossing pattern. At the snap, Stingley took five long strides downfield, then cut toward the middle at a forty-degree angle, seeking the seam between linebackers and DBs. He was open, but Grogan held the ball. As Stingley recalled, 94 Slant was a timing play, like thousands more to come in the late '70s, '80s, and beyond as offenses took advantage of the Blount Rule. "The ball had to be waiting for me when I planted my foot and turned in, or else the area would be jammed with defensive players. At last—maybe a second or a second and a half late—there was the ball . . . well over my head." Grogan should have eaten the ball or thrown elsewhere. Instead he threw too high just as the Raiders' rotating Cover Three zone brought Tatum speeding toward Stingley. According to Stingley, "I was looking Tatum dead in the eye . . . he was cocking his bone, his forearm, coming fast. . . . I dropped my head so I could duck the bone." The ball flew past as Tatum delivered a bone-hard hit to the back of Stingley's neck. Tatum and the Raiders would insist later that landing headfirst hurt Stingley more than the hit, but the tape shows that he went limp before he landed. Seconds later Tatum stood over him while Stingley lay still as a cat run over by a car, his right leg at an odd angle over his left. It could have been Swann, Stallworth, or another NFL receiver, but it wasn't. It was Darryl Stingley, born in Chicago in 1951, grown up to catch 110 passes for the Patriots from 1973 through '77, flat on the field with the strange feeling that his legs were gone.

Trainer Tom Healion jogged to his side. "Tom, am I all right?" Stingley asked Healion. "Am I all right? Am I gonna be all right?"

Five blue-clad trainers and assistants surrounded them. One tapped a rubber hammer on the reflex points on Stingley's knees. Once, twice. Nothing. He shook his head at Healion, who squeezed Stingley's hand, saying, "Sure, buddy, sure, you're okay." Stingley knew he wasn't. He couldn't feel Healion's hand. They wheeled him off on a gurney, his broken neck resting on a padded frame shaped like the bottom part of a guillotine. Trundled into an ambulance, half awake, Stingley followed a lights-and-sirens police escort to Eden Hospital in Castro Valley, fifteen minutes from the Coliseum, where "a nurse appeared. She cut off my football pants and all the tape, piece by piece, and my Patriots jersey with the big 84 on it. . . I passed out."

Dave Newhouse covered the Raiders for the *Oakland Tribune*. "After the game," he recalls, "the Patriots were all set to fly back to Boston. They were going to leave Stingley alone in the hospital till

John Madden stopped their plane. 'You've got to leave somebody with him,' he told them. So the Patriots sent a PR guy off the plane." The PR man drafted press releases updating Stingley's condition. *Darryl Stingley spent a restful night.... Stingley, recovering from a cervical spine fracture, remains in the intensive care unit. There has been little change in the condition of paralysis.... He remains in traction in a special circular orthopedic bed.* The reports made no mention of the absence of Patriots personnel in Stingley's hospital room, or the identity of a frequent visitor. "You know who spent the most time with him? Madden," says Newhouse. "John Madden spent hours and hours at Stingley's bedside. Even weeks later he was flying home from road games, driving from the airport to the hospital to sit up all night with Darryl Stingley. Madden and his wife, Virginia, became friends with Stingley's family, and there was no PR to it because nobody knew about it."

A day or two after the game, Stingley woke and tried to lift his head. He tried to see who else was in the room. As his vision cleared he saw "a hulking figure staring down at me. His eyes were red, and there were tears running down his cheeks." Madden gripped Stingley's numb hand "and touched my face, the way a father would." Later that day, Madden may have saved Stingley's life. The paralyzed patient was learning to keep track of his surroundings by moving only his eyes. He was struggling to breathe and saw Madden hurry to the door, yelling, "Nurse! Nurse!" A monitor was beeping; a plug that suctioned phlegm from Stingley's mouth had come loose. "The nurse stuck a tube down my throat and drew all the loose phlegm from my lungs. It hurt like crazy, and I started to cry," Stingley recalled. "Thank God for the coach. If he hadn't been there, I might have choked to death. At least that's what the nurse told me."

With some regret, Madden left the hospital to finish prepping his team for the 1978 season. He upped his Maalox intake, but his ulcers got worse. Jack Tatum never darkened the door of Stingley's hospital room, never phoned or sent a get-well card. When a reporter asked how he felt about Darryl Stingley, paralyzed for life, Tatum said, "You don't like to see any player get hurt, but football is a contact sport and that's a real dangerous pattern he ran."

The Raiders fell to Craig Morton and the Broncos in their '78 opener. A week later in San Diego they were less than a minute from starting the year 0-2. Trailing 20–14 with the ball on the Chargers' 14, they had time for one play. "Standing over center," Stabler recalled, "I was thinking, *Don't get caught with the ball*." He dropped back and kept dropping to the 24, where linebacker Woody Lowe wrapped him up for a game-ending sack. Or was it? As he fell, Stabler underhanded the ball toward the end zone. His last-ditch move was a forward lateral masquerading as a fumble. With no whistles or flags to stop the play, both teams took off after the bounding ball. Oakland's Pete Banaszak got there first and scooped the ball toward Casper, who used his right foot to nudge the football once, twice, three times to the goal line, where he fell on it. In the radio call of announcer Bill King, "The ball flipped forward—it's loose! A wild scramble, two seconds on the clock." The excitable King, sporting his trademark twirly mustache, voice rising, gaped at "Casper grabbing the ball. . . . It is ruled a fumble! The Oakland Raiders have scored on the most zany, unbelievable, absolutely impossible dream of a play! Madden is on the field. He wants to know if it's real. They said, 'Yes, get your big butt out of here!' He does! There's nothing real in the world anymore!"

If the fumbles were intentional, the play was illegal. Thirty-three years later Stabler says, "Sure, I fumbled on purpose. But the thing of it is, we wouldn't accept *not* getting to the end zone. That play defines our team—*find a way to win*."

After the season the Competition Committee passed a rule as

clumsily contrived as Oakland's 24-yard forward fumble. Hence-
forth, in the final two minutes of any half or overtime, or on any
fourth down, a forward fumble recovered by an offensive player
other than the fumbler would be spotted at the point where the
fumble occurred. The 1-1 Raiders would end up 9-7 and miss the '78
playoffs, but they had another crooked moment for their highlight
reel: the zany touchdown that entered Raiders lore as the Holy Roller
play. The Chargers called it the Immaculate Deception.

At a Santa Barbara bistro called Derf's, members of the Church of
Monday Night Football chanted commandments: "Honor thy holy
point spread, for it is right on" and "Thou shalt not covet thy neigh-
bor's beer." A 1979 Harris poll found that 70 percent of American
sports fans preferred football to baseball. At the same time a certain
malaise, to use President Jimmy Carter's term, infected the sport's
Monday-night showcase. "A sort of decadence set in," says a *Monday
Night Football* insider. The *MNF* stars squabbled between and even
during plays, with Howard Cosell insulting his boothmates on and
off the air. Cosell called Don Meredith "an imbecile." Meredith had
returned to the booth in 1977, replacing the overmatched Alex
Karras. ABC was now paying Meredith $400,000 a year, a 1,112 per-
cent raise over his starting salary of $33,000 eight seasons before,
but Dandy Don often sounded bored. He and Cosell sometimes got
soused during commercial breaks, leaving Frank Gifford to handle
more of the broadcast. Gifford, whom Cosell dismissed as "that man-
nequin," tried to improve by doing vocal and memory exercises, but
couldn't seem to get through a game without a gaffe. One night he
called the Cowboys' Dennis Thurman "Thurman Munson," mixing
him up with the Yankees catcher who'd just died in a plane crash. On
another Monday night a frustrated Gifford punched a production
assistant in the stomach.

Now and then a Monday-night game outshone the soap opera

in the booth. In November of 1978, Shula's 8-3 Dolphins faced a ready-for-prime-time Oilers club coached by Bum Phillips. A hero in Houston, Phillips had spurred an Oilers team that went 1-13 in both 1972 and '73 into contention in the AFC Central. His '78 Oilers were missing touchdown dancer Billy "White Shoes" Johnson, down with a bad knee, but had Dante Pastorini handing off to rookie sensation Earl Campbell, a Heisman winner out of Texas. Houston fans' cri de coeur, "Luv Ya Blue!" filled the Astrodome as Phillips strode out of the tunnel sporting his flat-top crew cut, rhinestone-studded boots, and a pop-art shirt covered with clouds of powder blue. Phillips generally topped his outfit with a ten-gallon hat, but left his white Stetson in the locker room during home games at the Astrodome. Bum's mother always told him not to wear a hat indoors.

Sixty-two thousand fans waving blue and white pom-poms seemed to raise the Astrodome's roof above its 208 feet as Phillips and his stars, Pastorini and Campbell, emerged from the tunnel. "A jubulant crowd here tonight," Gifford mispronounced. Quarterback Pastorini, a shaggy-haired Californian, had gone third overall behind Jim Plunkett and Archie Manning in the 1971 "Year of the Quarterback" draft. In '73 he married *Playboy* model June Wilkinson, known as the Bosom, whose measurements were said to be 44-23-36, almost a match for Carol Doda's. As an Oilers PR man told Roy Blount, "She may be why Pastorini is continually having abdominal pulls." But while Pastorini and Bum Phillips were the faces of the franchise, Earl Campbell was the legs. The bearded five-eleven, 232-pound rookie was already the NFL's premier power back, with O. J. Simpson speed, Lynn Swann balance, and a linebacker's taste for contact. Against the Rams he had cut through the line and encountered Rams linebacker Isiah Robertson. They were alone for a moment, a yard apart with nobody else in striking distance. Most runners would have put a move on the linebacker. Campbell drove his helmet into the 225-pound Robertson's chest. The impact was audible on TV. Robertson fell, and Campbell stepped over him.

That Monday night against Miami, Campbell took a pitchout from quarterback Pastorini. He stumbled at the 15, regained his footing, and veered right, dodging a tackler, turning downfield. "He outruns everybody!" Gifford said.

"He's gone, he's gone!" Cosell cried.

Campbell's 81-yard scamper was his fourth touchdown of the game. His 199-yard night gave him the NFL rushing lead and clinched the Rookie of the Year award. Dolphins quarterback Bob Griese, playing catch-up, squinting through Clark Kent glasses under his helmet, pleased the pass-happy Competition Committee by throwing for 349 yards, including a last-second touchdown, but the night went to Campbell and the Oilers, 35–30. "Earl Campbell had some head-on collisions with our players," Shula said after the game. "I think he won them all."

Miami and Houston met again in the playoffs. On Christmas Eve at the Orange Bowl, Shula's Dolphins stacked the line, holding Campbell to 84 yards on 26 carries, but while Campbell banged heads on play-action fakes, Pastorini threw for 306 yards. The once-perfect Dolphins fell short for the fifth straight season while Luv Ya Blue advanced to the second round against the AFC East–champ Patriots, who had been through a screwy holiday season of their own. It began with Coach Chuck Fairbanks's surprise announcement that he would jump to the University of Colorado the following year. Patriots owner Billy Sullivan, incensed, ordered Fairbanks out of the Patriots' locker room and handed the team over to a pair of assistants. The Pats sued the university. The school countersued. In court, Fairbanks testified that it never occurred to him that he needed to honor his four-year Patriots contract; after all, he'd had three college contracts before and had broken them all. In the end the suits were settled, with the Colorado Buffaloes boosters' club paying the Pats a $200,000 ransom for Fairbanks, equal to almost $1 million today. A school official grumbled, "My goal is to build a world-class university with a football program, not a world-class football program with a university." The orphaned Patriots lost their last two games in '78, including a postseason pasting by the Oilers that sent 12-6 Houston to the AFC Championship against the inevitable Steelers.

Oilers passer Pastorini, one of a few survivors of the team's 1-13 seasons, recalled running for his life during losses to Pittsburgh and Mean Joe Greene. "Greene could have ended my career several times, but he chose to hug me to the ground as opposed to nailing and burying me," Pastorini said. Now, with the Oilers standing between the Steelers and their third Super Bowl in five years, the QB was fair game.

Pittsburgh fans crowded into $15.25 bleacher seats under curtains of freezing rain on January 9, 1979. They waved soggy Terrible Towels and cheered their "Stillers" to a 14–3 lead. With less than a minute left in the first half, Pastorini hit running back Ronnie Coleman for a 15-yard gain. Steelers linebacker Jack Ham clocked Coleman and the ball came loose. Pittsburgh recovered. Bradshaw zipped a touchdown pass to Swann. Oilers speedster Johnnie Dirden fielded the ensuing kickoff. Running for daylight with no Steeler in his neighborhood, Dirden still somehow fumbled, the football popping from his hands like a jumping bean. The Steelers recovered. Seconds later, Bradshaw hit Stallworth for a touchdown. Bum Phillips kicked the plastic turf on the Oilers' sideline. "The behinder we got, the worse it got," Phillips said.

The Steelers held Earl Campbell to 62 yards in 22 tries. Houston's Coleman lost 5 yards on his only carry and fumbled again. Roy Gerela's field goal just before halftime capped a run of 17 Pittsburgh points in 48 seconds. The Oilers, behind 14–3 a minute before, trudged to their locker room trailing 31–3, and the second half was no better for Houston. Pastorini, sleet dripping off his helmet, threw 5 interceptions. The Steelers sacked him 4 times on a field that was part ice, part puddles. On one second-half play Bradshaw scrambled for 12 yards, slipped, and hydroplaned on his back for another 12. After the Steelers and the Oilers combined for a playoff-record dozen fumbles in Pittsburgh's ugly 34–5 victory, Pastorini cried, saying he felt "remorse, regret, everything bad."

Joe Greene could have told him not to take it so hard. "I knew they were in trouble before the game. They didn't have enough weapons."

As Roger Staubach saw it, only the Cowboys had enough weapons. "I was fired up to see the Steelers win because I didn't think we were as good as Pittsburgh," Staubach says. "I thought we were better."

11

THE SICKEST MAN
IN AMERICA

The league's leading brands were about to collide, winner take the decade. The thirteenth Super Bowl matched blue-collar Pittsburgh and upscale Dallas, Chuck Noll with his Motorola headset and Tom Landry under his crisp fedora, Pittburgh's Steel Curtain and Dallas's Doomsday Defense, balding Terry Bradshaw and gap-toothed Jack Lambert and Mean Joe Greene versus spotless Roger Staubach and America's Team. The Cowboys were defending champions, the first team to reach five Super Bowls, while the Steelers had won two of the last four. The victors would be the first three-time Super Bowl champs.

"A good old-fashioned showdown," Staubach called it.

The Steelers were 3½-point favorites. President Jimmy Carter and his eighty-year-old mother, Miss Lillian, bet $5 on the game; the president took Dallas. The first Super rematch was played on the same stiff Orange Bowl turf where the Steelers edged the Cowboys in Super Bowl X three years before. It featured nineteen All-Pro players, which made XIII the most talent-laden title game of all time. Fourteen players and both coaches would go on to the Hall of Fame.

The Steelers had nine of the future Hall of Famers. Pittsburgh had held opponents to 107.6 yards rushing per game to lead the NFL, while Dallas ranked second, allowing 7.2 inches more. Such a contest needed little buildup but got plenty, thanks largely to Thomas "Hollywood" Henderson. After predicting the Cowboys would shut out the Rams in the NFC Championship, the brash All-Pro linebacker capped their 28–0 win with a 68-yard interception return. Now Dallas's one-man publicity machine turned his spotlight on the Steelers. Henderson called Lambert, the maestro of middle linebackers, "a toothless chimpanzee." He claimed that Bradshaw was "so dumb he couldn't spell *cat* if you spotted him the *c* and the *t*." Henderson was no dummy. Believing that a black player wouldn't get noticed or paid for his talent like Bradshaw, Lambert, or his own team's white hero, Staubach, he made a conscious decision to get noticed for his mouth. "I was my own press agent," he recalls. Henderson rejected the stoic example of black stars from Jim Brown to Joe Greene in favor of a more colorful approach. "I was more like Muhammad Ali." Sporting a full-length mink coat while squiring Anita Pointer of the Pointer Sisters around Dallas, Henderson announced, "I have decided I am the best linebacker ever. Dick Butkus was just a lineman standing up." By popping off and daring opponents to shut him up, he set the pattern for successors such as Deion Sanders, Randy Moss, and Terrell Owens.

The Steelers ignored him. They considered Hollywood Henderson the consummate Cowboy: loud, slick, and overrated. They didn't know he was also a serious coke user. In the late '70s Henderson progressed from sniffing lines in hotel rooms to snorting liquid cocaine during games. He kept the drug in a plastic inhaler the size of a ChapStick tube, hidden in his uniform pants.

Henderson swears he wasn't getting high, at least during games. "I didn't do it to feel good. It was anesthetic," he says. "I'd gotten a deviated septum from snorting ungrinded coke, and it *hurt*. I had constant headaches. But I couldn't exactly go to the team doctor and say, 'Doc, can you give me a novocaine shot in my nose?' So I kept the inhaler with the liquid cocaine hidden in my thigh pad. To stop the headaches."

Before the game, Chuck Noll told the Steelers they were going to win Super Bowl XIII because they were tougher than the Cowboys. "They are afraid to play smashmouth football with us," he said. They'd prove it by resorting to trickery. "They will reach into their bag of tricks, and that's when the game's over. We will have won at that moment."

NBC led off Super Sunday with the TV premiere of *Black Sunday*, the Hollywood thriller with action sequences shot during Super Bowl X between the Steelers and the Cowboys. After the movie, air force fighter jets roared overhead, carrying on a tradition launched at Super Bowl II. The Cowboys Cheerleaders covered their hearts with their pom-poms during a national anthem sung by the toothy Colgate Thirteen. Then an antique Packard convertible chugged onto the field. Rusty-jointed George Halas climbed out at midfield. Halas, eighty-three, flipped an 1820 gold piece. Dallas captain Staubach called heads. The gold coin came up heads. The coin flip was the one facet of the game the Cowboys dominated—they'd called heads and won the toss in Super Bowls X, XII, and XIII. "We'll receive," Staubach said.

As in Super Bowl X, when Henderson took a reverse 48 yards on the opening kickoff, the Cowboys got flashy in their first possession. After a pair of first downs that saw Tony Dorsett cutting laser holes through the Steel Curtain, Landry called for a double reverse. The stern Dallas coach served as his own offensive coordinator, indulging a go-for-broke gambler's weakness for trick plays. "He'd been a defensive coordinator," Staubach says, "so Landry was always thinking from that side of the ball. Our game plan was always about screwing up the other guys' defense." But this double reverse—

Dorsett and Drew Pearson crossing in the backfield, Dorsett about to hand off to Pearson, who could run the ball or throw it—didn't surprise the Steelers. Noll had predicted it. The Steelers had practiced defending it. Now the Cowboys' double reverse was playing out as they'd expected. But as Noll watched, his heart sank. They were blowing the coverage! Pittsburgh had nobody near tight end Billy Joe DuPree. Noll stepped toward the field as if to cover DuPree himself. This was a nightmare: coverage blown, the outcoached Cowboys on the brink of a 7–0 lead—until Dorsett and Pearson botched the handoff. The ball bounced free. Pittsburgh came up with it. Seven plays later, Bradshaw found John Stallworth between Dallas defenders for a 28-yard touchdown and a 7–0 lead for the Steelers.

Hollywood Henderson recalls, "We could have gotten down after that. Instead we got up. We got after 'em." Henderson blitzed and pinned Bradshaw's arms to his sides, forcing a fumble. Soon Bradshaw fumbled again. The Dallas offense turned those blunders into 14 points. Minutes later Bradshaw hit Stallworth for 15 yards, a routine first down until Stallworth slipped a tackle and loped 60 more yards for a touchdown that knotted the score. Steelers 14, Cowboys 14.

Late in the half, Staubach moved Dallas to the Steelers' 32. "We had a chance to take the lead at halftime," he says. Seeing Pearson cut across the middle, Staubach fired without flicking an eye toward cornerback Mel Blount. He had watched enough film to know how Blount reacted to this play. Film study had evolved by leaps since the 1950s, when Giants assistant Vince Lombardi installed a Polaroid camera in the press box. Giants vice president Wellington Mara, the owner's son, would photograph opposition defenses, stick the instant photos in a sock tied to a string, and lower the sock to Lombardi. In the '60s Sid Gillman spliced celluloid game film into reels devoted to particular positions or formations. It was a far cry from the laptop libraries today's coaches and players use to study virtually any instant of any game from any angle, but by 1978, after hundreds of hours watching the Steelers on clickety 16 mm film and first-generation videotape, Staubach knew what Mel Blount would do before he did it. After watching Blount backpedal time after time on plays like this, Staubach saved a split second by throwing without looking for the cornerback. He knew Blount would be ten yards behind the spot Pearson was approaching.

Only this time, Blount played a hunch. Instead of backpedaling, he ran forward—a move that could make him a Super goat if Staubach threw over his head—and popped into Staubach's field of vision like a video-game gremlin. "That pass haunts me," Staubach says. "I never saw him." Blount stepped between Pearson and the ball. Blount's interception led to a Bradshaw-to–Rocky Bleier flip that gave Pittsburgh a 21–14 edge at halftime.

"We'd just played the biggest what-if half you could play," Staubach says. "What if Pearson hadn't fumbled on the double reverse? What if Blount had guessed wrong about Pearson's pattern? The score could have been Cowboys 28, Steelers 7. "Every game's like that to some degree, but this one—man! We figured, 'We're still the best team.' So we had our heads high in the locker room. We just had a stretch when every frickin' thing went wrong, we were only down seven and we had thirty minutes to play."

Hollywood Henderson had his head down. He was in the bathroom, sniffing a hit of liquid cocaine. He recalls feeling "*ready*. Ready to show Mean Joe and Bradshaw who was better. And Franco, too, that bitch." He despised Franco Harris for being overrated—a decent runner, maybe, but a timid, useless blocker—and for being more famous than Hollywood Henderson.

On the field, workers rolled out a blue tarp representing the Atlantic Ocean. The "Caribbean Carnival" halftime show featured a boat-shaped float that crept over the tarp, "sailing" between Jamaica, Puerto Rico, and the Bahamas. Musicians were supposed to play indigenous music at each port of call, but the Haitian band didn't show up. The tarp got snarled on the base of a goalpost, tearing the ocean, and the float's lawn-mower motor conked out off San Juan.

The first twelve minutes of the third quarter were all Steel and Doomsday. Then Dallas advanced to the Steelers' 10-yard line. Landry called for a two-tight-end set. That brought DuPree's backup into the game. Jackie Smith, thirty-eight, was a future Hall of Famer who'd retired after fifteen years with the Cardinals only to let Landry talk him out of retirement to join what promised to be the best Cowboys team in franchise history. The sticky-handed Smith was roster depth for the playoffs, nothing more. He hadn't caught a pass all season. Yet here he was lining up with the starters in the third quarter of a Super Bowl that would be hailed as one of the best ever. The Cowboys sent Dorsett in motion, drawing linebacker coverage. Smith slipped into the end zone unnoticed. Crisscrossing Steelers ignored him. There wasn't a black jersey within five yards. Eighty thousand ticket-buyers and 100 million TV viewers saw Smith waiting for the 10-yard gimme that would tie the Super Bowl and cap his Hall of Fame career.

"Roger back to throw," said radio announcer Verne Lundquist, *"finds a man open in the end zone. Caught! Touchdown! . . . DROPPED! Dropped in the end zone! Jackie Smith all by himself. Oh, bless his heart, he's got to be the sickest man in America."*

Smith writhed in the end zone, staring at his suddenly buttery fingers. Dallas settled for a Rafael Septien field goal that cut the deficit to four, 21–17. Next came a crucial intervention. Bradshaw lofted a deep ball to Swann, who ran up cornerback Benny Barnes's legs as both men chased the pass. Back judge Pat Knight, standing within spitting distance of the play, signaled incomplete. Field judge Fred Swearingen, jogging in from twenty yards away, flung his flag, calling interference—on Barnes. This was the same Swearingen who midwifed the Immaculate Reception seven years before, when he ruled Franco Harris's shoestring grab a legal catch. (Oddly enough, there is no Swearingen statue in Pittsburgh.) His flag turned a punting situation into a Steelers first down at the Dallas 23. Three plays later, with Bradshaw facing third-and-4 from the 17, the Cowboys blitzed. "I got sacked by Hollywood Henderson," Bradshaw recalled. "Maybe he hit me a little extra hard and just a smidgen too late. Or maybe that was a solid-lead cloud that fell out of the sky on my head."

As Henderson glowered down at the fallen quarterback, Harris shoved him. Normally the calmest man on the field, Franco loathed Henderson, his opposite, loud and selfish, all ego. "Get away," he said. In the Steelers' version of their squabble, Henderson shot back, "Fuck you in your ass, and your mama, too."

"Come on—who talks like that?" Henderson asks today. "What I said was 'Fuck you, you soft fucking bitch. Why didn't you block me? Because you *can't block*.' Which happened to be true."

After the sack was nullified by a pre-snap penalty on the Steelers, Pittsburgh faced third-and-9. Harris seldom spoke in the huddle, but now he glared at Bradshaw and said, "Give me the ball." Bradshaw nodded. Passing down or not, he was listening to Franco. He called 93 Tackle Trap, one of the Steelers' trademark running plays.

The Cowboys showed blitz. On their own initiative, with no signal from Landry or his assistants, free safety Cliff "Captain Crash" Harris and strong safety Charlie Waters were trying to outsmart Bradshaw. Sneaking toward the line, they hoped to lure him into calling an audible—a pass they'd fall back and intercept. But after nine years in the league even a country boy from Shreveport could smell a couple of Dallas rats. "I was supposed to *believe* they were blitzing and change the play at the line," Bradshaw remembered. "But Franco wanted the ball." And by showing blitz and then retreating, the safeties outsmarted themselves. "They were completely out of position."

Franco Harris barreled through the line. One Cowboy had a shot at him—Cliff Harris, cursing as he closed the gap—but collided with a wrong-footed official who stumbled into his path. (Umpire Art Demmas, not Swearingen.) The Harrises were at cross-purposes, two yards apart, Cliff stopping the ref for no gain while Franco went 22 yards on his screw-you-Hollywood ramble to the end zone. Bradshaw recalled the play in five words: "Touchdown! Ball game! Super Bowl!"

Staubach disagreed. "It looked bad, but we weren't done." With 7:05 left in the last Super Bowl played in the '70s, the Cowboys trailed 28–17.

"Kick it deep," Noll instructed Roy Gerela, who tried to pummel the ball, slipped, and almost whiffed a kickoff for the second time in his postseason career. His duffed kick hopped toward All-Pro tackle Randy White, who was on the kickoff return team as a blocker. The last man any coach would want on his "hands team," White had a gnarled meat hook for a right hand and a cast on his broken left. His cast, Gerela's bouncing kick, and Tony Dungy all arrived at the same spot at the same instant. Dungy, a second-string defensive back who would coach the Colts to a Super Bowl victory twenty-eight years later, knocked the ball loose, the Steelers recovered, and the next play was a Bradshaw–Swann bullet that extended their lead to 35–17.

"We *still* weren't done," recalls Staubach, still defiant. In the next four minutes he threw for 24 yards, ran for 18, handed off to Dorsett for 29 more, and found DuPree open in the end zone. The score was 35–24. Dallas lined up for an onside kick that bounded to Dungy, one of the surest-handed Steelers. Dungy fumbled. Dallas recovered. Staubach hit Drew Pearson for 22 yards, Pearson for 25 more, Butch Johnson for 4 yards and 6 points. The score was 35–30. With no 2-point conversion available—the league didn't get around to that until 1994—Septien kicked a PAT that made it 35–31 with 22 seconds on the clock. The Cowboys needed another Hail Mary. But first they needed the ball.

Septien bunted another onside kick. This one zigzagged toward Vietnam vet Rocky Bleier, who watched it coming closer, his body tensed from head to shrapnel-scarred foot, until the ball seemed to select him, bounced right at him, and he fell on it as if it were a live grenade.

Bradshaw thrust a forefinger at the Florida sky. He had thrown for 318 yards, the first 300-yard performance of his career, eclipsing Bart Starr's Super Bowl record by 68 yards, completing the Steelers' shift from a turf-eating, run-first offense to an aerial attack that revolved around Bradshaw, Swann, and Stallworth. (Aside from his touchdown romp, Franco Harris had gained only 46 yards in 19 carries.) The moody quarterback still suffered spells that would later be diagnosed as clinical depression, but not that day, not after shaking off his first-half fumbles and connecting on 8 out of 9 third-down throws. A unanimous choice as Super Bowl MVP, Bradshaw hoisted the Lombardi Trophy and sent out a three-letter word to Hollywood Henderson: *"C-O-T!"*

While the losers showered and dressed, Landry blamed the refs. Swearingen's interference call on Barnes, he said, "was the kiss of death. I'd say it was the ball game for Pittsburgh." Chuck Noll got a kick out of that. For years he joked that the Steelers' Super Bowl XIII rings "have a button on the side. You push the button, there's a tiny tape recorder, and you get to hear Tom Landry bitching."

Super Bowl XIII made Hollywood Henderson "sick. Sicker than sick. Because it was tragic. That game defined our era, and it made the Pittsburgh Steelers the team of the decade."

In one sense the Cowboys were the decade's best: they won the most games. But they met Pittsburgh twice in the ultimate game and lost twice. Both games were busting with what-ifs. If DuPree

. . . If Jackie Smith . . . If Blount . . . If broken-handed Randy White . . . If Harris or Harris or Swearingen . . . One or two ifs and Dallas, not Pittsburgh, might have been the '70s' team. Instead the Cowboys were "the almost team," Henderson says. "The team that fucked up—nobody more than me. And the game only gives you so many chances."

12

APOCALYPSE NOW

Pete Rozelle convened the forty-fourth annual NFL draft on Thursday, the third of May, 1979. The draft was not televised. Only one player was present. Rozelle, fit and tanned in a gray banker's suit, greeted league and club officials and a handful of reporters in the Starlight Roof at New York's Waldorf-Astoria hotel, a ballroom lined with cafeteria-style tables. The tables held phones connected to twenty-eight war rooms in NFL cities. A roped-off corral behind the tables held more than two hundred fans—"draftniks," the *Times* called them—who'd come to cheer or heckle the Giants' and Jets' picks.

Three thousand miles to the west, the 49ers brain trust sat in a cramped room at 711 Nevada Street in Redwood City, California. The Niners' headquarters, a converted tract home, resembled a sleep-cheap motel. Inside, white-haired Bill Walsh stood ready to phone San Francisco's choices to New York—but only after twenty-eight names came off the wall in front of coach Walsh. His last-place 49ers had no first-round pick. Joe Thomas, their previous general manager, had completed his destruction of a mediocre franchise a year before by trading the team's first-round choice in this draft to the Bills for O. J. Simpson. The thirty-one-year-old Juice was pulp, his knees creaky and painful after ten years in the league. Simpson had gained 593 yards and scored a single touchdown in '78 as the Niners went 2-14. Their league-worst record earned the top choice in the 1979 draft—for Buffalo.

Rozelle cleared his throat. *"The Buffalo Bills select ... Tom Cousineau, linebacker, Ohio State."* Curly-haired Cousineau, his bulging muscles testing the weave of his Bills-blue suit, stepped from behind a curtain to shake the commissioner's hand. The Bills had flown their number one pick to New York; every other draftee would get the news by phone.

In the 49er war room a sticky nameplate reading TOM COUSINEAU came off the wall. Next came Colorado State defensive end MIKE BELL, who went to the Chiefs. No surprises yet. The Niners needed a quarterback, but Walsh knew the top three passers would be gone before his turn came. Jack Thompson, the "throwin' Samoan" who'd set an NCAA record by throwing for 7,818 passing yards for Washington State, went third overall to Paul Brown's Bengals. Morehead State's little-known Phil Simms went seventh overall to the Giants, whose fans at the Waldorf-Astoria yelled "Boo!" and "Who?" The Chiefs made Clemson's Steve Fuller the twenty-third selection. Finally, with the first choice of the second round, the 49ers chose UCLA speedster James Owens, the best athlete left on the board.

Niners quarterback Steve DeBerg was safe for another year. DeBerg was no star, a 45-percent passer with 8 touchdown throws and 22 interceptions in 1978, but with the viable quarterback prospects off the board, he'd get another chance in '79.

The 49ers had two hours to prepare for their next pick, the final choice of the third round, eighty-second overall. Tony Razzano, the team's new scouting director, had pestered Walsh about a kid Razzano loved, a skinny quarterback who'd spent most of his college career trying to win a starting job at Notre Dame. When scouts graded quarterbacks' arm strength at a tryout camp for NFL prospects, Throwin' Samoan Jack Thompson topped the scale at 8, while the Notre Dame kid got a 6. But the more Razzano talked about Joe Montana, the more Walsh liked what he heard.

Bill Walsh, forty-seven, his white hair earned in eight years as Paul Brown's offensive coordinator in Cincinnati, was hungry to make his mark on the league. Walsh, not Brown, called the Bengals' plays all those years, pioneering the short-passing attack that would be known as the West Coast Offense. Nobody confused football coaches with Newton and Einstein in those days, but Walsh wouldn't have blushed if you called him a genius. A former boxer with a head for numbers and angles, he was so X-and-O-minded that he once grabbed a pen from a waiter in a restaurant and diagrammed a play on his wife's arm. In Cincinnati, Walsh had built an offense around rag-armed quarterback Virgil Carter: he drew up plays that called for Carter to take a short, three-step drop and flip short passes for 5- or 7- or 10-yard gains. After the undermanned Bengals surprised the league with an 8-6 record in 1972, Walsh waited for head-coaching offers. None came. He expected to get the Bengals job once the sixty-eight-year-old Brown retired, but when the owner-coach stepped down three years later, he named offensive line coach Bill "Tiger" Johnson to succeed him. Walsh, astonished and crushed, sat in Brown's office with his head in his hands. Eight-plus years of loyalty to the legendary coach ("Brown-nosing," Cincy wags called it), and for what? Yet if Walsh felt betrayed then, he didn't know the half of it. Later he learned that several owners and club executives had called Brown over the years, asking permission to interview Walsh for head-coaching positions. Brown told them his assistant was overrated, a screwup. "If I were you, I wouldn't touch him with a ten-foot pole," he said. "He'll wreck your team."

When Brown told Walsh that Tiger Johnson would be the Bengals' head coach in 1976, Walsh stood up and left the room. "Wait here. You wait!" Brown shouted. But Walsh didn't wait. He went West—to San Francisco by way of San Diego, where he helped Sid Gillman refine the Chargers' passing attack, and Palo Alto, where Walsh's Stanford teams overachieved for two seasons. Then, still burning to prove himself in the NFL, he accepted Eddie DeBartolo's offer to coach the last-place 49ers.

On New Year's Day, 1979, a day after his Stanford team beat Georgia in the Bluebonnet Bowl, Walsh was waiting for his flight home. He stood under a TV at the Houston airport, watching Notre Dame's skinny quarterback rally the Fighting Irish to a 23-point comeback and a 1-point victory in the Cotton Bowl. *That kid's got something,* he thought. Great feet, for one thing. In the offense Walsh was developing—a sustained series of surgical strikes that would exploit the NFL's move toward pass-friendly rules—the ideal quarterback would set up fast, duck a tackle or two, scan the field at a glance, and choose among receivers cutting into zones of opportunity. Joe Montana fit the bill. Montana had the feet, the discerning eye, and more. He had presence. Hailing from western Pennsylvania's cradle of quarterbacks including Johnny Lujack, Johnny Unitas, Joe Namath, and Terry Hanratty (and preceding Jim Kelly and Dan Marino), Montana seemed born to the role. Like his boyhood hero Hanratty, he had gone from Pennsylvania coal country to Notre Dame, where his unflappability earned him the nickname Joe Cool.

Four months after his Cotton Bowl comeback, JOE MONTANA was still stuck to the wall in the 49ers war room. The third round dragged on. The Cowboys were up next with the seventy-sixth pick. That worried Walsh. Tex Schramm, Gil Brandt, and Tom Landry were shrewd judges of talent. The question was, would they take a quarterback? Roger Staubach had told Landry he was thinking of retiring, but Dallas had an understudy in place: Danny White, who would lead the Cowboys downhill in the '80s. Still, Dallas usually took the best player on the board. In the third round, with seventy-five players gone, Montana was at the top of their list.

Landry conferred with Schramm and Brandt in the Cowboys' war room, a few floors above the Dallas Playboy Club in a high-rise on the North Central Expressway. "We don't need another quarterback," Landry said.

In New York, Rozelle announced the draft's seventy-sixth selection: "*The Dallas Cowboys select . . . Doug Cosbie, tight end, Santa Clara University.*" Cosbie would go on to a fine career—fine times three, even. He would finish with precisely 300 catches, 30 touchdowns, and 3 Pro-Bowl appearances, but he wouldn't match the kid who fell to San Francisco.

Just before the Niners' turn in the third round, six-footer Walsh bent down to five-seven owner DeBartolo, who had graduated from Notre Dame when Hanratty was the Irish quarterback. "Are you ready for another Golden Domer?" Walsh asked.

"Go for it."

Rozelle said, "*The San Francisco Forty-Niners select Joe Montana, quarterback, Notre Dame.*" The draftniks in the ballroom shrugged.

When Walsh addressed local reporters at the last-place Niners' sparsely attended news conference, he praised top pick Owens, an Olympic hurdler who would go on to score 10 NFL touchdowns in a six-year career. Third-rounder Joe Montana, he added, had a chance to be "pretty good."

The team's tenth-round pick went unnoticed. Gangly receiver Dwight Clark had caught 33 passes in four years at Clemson. Clark was slow but had great timing, particularly when it came to answering the phone. Months before, when Walsh called Clemson to talk to Steve Fuller—the '79 draft's third-ranked passer after Jack Thompson and Phil Simms—it was Fuller's roommate who answered the phone.

"You want Steve?" he asked the 49ers coach. "Hold on."

"Wait. Who's this?" Walsh asked.

"Dwight Clark."

"Didn't you play receiver?" Walsh had a favor to ask. He was coming to Clemson to see Fuller, he said. Could Clark run pass routes for him?

"Sure. Why not?" It might be the pass-catching equivalent of serving as a tackling dummy, but Clark wasn't turning down any requests from NFL coaches. He went along, and Walsh made a mental note of Clark's footwork and fingertip grabs. He asked Clemson for film of Clark's catches during his senior season. All 11 of them. And in the tenth round of the '79 draft, 226 picks after the Chiefs selected Fuller, Walsh made Dwight Clark a 49er.

A month later Clark was sitting at a Howard Johnson's lunch counter in Redwood City when a thin, hippie-looking kid sauntered in. "He's got long blond hair and a Fu Manchu mustache, and his legs are twigs," Clark remembered. "I'm thinking, 'If he's a player, he's got to be a kicker. With that scrawny body, there's no way he can be a football player.'"

The pass-catcher stuck out his hand. "I'm Dwight Clark."

"Howyadoin'?" the blond kid said. "Joe Montana."

They practiced and partied their way through minicamp in Santa Clara. Montana and Clark ran plays with other scrubs on the practice field, learning the gears of San Francisco's ball-control offense, memorizing what Walsh called his inventory of plays. In the evenings they bummed quarters to feed pinball machines in a bar. Montana was a prankster. "Nothing nasty," he recalls, "but I liked to have fun." He would "borrow" veterans' bicycles—the preferred mode of transport at the Niners' sprawling training camp—and hang them in treetops. Once, when asked to address the team, Montana sucked helium beforehand and sounded like a duck. But the rookie was all business in practice, and his quick feet and eyes were ideal for Walsh's innovative attack. The West Coast Offense employed short drops of three or five steps rather than the traditional seven. The quarterback looked for receivers running tightly timed patterns, often quick slants that went for 4 or 5 yards—though the receiver could gain 10 or 20 if he broke a tackle. The geometry of this offense was horizontal rather than vertical. It forced defenses to cover the field from sideline to sideline, often with linebackers who were slower than the receivers. It flooded the field with receivers and running backs, giving the passer multiple targets as long as he could dodge pass rushers, who often went unblocked. Walsh's offense owed its existence to rules introduced in the '70s, the Mel Blount Rule in particular: With defenders no longer jamming receivers at will, disrupting their timing, a passer could find his receivers where he expected them to be. An offense could run more like clockwork.

"Pass first, run later," Walsh said, inverting the wisdom of Lombardi and other field marshals of an older generation. His approach was made for a passer like Montana: Drop three steps, survey the field, and release the ball before the defense reacts. In Walsh's scheme the quarterback might have three or four potential targets breaking different ways—sometimes all on the same side of the field, so he didn't have to turn his head. Montana saw his receivers cutting almost before they made their cuts, the way basketball's Larry Bird and Magic Johnson saw pick-and-rolls unfold in advance. (As Magic put it, "I know what the guys are thinking—it's like we've got ESPN.") Brian Billick, an aide to Walsh in those days, recalls Montana's "otherworldly vision. Joe saw the whole field at once." An underrated athlete who could stand flat-footed and dunk a basketball, Montana was a cool customer in the huddle, a natural leader. From the day he arrived in camp, Steve DeBerg's snaps were numbered.

If Miami's Bob Griese was Don Shula's field general, Montana would be Walsh's on-field avatar. In Walsh's plan the quarterback was literally programmed by the coach. Walsh had scripted plays in Cincinnati, prearranging the first five calls of each game for Virgil

Carter. In 1976, as Gillman's offensive coordinator in San Diego, he added several more per game for Dan Fouts. In San Francisco he began scripting the first twelve to fifteen plays of each game, a total that would rise to twenty-five, with contingency plans for various outcomes. "Bill's system was complicated, but the basics were simple," Montana recalls. "He said, 'Memorize them.'" Play-callers such as Griese might chafe at such a system. Old-school throwers such as Stabler and Bradshaw would hate it. They saw themselves as leaders, not robots. "Scripts are for stage plays," Stabler says. Montana had a different view. "Defenses were getting more complex," he says. "The whole game was. Pretty soon I was the first quarterback with headphones in my helmet, getting plays radioed in."

"The great Steelers and Raiders teams of the seventies were dinosaurs," says ex-Raider Matt Millen. "They ruled the last era when NFL football was decided mostly on the field. Ever since then, it's been decided mostly on the sidelines." Decided by coaches and their staffs studying digital film by the terabyte, devising game plans, scripting plays, printing the plays on color-coded, weatherproof, laminated play cards and depth charts, conferring over multichannel headsets to make in-game decisions—until their best-laid plans break down and the men on the field make something happen.

"I got my Hunky back!" Shula was referring to Larry Csonka, who shared his Hungarian heritage. Returning to Miami after his WFL adventure and three years with the Giants, the thirty-two-year-old Csonka chugged for 837 yards and a dozen touchdowns for the 1979 Dolphins, while Griese, efficient as ever at age thirty-four, hit on 57 percent of his passes for 14 scores. Miami won the AFC East for the sixth time since '71 only to fall to perpetual AFC Central champion Pittsburgh in the playoffs. The Steelers bounced Luv Ya Blue Houston and league MVP Earl Campbell in the next round, holding rushing champ Campbell to 15 yards in 17 carries. The dinosaurs from Three Rivers outscored their playoff foes 61–27 en route to their fourth Super Bowl in six seasons. They were 11½-point favorites against the unexpected Los Angeles Rams, who had won a weak NFC West with a record of 9-7. Among the Rams' losses was a 30–6 drubbing in Dallas, but LA got back at the Cowboys in the postseason, slipping past Landry's team, 21–19, in what would be Roger Staubach's last game.

Staubach had his sixth All-Pro season in 1979. He completed 58 percent of his passes, threw for a career-high 27 touchdowns, and led the league with a 92.3 quarterback rating. He applauded the latest rule to protect passers, who no longer had to go down to be considered down: starting in '79, a play was ruled dead if the quarterback was "in the grasp" of a defender. ("People don't want to see the quarterback on a stretcher," Competition Committee member Shula explained.) Still Staubach felt too vulnerable to suit up again. "I was thirty-eight, with more concussions than I needed," he recalls. "One in high school, one in college, seven or eight with the Cowboys, and those are the ones I remembered." That off-season he submitted to an exam by Dr. Fred Plum, the Cornell neurologist who coined the terms *persistent vegetative state* and *locked-in syndrome*. Plum found that while the Cowboys' captain showed no signs of anything so drastic, he wasn't quite normal, either. "He found a reflex on my right side that was a little different from the one on the left. That made me stop and think. If I'd been thirty-two or thirty-three, I would have kept playing, but I had five kids and wanted to be a dad to them. So I said good-bye."

Twenty-nine hours after Staubach's last snap, the '80s began.

Art Rooney, seventy-eight, funereal in his dark suit on a Pasadena afternoon, flipped the ceremonial coin at Super Bowl XIV. The Steeler owner's toss called to mind another coin flip a decade before, the one that earned Pittsburgh the right to draft Terry Bradshaw. Rooney's old doormats had won three titles since then, including the one that cost President Jimmy Carter $5, while Carter's bad luck held:

The president's approval rating slipped to 31 percent after Islamic militants overran the US embassy in Iran, taking fifty-two hostages. On day seventy-eight of the crisis ABC News billed as America Held Hostage, the Rams won Rooney's coin toss. They chose to receive and proceeded to knock the proud Steelers onto their heels behind an offensive line averaging six-four and 262. At the half, with the Rams leading 13–10, 80 million viewers saw a Coca-Cola commercial that many consider the best ever: A boy gives a menacing, limping Mean Joe Greene his Coke, which Greene guzzles before tossing the boy his jersey, saying, "Hey, kid—catch!" Viewers never saw the first take, in which Greene, who actually downed the whole Coke, got as far as "Hey, kid" before he let out a booming burp.

After Up with People's halftime "Salute to the Big Band Era," which one review called "gruesomely peppy," Bradshaw sent a third-quarter bomb Lynn Swann's way. Rams safety Nolan Cromwell got fingers on the ball, but Swann made a fast-twitch adjustment and cradled it on his way to a touchdown that put the Steelers ahead 17–13. Vince Ferragamo, the Rams' Hollywood-handsome quarterback, struck back with a 50-yarder to Bill Waddy. Then Bud Carson, Lionel Taylor, and Dan Radakovich—all ex-Steelers assistants under Chuck Noll, now working for Rams coach Ray Malavasi—figured they'd double-cross their old boss. The Rams sent running back Lawrence McCutcheon on a sweep, just as Noll and the Steelers expected. It was one of LA's favorite plays. Pittsburgh's defenders took beelines toward McCutcheon, who suddenly stopped, yanked the ball behind his ear, and uncorked the third pass of his seven-year NFL career, and the first completion, a floater to Ron Smith for 6 points that put the Rams ahead again.

Late in the quarter, Bradshaw looked deep for Swann. Number 88 was covered. "I figured I could gun it in there," recalled Bradshaw. Cromwell, the safety, hesitated for an instant to make the receiver look more open than he was, tempting Bradshaw to throw. Here came the ball, Cromwell stepping in front of Swann with nothing but air between him and the end zone. "The pass hit Nolan right between the numbers," recalled Rams defensive end Jack Youngblood, who was playing on a broken leg, hobbling toward the nearest Steeler to set a block for Cromwell. "If you throw that ball a hundred times, he catches ninety-nine." This was the one Cromwell dropped. Like Jackie Smith in Super Bowl XIII a year before, Cromwell stared in disbelief at his empty hands. The Rams still led, 19-17, but they should have been up by 9.

Three minutes into the final quarter, the Steelers facing third-and-8 from their own 27, Noll channeled his inner riverboat gambler. He was going to cross up the double-crossers with a game-breaker. He sent a play to the huddle: 60 prevent slot hook-and-go. The play called for Stallworth to fake a turn-in route and then break deep. Bradshaw was about to veto it in the huddle, switching to a play of his own, if only to prove who calls the plays around here, when Stallworth said, "Brad, it'll work."

Lining up in the left slot, Stallworth took a breath. At the snap he loped ten yards downfield before planting his right, inside foot, faking the turn-in. Then he pushed off that foot and bolted for the NFL logo at midfield.

Bud Carson saw it coming. The Steelers' former defensive coordinator, now working for the Rams, figured Noll would try to turn the game in one stroke. His defense had practiced against this play. The Rams were ready; they had cornerback Rod Perry underneath and safety Eddie Brown on top, sandwiching Stallworth as he hooked and went. But in one of the array of details that change games and careers, Brown went for the fake. He broke Carson's coverage, leaving Perry to cover Stallworth alone.

Carson made a mental note to cut Eddie Brown or shoot him. But it looked as if the Rams would get away with Brown's mistake. Stallworth took off, Bradshaw let fly, but the ball was out of reach.

Stallworth thought, *Dammit, Bradshaw, you've overthrown me.* If the ball fell, the Steelers would be punting from their own 14. A Rams score after that could put LA ahead by 9. Stallworth took a long last step as Perry leaped and swatted at the ball, coming within a hair of tipping it away. In the end, Noll's call, Stallworth's lobbying in the huddle, Brown's blunder, Bradshaw's arm, Perry's not-quite-long-enough arms, Stallworth's long stride, and his sticky fingers combined to turn third-and-8 into a 73-yard reception. Touchdown.

Brown, the beaten safety, told Carson he was sorry—he'd thought they were in dime coverage, with a sixth defensive back behind him, instead of the five-DB nickel they were in. For want of a dime, the Rams fell behind, 24–19.

With time dwindling, Ferragamo moved the Rams to the Steelers' 20. Middle linebacker Lambert, spitting and cursing through the gap in his teeth on his way to a game-high 13 tackles, sniffed out Ferragamo's pass to wideout Ron Smith with five and a half minutes left. Covering fifteen yards in great gulping strides, Lambert cut past Smith for an interception at the Steelers' 14. Ferragamo couldn't believe his eyes. "I underestimated Lambert's range," he said after the game.

In the owner's box, Art Rooney lit a cigar and started for the elevator. "Where are you going?" his son Dan asked. "The game's not over."

"It's over," the Chief said.

With five minutes to play, Pittsburgh led by 5. Pittsburgh had the ball. Two running plays went nowhere. It was third-and-long again. Bradshaw, calling signals, saw the Rams in dime coverage, for real this time. He shot the ball to Stallworth underneath. The ball was behind him. *Bradshaw, you've underthrown me,* thought Stallworth. Still he reached back for the catch, then sprinted 45 yards past twice-beaten cornerback Perry. Two plays later, a pass-interference call gave the Steelers a first down at the Rams' 1-yard line. But

LA's middle linebacker, Jack "Hacksaw" Reynolds, wasn't going down without a fight. He downed Rocky Bleier for no gain. After the two-minute warning and a beer commercial, Reynolds sliced through the line to stop Franco Harris. The Chief puffed harder on his stogie. If the Rams held, they were alive. On the next play Harris took Bradshaw's handoff and slid off-tackle into the gold-painted end zone, just under the stenciled word RAMS. Eight years after the Immaculate Reception, the first team to win three Super Bowls was about to win its fourth.

The Steelers got the ball back with 39 seconds left. The Rams were out of time-outs. "We had it won," Bradshaw remembered. "Usually an athlete is so focused on what needs to be done that it's impossible to savor it. But just this one time, when we broke the huddle, I wanted to pack it away in my mind forever. For this bunch of Steelers, the run was over."

He was prescient: The Steelers, four-time champions in half a dozen years, wouldn't play on another Super Sunday until 1996. They wouldn't win again until 2006.

Bradshaw looked up at the crowd, the cameras, the Rams, the sky. He took the snap from center Mike Webster. "You walk up to the line of scrimmage with the Super Bowl won—that's pretty cool. So I stood there a moment and absorbed it." Then he took a knee. The gun sounded, triggering amber waves of Terrible Towels in the cheap seats. (The cherry on top for Pittsburgh fans was a final score of 31–19. The Steelers, favored by 11½, covered.) The Steelers hugged. They shook hands with Ferragamo and the Rams. At last Bradshaw, Noll, Greene, Lambert, Franco and Bleier, Swann and Stallworth, made their way to the tunnel that led to the locker room, where Art Rooney was waiting. Pete Rozelle was down there, too, waiting to hand Rooney the Lombardi Trophy. Again.

A decade and a half into the Super Bowl era, Rozelle couldn't have been happier with the product. Except for the halftime show.

The fifty-three-year-old commissioner's musical tastes were square enough to fit in an elevator—he dug Mantovani and Tony Bennett, maybe a little Tom Jones after a couple of drinks—but knew he was out of sync with the coming generation of NFL fans, and that could be bad for business. According to Michael MacCambridge's *America's Game*, Rozelle met with his staff on the day after Super Bowl XIV and said, "There are three words I never want to hear again: Up with People." Thus began the revamping of the Super Bowl half-time show from a wholesome sing-along to a multimedia spectacle featuring lasers, "alien" invaders, the world's most talked-about commercials, Michael Jackson, Britney Spears, the Rolling Stones, U2, the Who, Prince's phallic guitar, Janet Jackson's wardrobe mal-function, M.I.A. upstaging Madonna, and Nicki Minaj shooting a bird that made more news than the pigeons at Super Bowl I.

Two months into the '80s, Al Davis fired a cannon shot at Rozelle. Dressed in black, silver, and shades, Davis stood beside Los Angeles mayor Tom Bradley and announced his plan to move the Raiders to LA. League bylaws required a vote of the owners to approve such a move. The vote was 22-0 against, with 5 abstentions. Davis ignored it. Over the next two years he stalked Rozelle and the NFL through local and federal courts until he won an antitrust case allowing him to move the team. Rozelle called the crisis "apocalypse now . . . the issue is anarchy." The move couldn't happen right away—not for two seasons, as it turned out, while the Raiders fought the NFL in court and sought a stadium lease in LA—but Davis's latest skirmish with his archenemy would alter the future of his franchise and the league. In the short term it made lame ducks of the Raiders, whose fans branded them the Oakland Traitors.

"That club wasn't the same Raiders anyway," Stabler says. "I was on my way out—a bunch of us were. John Madden was gone."

A decade of fighting ulcers, guzzling Maalox, and riding out bumpy team flights despite his terror of flying had worn Madden out. "I can't do this forever," he said. "Hey, Vince Lombardi only coached ten years." Lombardi died of cancer; Madden wanted out before a heart attack or stroke brought him down. After Oakland missed the 1978 playoffs, he retired at the age of forty-two. The youngest coach ever to reach 100 NFL victories, Madden is still the winningest coach in Raiders history. He never had a losing season. Most impressive of all, perhaps, was his 36-16-2 record against other future Hall of Fame coaches.

Handing the reins to Tom Flores, Madden moved upstairs to the broadcast booth. "John was colorful and I was boring, but I knew the Raider way," says Flores. The Raider way tolerated weirdness. When quirky tight end Todd Christensen quoted Thoreau on the practice field, Flores shot back, *Get your ass in the huddle*—that's a quote from Tennessee Williams."

Marooned in Oakland, sometimes booed at home by their unruly fans ("beyond doubt the sleaziest and rudest and most sinister mob of thugs and whackos ever assembled in such numbers," Hunter Thompson called Raider fans), the Raiders were also breaking in a new quarterback. After Stabler held out for a raise on his $275,000 salary, Davis traded the Snake to Houston for June Wilkinson's husband, the strong-armed, muscle-pull-prone Dan Pastorini. Stabler didn't mind. Flores was stricter about curfews than Madden had been. "Oakland wasn't so fun anymore," Stabler says. Cliff Branch was out of football, along with three-quarters of the Soul Patrol. Of the forty-three Raiders who won Super Bowl XI, thirty-one were gone three years later. Fred Biletnikoff, three years removed from his MVP heroics against the Vikings, was sitting at home in San Diego, drawing $400 a month in state unemployment benefits. That was more than he could expect from his NFL pension. If six-time All-Pro Biletnikoff waited for ten years and started taking his pension at age forty-five, it would amount to about

$150 a month. Ten years after that came a pension boost: as of 1998, veterans who'd lasted ten years in the NFL received $4,250 a month, still less than a third of what a ten-year major-league-baseball player received. A new collective-bargaining agreement in 2011 added a $600 million Legacy Fund for retirees. "That sounds like a lot until you put a pencil to it," says Conrad Dobler, who retired in 1981 after ten years with the Cardinals, Saints, and Bills. "It averages out to something like sixty-two hundred and fifty a year per man, or five hundred and twenty dollars a month. Today's players pay their limo drivers more than that. And of course it's not too helpful for the ones who are dead."

Phil Villapiano was still a Raider in '79. "But it wasn't the same," he says. The veteran linebacker adapted reluctantly to late-'70s defensive schemes. "The coaches were taking control. Everything was getting complicated. There was more and more platooning." After playing every down for most of his career, Villapiano, thirty-one, found himself shuttling in and out depending on down and distance. On third-and-long the Raiders would shift to a nickel defense—a 4-2-5 alignment of four pass rushers, two linebackers, and the five defensive backs who gave the formation its name. The first time Oakland went to nickel coverage on third down, Villapiano and Ted Hendricks came off the field holding hands. "Look, Coach, we're *girls*," the two Pro Bowlers said. "We can't play every down like *real* football players!"

Villapiano blew out a knee in Pittsburgh—where else? His foot caught a seam in the artificial turf, twisting his left leg at a weird angle just in time for a blocker to total it. His knee made a snapping sound that turned his stomach. He spent a year rehabbing on first-generation Cybex machines. "Those suckers were great! You could work one muscle group at a time," he recalls. "I was never going to be the same. I had knee ligaments torn in half. But I still wanted to come back and play every down. I wanted the game to be like it used to be." Villapiano started all thirty-two games the Raiders played in 1978 and '79. In the spring of 1980, after the Raiders missed the '79 playoffs, he came home from church with his wife and heard his phone ringing.

"Phil, it's Al Davis," the Raiders' owner said. "How you doing?"

"Good, Al. The knee feels great."

"We're looking at a kid in Buffalo. Bobby Chandler," Davis said.

"Chandler's good."

"With Freddie retired, we need a receiver. But I can't screw up here. You think he's *Biletnikoff* good?"

"Chandler can play. He's got great hands. It'll be tough to get him," Villapiano said. "What would you have to give up?"

"You."

"What? Al, c'mon. You're joking."

"Phil, I think you'll like Buffalo. Chuck Knox is gonna call you in ten minutes."

A four-time All-Pro who thought of himself as a born Raider, Villapiano joined the Buffalo Bills in 1980.

It was an election year. President Carter and Republican nominee, Ronald Reagan, were scheduled to debate on national TV that fall, but when the candidates and their advisers realized that the debate would conflict with *Monday Night Football*, they rescheduled.

MNF was still ABC Sports' five-hundred-pound gorilla, but like the evolving NFL it was a different animal from the one that remade TV sports in the early '70s. Still a Top 20 show in the ratings— barely—the brand had been diluted by "special" Thursday- and Saturday- and Sunday-night editions. "Our act was getting a little stale. We'd been on for a decade," says producer Dennis Lewin. "Ratings were down. Some of the sniping in the booth was real." Howard Cosell ripped producer Lewin's every move. Cosell interrupted and corrected Meredith's occasional replacement, Fran Tarkenton, the erstwhile Vikings scrambler whose on-field improv skills didn't translate to the booth. John Madden had been a candidate to join the Monday-night team, but *MNF* guru Roone Arledge didn't think much of Madden's TV talent. Nor did Cosell, who saw Madden as a clown, "not remotely qualified to restore the luster of *Monday Night Football*. To call him a prime-time performer is to know nothing about television." (Cosell also called O. J. Simpson "a kind, thoughtful, sensitive man who cares about people.") And so, while Madden punctuated his first CBS broadcasts with *bams* and *booms* and fresh, unrehearsed analysis, *Monday Night Football* played it safe. Football was a game of inches, Tarkenton announced, and when the going got tough, the tough did exactly what you'd expect.

Cosell, sixty-two, embittered by the failure of his variety show, often emptied his Monday-night bottle of vodka by the fourth quarter. Still, he was the only real journalist in the booth. "Howard was difficult, but brilliant in his way," recalls Don Ohlmeyer. "He still transcended sports." Thus it was Cosell who cut into a Dolphins-Patriots game on December 8, 1980, with breaking news: "An un*speak*able tragedy confirmed to us by ABC News," Cosell began, the gravity of his voice clashing with his carny-barker cadence. "John *Lennon*, outside his a*part*ment building on the *West* Side of *New* York City, the most *famous* perhaps of all the Beatles, shot *twice* in the back, *rushed* to Roosevelt Hospital, dead . . . on . . . arrival."

Cosell and Frank Gifford—the Giffer, in Lennon's fond sign-off the night Lennon visited the booth—felt awkward going on with a football telecast after such news, yet on they went, voices rising as Dolphins rookie David Woodley threw to Nat Moore to get Miami into overtime. Woodley had replaced Bob Griese when Griese tore up his throwing shoulder that fall. The thirty-five-year-old veteran would never play another down. Griese pumped his pallid fist as Uwe von Schamann, Garo Yepremian's soccer-style successor, sent a 23-yard field goal through the uprights for a 3-point victory that would help knock the Patriots out of the playoffs. New England, coached by

Ron Erhardt, went on to finish 10-6. Erhardt had been one of the co-coaches who subbed for Chuck Fairbanks in '78, when Fairbanks broke his contract and skipped to Colorado. Now, even with seven Pro Bowlers in the lineup and a coaching staff featuring Hall of Famers Raymond Berry and Jim Ringo as well as special-teams coach Gino Cappelletti and linebackers coach Bill Parcells, his Pats lost the AFC East to the 11-5 Bills, Villapiano's new team. New England missed out on wild-card bids, which went to the 11-5 Raiders, who got 49 catches and 10 touchdowns from Bobby Chandler, and the 11-5 Oilers, who got 1,934 rushing yards from Earl Campbell and 3,202 in the air from their scraggly-bearded quarterback, Ken Stabler.

The Bills flew to San Francisco needing a Week Sixteen victory over the 49ers to win the East. They knew the Niners were dangerous for a 6-9 team. Coming off the back-to-back 2-14 years that spurred Eddie DeBartolo to hire Bill Walsh, they'd started the season by beating the Saints, Cardinals, and Jets. Their low point came in Week Six at Texas Stadium. If God was peering down to watch His favorite team that week, as Dallas fans claimed, He saw the Cowboys bullying the Niners, prancing and taunting them. Walsh was convinced that Tom Landry was running up the score. Steve DeBerg threw 5 interceptions while Montana sat on the bench, looking every which way but at Walsh. "I was scared he'd send me in," he said years later. Walsh waited until after the 59–14 defeat to name Montana his new quarterback. But after three more losses the panicky coach reinstated DeBerg, who promptly lost to the Packers. A week later, against Shula's Dolphins in the Orange Bowl, DeBerg completed 29 of 41 for 225 yards, an average of 7.8 yards per completion, 5.5 yards per throw. He was running Walsh's offense well enough, but nothing went right in the Niners' eighth straight loss. On one critical series, they kicked a field goal only to have it nullified by a penalty. They kicked another field goal only to have that one called back, too, then made a miracle first down only to watch the referees spot the ball an inch short. The refs explained each call to Shula but ignored Walsh. Like many others around the league, Walsh thought NFL officials kowtowed to Shula, a cochairman of the Competition Committee. "They figured the Dolphins were a power in the league, and the Forty-Niners were just another team on the schedule," Walsh told writer David Harris. Walsh wept on the flight home.

Montana had come off the bench to connect on 3 slants for 17 yards against the Dolphins. With nothing to lose, Walsh made him his starter. "For good this time," Walsh said. With the spindly twenty-four-year-old under center, taking three-step drops and clicking through his options with bullet-point precision, the 49ers scraped out wins over the Giants (Simms 15-28, 118 yards, no touchdowns, and 1 interception; Montana 9-15, 151, 1 and 2) and Patriots (Grogan 16-32, 274, 0 and 6; Montana 14-23, 123, 3 and 1). In Week Fourteen the 5-8 Niners hosted the New Orleans Saints, aka Aints, losers of thirteen in a row. The Saints were quarterbacked by Archie Manning, a redheaded, freckle-faced regional hero. Manning had been such a star at Ole Miss that the state legislature allotted $150,000 to improve the lights at the Rebels' stadium so he'd look better on TV. Sportswriters called him "Huck Finn in hip pads." A country tune called "The Ballad of Archie Who" sold fifty thousand copies. The Saints had taken Manning second overall in the Great Quarterback Draft of '71, between top pick Jim Plunkett of Stanford and Santa Clara's Pastorini. (Ken Anderson went sixty-seventh that year, Joe Theismann ninety-ninth.) Eight years later he was the best-paid player in the league at $750,000 a year. A two-time Pro Bowler who completed 60-plus percent of his passes for a team whose long-suffering fans wore paper bags over their heads, Manning had a four-year-old son he swore was more accurate yet. Archie said Little Peyton could peg a pebble through a Cheerio. Archie's wife, Olivia, was now eight months pregnant with a boy they planned to give Archie's real first name, Elisha.

At Candlestick Park, Manning scrambled and shredded the 49ers for 377 yards through the air. His 3 touchdown passes helped give the 0-13 Saints a 35–7 lead at halftime. "We looked lost. Joe looked overmatched, but Bill stuck with him," says Billick.

Montana was nervous. "Scared," he says again—a word no one else ever used to describe him. He rallied Walsh's team to a 35–35 tie at the end of regulation. The Niners gained a record 409 yards in the second half and 73 more on an overtime drive to a game-winning field goal. "That," says Billick, "was Joe's coming-out party. And the seminal moment for the West Coast Offense—the next stage in NFL football."

Walsh called the overtime victory "the start of modern Forty-Niners history." If so, it was a stutter start, halted two weeks later by an 18–13 loss to the Buffalo Bills that closed the Niners' fourth straight losing season.

The Bills didn't last long in the playoffs. "We were gone before you could get your TV aerial adjusted," says Villapiano. San Diego's 11-5 Chargers beat Buffalo and awaited the winner of the next day's divisional playoff between the AFC Central champion Browns and a wild-card club that hadn't made the postseason since '77, the Raiders.

Still stuck in Oakland pending litigation, with Tom Flores as head coach and Dan Pastorini at quarterback, the 1980 Raiders had opened the season 3-3. At a team meeting, Dave Casper blew his stack. "I'm sick of hearing, 'We have to play better.'" He wasn't perfect, he said. "But Gene Upshaw is playing like crap. So are some other people. I'm sick of this *we* shit." Madden might have applauded Casper's fire or chewed him out for ripping Upshaw. Flores stood by while Al Davis traded the Ghost to Houston for a couple of draft picks. This was a new Raider way: playing for the future in LA. It made sense given Oakland's predicament at quarterback.

Pastorini was no Stabler. Stronger arm, classic footwork, movie-star looks, but you couldn't picture Dante Anthony Pastorini descending into the huddle with frozen blood and snot hanging off his nose. "Dan just didn't work out as a Raider," says Flores, who loved Pastorini's arm but came to doubt his guts. "Even if he hadn't got hurt, we were going to make a move." When Pastorini broke his leg against the Chiefs, his backup took over: the one guy drafted ahead of Pastorini and Manning in the Great Quarterback Draft of '71. Jim Plunkett had flopped with the Patriots and 49ers before signing with Oakland. But he was resilient, a Mexican-American who'd grown up poor, working at a gas station and a supermarket to support two blind parents, before his golden arm carried him to a Heisman Trophy at Stanford. Once installed as the Raiders' starter, the doughy thirty-two-year-old they called Chunky engineered a 38–24 win over the high-powered Chargers, followed by a 45–34 Monday-night thrashing of the Steelers that suggested Pittsburgh's decade was over.

The Raiders finished 11-5 to score a wild-card berth and hosted none other than the 11-5 Houston Oilers in the postseason. With ex-Raiders Stabler, Casper, and Jack Tatum dressed in Houston white and baby blue returning to Oakland to face the Plunkett-led silver and black, colors and loyalties were all mixed up. At the Oakland Coliseum, hosting its last NFL playoff game until the year 2000, a banner read SACK THE SNAKE. *Sic transit* the Raider Way. The Raiders blitzed Stabler from the weak side, the left-handed Snake's blind side. Cornerback Lester Hayes, his hands glommed with Kwik Grip stickum—a habit he'd picked up from Biletnikoff—leveled Stabler twice and picked him off twice more. Stabler still threw for 243 yards to Plunkett's 168, but the Raiders whipped Snake and the Oilers, 27–7. After the game a woozy, bruised Stabler said, "They play better defense than they used to."

A week later in Cleveland, snow flurries off Lake Erie froze parts of the field on the coldest football Sunday since the Packers-

Cowboys Ice Bowl of 1967. Game-time temperature for the Raiders and Browns' second-round playoff game at Cleveland Stadium was four degrees, the windchill thirty-six below. Lester Hayes's stickum froze solid. Before the game Raiders coach Flores, wearing long underwear under layers of sweaters and pants, lumbering along the sideline like an astronaut, saw wet grass at the open end of Cleveland Stadium, facing the lake. The rest of the field was frozen, but the wind blew the grass at that end of the field. "That's why we chose to defend rather than receive when we won the flip," Flores says. "To avoid that end in the second half."

Oakland led 14–12 with less than a minute left in the game. The Browns had the ball on the Raiders' 13-yard line. Forty-one seconds on the clock. Second down, 9 yards to go. Cleveland coach Sam Rutigliano conferred with quarterback Brian Sipe. A field goal right now would send the Browns to the AFC Championship, their first in the postmerger era, but kicker Don Cockroft had already missed twice and blown two crucial extra points in the cold, swirling gale. So Rutigliano called a pass play, Red Right 88, warning Sipe to "throw it in the lake" unless his receiver was wide open. They had time for two more plays. But Sipe forced the issue. He wanted to beat the Raiders now, not wait for a field goal. Sipe forced the ball to tight end Ozzie Newsome. The wind may have slowed the pass; Newsome never had a chance. Oakland safety Mike Davis intercepted and the Raiders rolled to San Diego, where they got a 65-yard touchdown when Plunkett's deflected pass fell into Raymond Chester's hands. Oakland held on to win the AFC Championship, 34–27. So much for planning for the future—the lame-duck Raiders were going to the Super Bowl.

Al Davis, sporting a black jacket and silver turtleneck, said he'd gladly accept another trophy from Rozelle if Oakland won. "I have the same amount of respect for the commissioner I've always had."

Philadelphia Eagles coach Dick Vermeil kept his NFC champions buttoned up in the team's New Orleans hotel during Super Bowl week, while Flores let his Raiders loose on the French Quarter. One night John Matuszak stayed out till 3:00 a.m., dancing with half-naked women and, in one witness's words, "drinking Bourbon Street dry."

Vermeil was appalled. "If he were on the Eagles," he said, "he'd be on a plane back to Philadelphia right now."

The next day, Coach Flores asked Matuszak what he'd been thinking. "You're six-eight, 315 pounds. You think nobody's gonna notice you?"

"Aw, Coach," Matuszak said, "I was makin' sure everybody else made curfew."

Flores bit his lip. Good answer, he thought. Good enough to get the Tooz back onto the practice field, where the Raiders again cut their final Super practice short. They were ready and felt readier yet when Sunday came at last and they got a look at the Eagles during pregame warm-ups. "We were loose," recalls Oakland's Cedric Hardman, "and they looked too tight to spit."

January 25, 1981, the fifteenth Super Sunday: a mammoth yellow ribbon, eighty feet long and ten yards wide, adorned the gray cement shell of New Orleans' seventy-thousand-seat Superdome. Five days earlier, on the day President Ronald Reagan succeeded Jimmy Carter, Iran had released America's hostages after 444 days of captivity. Yellow ribbons sprang up from Seattle to New Orleans, where Super Bowl XV kicked off at 5:00 p.m. and was effectively over at 6:00. By that time Eagles quarterback Ron Jaworski had thrown his first pass to Raiders linebacker Rod Martin, who returned the interception to the Philadelphia 30. Plunkett hit Cliff Branch to give Oakland a 7–0 lead. Jaworski then connected on a 40-yard bomb only to see the play called back on an illegal-motion penalty. ("Doggone rotten touchdown called back!" Eagles assistant Dick Coury yelled.) In the third quarter the Eagles had Plunkett as good as sacked until the chubby Oakland passer slipped the rush and flipped the ball over the outstretched hand of cornerback Herman Edwards—the future NFL coach and ESPN shouter—to Kenny King, who went 80 yards. Raiders 27, Eagles 10. Plunkett, who finished 13-21 for 261 yards and 3 touchdowns, doubled as Super Bowl MVP and Comeback Player of the Year. The next morning a happy, sleepless Flores was summoned to a TV studio for an interview with Bryant Gumbel. He was waiting outside the studio when a familiar shadow loomed over him.

"Tom!" John Madden said. "Congratulations!" Gumbel would have to wait; the only Raider coaches who ever won a Super Bowl were going out for coffee.

The Raiders and Forty-Niners were like the cities themselves," says Cedric Hardman, who played for both teams. "Oakland was rowdier. San Francisco was a little more calculating."

Calculating or not, the 49ers went 8-24 in Bill Walsh's first two years as coach. They weren't getting better. Bay Area boobirds cawed for Walsh's head. "We knew how they felt. We were bad," says Montana, "but it's not like we totally sucked. There were indications we were on the right track." One was Montana's line in the season-ending Buffalo game: 25 completions in 36 throws for 163 yards, a mere 6.5 yards per completion. Such stats didn't compute for a long-baller such as Bradshaw, who averaged a league-leading 15.3 yards per completion that year. "I was embarrassed to complete a dinky five-yard pass," Bradshaw said. But Bradshaw didn't see the revolution coming. Six and a half yards might sound dinky for a pass play, but it was two and a half yards better than the league-average running play.

"I took what they gave me," Montana says.

"There was a perfect storm brewing," says Billick. "You had ten years of rules changes favoring offense. Pass-blockers could use their hands. Defenders couldn't jam receivers. The media was changing, too, turning helmets into TV stars. Joe Montana was blond and blue-eyed. When he took off his helmet, he looked like a movie star, and he made football look easy. Of course it *wasn't* easy, and it was getting harder all the time. Players were bigger and faster. The money kept getting bigger. The price of poker was going up, and when you raise the stakes, you draw better players and more brainpower. That was the Niners' advantage. In the front office and on the sideline, it was Bill Walsh's time. On the field, it was Joe's time."

13

SPRINT OPTION

Walsh wanted to be like Paul Brown, the father figure who'd chosen Tiger Johnson over him. Brown had been the first to time players in the 40-yard dash, the first to record the result of every play of every game, the first to screen game film in classroom-style team meetings. In the 1940s Brown ran scores of clinics attended by more than two thousand coaches and aspiring coaches. To succeed, he told them, they'd have to be like him. "You must be an all-out person," Brown said. "I compare it to the commitment a man makes when he becomes a priest. You have to be a football crackpot."

Forty years later, Brown was still around. Long after he retired from coaching, the seventy-three-year-old Bengals owner attended every practice. "You'd look up and there he was, watching you with steely blue eyes," recalls linebacker Reggie Williams. "The coaches were scared of him. Everybody was. This was the notorious Paul Brown, who once cut a kicker at halftime."

Unlike his mentor, Walsh was never "Coach" to his players. He insisted that they call him Bill. But like Brown he was an all-out person, an innovator and football crackpot. His 8-24 record going into his third season made him sick to his stomach. Nobody expected the 49ers to win the NFC West, a division owned by the Rams. But an 8-8 record in 1981 sounded doable. "I just wanted our team to be competitive and start gaining some respect around the NFL, because we had lost for so long," Walsh recalled. He had an odd way of going about it, at least by the NFL standards of the day. It started with training camp. Most coaches saw camp as a time for harsh, sweat-drenched drills that would toughen their players for the season to come. Walsh thought that was stupid. Too many players got hurt at camp, too many others wore down before the season began. Rejecting old-school coaching based on military boot camps, "coaching that forces a player to test his courage or prove he's a man," Walsh based his system on players' "thinking" and even their "self-esteem." He thought his 1981 Niners looked like a .500 or better team thanks partly to a pair of newcomers at key spots on defense. Cornerback Ronnie Lott, a rookie from USC, would solidify the secondary, while Jack "Hacksaw" Reynolds, a veteran from LA by way of another universe, played middle linebacker. In addition to cutting a Chevy Bel Air in half—with a handsaw, not a chain saw—Reynolds had "surfed trees" while growing up in Ohio. "You climb a tree, then another guy cuts it down and you crash." After the Rams decided he was past his prime at thirty-three, Reynolds brought his gnarly attitude to a town and a team that welcomed it. Rather than waste time finding an apartment, he spent his first few weeks as a 49er living out of his locker, and once the season began, Reynolds showed up for game-day breakfasts at the team hotel in full uniform, clanking down the hallway in cleats, pads, and eye-black. After breakfast he put on his helmet and drove his dented, backfiring 1970 Lincoln Continental to the stadium.

The 49ers lost at Detroit to open the 1981 season. After beating the Bears they suffered a strafing by a strong Falcons club that intercepted two Montana misfires, running one back from a yard deep in the end zone for a 101-yard touchdown. The losses ate at Walsh. Nine and 26 as a head coach, too frustrated to eat or sleep, he still believed his approach was right for the times. As Schramm, Shula, and the rest of the Competition Committee gradually turned a smashmouth sport into something more telegenic and potentially more complex, scoring rose from 34 points per game in 1977 to 41 per game three years later. Forty-seven percent of NFL plays were now passes, up from 38 percent in '77. Walsh was sure his pass-first attack represented the next step in the sport's progress, with the quick-step drop and short pass serving as what he termed "a long handoff." The *San Francisco Examiner*, detecting progress, hailed him as "a great coach," but his assistants wondered aloud if the 49ers would win another game all year. After a sloppy victory over Manning and the Saints, Walsh went shopping for more defense. He traded draft picks to the Chargers for Pro Bowl defensive end Fred Dean. At six-two and 227 Dean was small for the position, a pack-a-day smoker of Kools who'd burned his bridges in San Diego by holding out for a raise on his $75,000 salary. Walsh, who loved Dean's get-offs, doubled his pay.

A convincing win over the Redskins at RFK Stadium got the Niners to 3-2. They hosted Dallas the following week. Plenty of teams disliked Tom Landry's Cowboys, but for the Niners, still smarting from their blowout loss the year before—the Cowboys laughing while Landry ran up the score—it was personal. "San Francisco hated Dallas for looking down on them," says Hollywood Henderson, one of Walsh's failed projects. Intrigued by Henderson's athleticism, he'd sent the Cowboys a 1980 draft pick for him, only to cut him after Hollywood snorted so much cocaine—before, during, and after practices, meetings, and meals—that he couldn't stay on the field for more than a few plays.

Cowboys quarterback Danny White spent much of Week Six in '81 looking up at Fred Dean, who blew through tag-team blocking to sack White 4 times in a 45–14 defeat that left Tom Landry looking as if he were sucking lemons. *Sports Illustrated* wondered "if those funny little fellows from San Francisco could possibly be for real." *Monday Night Football* seemed to think not. The 49ers had never appeared in Cosell's halftime highlights, and Howard ignored them again the next night. Walsh, who often blew off steam by shadowboxing, used a Tuesday-morning press briefing to take a few shots at the rest of the league. "We're not accepted nationally. Football elitists don't consider us," he announced, lumping Cosell and *MNF* in with what he called "influence sources" in the NFL, "forty-five-year-old men who are football groupies who prefer that we do not exist." In New York, Pete Rozelle was taking an aspirin. As if Al Davis weren't trouble enough, here was another left-coast loose cannon with a persecution complex.

Groupies of all sorts noticed when the 49ers outslugged Pittsburgh at Three Rivers, 17–14, dealing the Steelers their first home loss to an NFC opponent in ten years. Montana was off and on that day, picked off by Mel Blount and Jack Lambert but on target to Dwight Clark 7 times. Clark was on his way to 85 catches for the season, 52 more than in his entire college career. The secondary, led by safety Dwight Hicks, put the clamps on the Steelers' receivers. Hicks, cut by the Eagles, had been working in a health-food store when Walsh signed him; three years later the San Francisco secondary, known as Dwight Hicks and His Hot Licks in a nod to singer Dan Hicks's band, intercepted Bradshaw 3 times as the 49ers improved to 7-2 on the season. They led the NFC West by 2 games. Owner Eddie DeBartolo waded through his players, jumping to high-five them in the beery, happy visitors' locker room at Three Rivers, where Madden's Raiders had hung their heads after the Immaculate Reception. "These kids are amazing!" DeBartolo shouted, adding, "I don't want to get too excited. It's going to take another draft, another year, to have a real contending club." He was wrong about that.

On the sixth of December 1981, the 49ers took on the Bengals at Riverfront Stadium. It was Walsh's first visit to Cincinnati since he'd walked out on Brown six years before. Earlier that year the new-look Bengals unveiled their tiger-stripe helmets and introduced a new coach, Forrest Gregg, an offensive tackle for Lombardi's golden-age Packers, but the franchise still belonged to Brown. The owner stalked the sidelines at practice. He lectured Gregg. During home games, Brown peered down from his private box above the field. He and Walsh pooh-poohed talk of any grudge between them, but the players knew better. "Bill Walsh wanted that game. A lot," Montana recalls. Gregg had the AFC Central–leading Bengals on a 5-game win streak, while the 10-3 49ers had already clinched the NFL West. Walsh could have rested his starters against Cincinnati, just as Madden could have done in '76. Again it didn't happen.

Montana completed 23 of 36 throws for 187 yards against the Bengals, averaging 8.1 yards per completion and just 5.2 per attempt. Reporters accustomed to seeing Bradshaw and Stabler go for broke were unimpressed. "Montana and Dwight Clark gave an exhibition of what has come to be called 'dinking,'" wrote one. "Pro football has a vocabulary of its own, blitz and sack being examples, and 'to dink' is the new verb." Bradshaw would disparage Montana's dinky throws (and failure to call his own plays), but according to Bengals linebacker Williams, who chased him around that day, "Montana was deadly. He would find a way to foil you. He'd dodge, or let you get *this close* and then flick the ball away. We thought he was lucky at first, but he kept doing it. Finally you say he's just special, a true nemesis, the guy who makes you lose."

In his third pro season, Montana was finding his rhythm. His 63.7 percent completion rate was best in the league. He broke John

Brodie's club record for consecutive throws without an interception. Yet there was always more to Montana than his stats. Teammates spoke of his serenity under pressure. A master of the hot read—the art of hitting a receiver who purposely cuts his route short, so the passer can throw before the rush arrives—he foiled blitzes almost before they started, zipping the ball to Clark or Freddie Solomon in the space a blitzing linebacker left behind. Twenty-one guys named Joe were in the league in 1981, but only one Joe Cool. Others got flustered when the clock ran down or the pocket collapsed. For Montana, as for other special athletes such as Magic Johnson, Larry Bird, and Wayne Gretzky, time seemed to slow down when it mattered most. Like them he had abundant self-assurance, keen vision, and a geometric sense of players' movements. Like them he saw the next moment before anyone else. Montana never claimed to know how he did it. "I could make hot reads in a hurry," he allows. "Other than that, I was trying to stay alive and find somebody open."

Staubach, who had some of the same magic, has an idea of where it comes from. "You feel you've put in the work, paid the price, to get to that key moment. Now you *deserve* to have it go your way. And it does. Because you prepared, but also because there was no shred of doubt holding you back. But even that isn't enough. In a team sport, you've got to transfer that feeling to your teammates. That's what the great ones do." More than leadership, such contagious confidence is an act of will. It says, *Follow me.*

After Cincinnati cut the 49ers' lead to 7–3, the Niners huddled. "We are gonna get this done," Montana told them. Then he led a drive that ended with a 15-yard touchdown pass to Clark. Bengals quarterback Ken Anderson went out with a sprained toe and was replaced by none other than Jack Thompson, the throwin' Samoan who'd gone third overall in the 1979 draft, seventy-nine picks ahead of Montana. Thompson would throw for 33 career touchdowns to Montana's 273. As Anderson's backup he completed 10 of 18 passes and watched Montana throw for 2 touchdowns and run 5 yards for another—a fourth-quarter score that put the game away.

As the Niners' charter banked west over Cincinnati that night, Walsh felt he'd gotten even with Brown. Even better than even: one up. "It was snowing down there. Lights on," he recalled, "and I just sat there quietly, looking down, feeling euphoric." Ahead lay the 49ers' first trip to the postseason since 1972.

Phil Villapiano was freezing his butt off in Buffalo. During training camp in '81, his first year with the Bills, Villapiano tutored a young linebacker named Lucius Sanford. When the season began, Coach Chuck Knox named Sanford the starter. "Phil, I need you off the bench. You'll play middle or outside when somebody goes down," Knox said.

Too hyper to sit, Villapiano asked to play special teams. Knox made him captain of the young kamikazes on the kickoff- and punt-return units, and the ten-year veteran found himself sprinting toward contact, surrounded by "maniacs and explosions." He relished every play. Between games he pumped iron and partied with a new favorite running mate, Conrad Dobler, the saturnine offensive guard known for holding, tripping, cut-blocking, leg-whipping, and gouging opponents. *Sports Illustrated* put Dobler on its cover under the headline "Pro Football's Dirtiest Player." A Fu Manchu'd three-time Pro Bowler, he admitted biting the Vikings' Doug Sutherland.

"Sutherland put his fingers in my mouth," Dobler says today. "What did he expect? I don't think he was trying to stroke my mustache." According to *Sports Illustrated*'s Paul Zimmerman, "Dobler made teams that he played on better. He played hurt, didn't complain, but he was a filthy, filthy player." Another *SI* writer claimed Dobler "makes even Oakland's George Atkinson look like Mr. Clean." To columnist Jim Murray, he was "troglodytic." Once, when Philadelphia's Bill Bergey asked to see the cast on his broken hand,

Dobler gave Bergey a close look at the cast before smashing him in the mouth with it. And while Dobler relished his thuggish reputation, he insisted he was a thinking man's goon. On an NFL survey asking players, "Did you take up football for any particular reason?" he wrote, "It is the only sport where there is controlled violence mixed with careful technical planning." When St. Louis traded him to New Orleans, he said, "Religiously speaking, it's an advancement from a Cardinal to a Saint." By 1981 he and Villapiano were thirty-one and thirty-two years old, respectively, slower and gimpier than in the Raiders-Cardinals battles of the '70s. During one of those games Dobler, hearing that Villapiano was playing with injured ribs, punched him in the chest. As teammates in Buffalo they laughed about that. They also shared an affinity for a B-vitamin elixir called red juice. "We took turns injecting each other in the ass," Villapiano says. "I shot Conrad, he shot me, and we laughed."

"Yeah, till the stuff made Phil's legs swell up. It gave him gout," Dobler recalls.

"We were old-time football," says Villapiano. "We played for keeps, then we'd drink and raise hell. After the war, you party."

With Dobler and his linemates protecting quarterback Joe Ferguson, who threw for 3,652 regular-season yards and 24 touchdowns, the 10-6 Bills advanced to the wild-card round of the playoffs. There they met the Jets, making their first playoff appearance since 1969, in a cold rain at Shea Stadium. New York had 56-percent passer Richard Todd and 623-yard rusher Freeman McNeil in the backfield and fire-breathing bookends Joe Klecko and Marc Gastineau on the defensive line. Villapiano joined Lucius Sanford in Knox's 3-4 alignment for the Bills. Less reckless than in his Raider days, Villapiano was beginning to feel all of his thirty-two years. He started getting stingers, sudden pain and tingling after impact. The first time it happened, a pain like bee stings going up and down his left arm, he was afraid he'd broken his neck. Growing leery of headfirst contact, he did more arm-tackling. "Lucius," he told Sanford, "you'll know you're getting old when it hurts *you* to make the tackle." Villapiano stung Todd with an interception during Buffalo's 31–27 upset, and the Bills were off to Cincinnati for the second week of the playoffs.

Brown's Bengals had progressed from the original dink-and-dunk days of Virgil Carter to a more sophisticated attack featuring Ken Anderson, another Walsh protégé. (All three quarterbacks Walsh tutored in Cincinnati went on to lead the NFL in completion percentage.) In 1975, Walsh's last year with the Bengals, he'd tutored Anderson to a Pro Bowl season. "Bill Walsh made me," Anderson said. Now the tiger-striped quarterback was a 63 percent passer, the league's MVP, starring with thousand-yard rusher Pete Johnson behind a line cemented by second-year left tackle Anthony Muñoz. One of the best blockers ever, Muñoz protected his quarterback's blind side while Anderson fired lazy spirals to wide receivers Isaac Curtis and Cris Collinsworth, a beanpole rookie whose 16-yard touchdown catch put the Bengals ahead in their playoff tilt against Buffalo. Cincinnati held on for the first postseason victory in franchise history, eliminating the Bills in what would be Conrad Dobler's final game. Knees shot, mustache going gray, the "dirtiest player" retired, hobbling toward the next in a series of knee surgeries that would ultimately total thirty-two: thirty-two operations, nine knee replacements.

In the '81 NFC playoffs, Dallas's Flex defense spelled doom for the Tampa Bay Bucs, 38–0, while the Giants upset Ron Jaworski and the Eagles to earn a divisional-round date with San Francisco. The 49ers' offense was still novel enough to be described around the league as "college-y" or, worse, "sissy football." The Raiders had their own name for it: "Montana and the chickenshits." The 9–7 Giants were said to be tougher. "More traditional," said their linebackers coach, Bill Belichick. Along with defensive coordinator Bill Parcells, Belichick helped head coach Ray Perkins orchestrate the Giants' punishing defense, which wasn't so traditional at right outside linebacker. That was where a rookie out of North Carolina was reinventing the position. Six-three and 240 pounds with 4.4 speed and a squeaky, adenoidal voice, Lawrence Taylor was a Tasmanian devil in pads and a helmet, a defensive force unlike any since Joe Greene. In the preseason, on the first play of his first pro practice, Taylor blew through veteran blockers and sacked the passer. The offense regrouped and snapped the ball again. Taylor sacked the passer again. "This happened *six times in a row*," the Giants' Phil Simms recalled. Other outside linebackers played the run or dropped into pass coverage. Taylor, the 1981 Rookie of the Year and Defensive Player of the Year, spun past or through blockers to hunt quarterbacks. The 49ers were lucky to have subterranean help against Taylor. Their home field at Candlestick Park was below sea level. "When the tide comes in from the bay, the water rises right up through the ground," Clark recalled. The two teams had met in the regular season, a hard-fought battle at Candlestick Park in which the quarterbacks made the difference. Montana hit 27 of 39 passes for 234 yards while Scott Brunner was 13 for 34 with 3 interceptions. The Niners held on, 17–10, forcing the Giants to win three in a row to reach the playoffs. Now, five weeks later, with rain pelting sodden Candlestick on the third day of 1982, Taylor and the Giants slipped and skidded while the 49ers, wearing extralong cleats for better footing, held their ground. They sent half a dozen blockers from all angles to get in Taylor's way.

On the Niners' first play from scrimmage, Montana took a three-step drop and flung a dart to Clark. First down. Two penalties that slowed their opening drive contributed to the playoff game's first statistical quirk: the 8-yard pass that gave San Francisco a 7–0 lead also gave Montana 111 yards passing on a single scoring drive, a record that still stands.

Rather than outslog the Giants, Walsh intended to outsmart

Perkins, Parcells, and Belichick with motion and multiple sets including one that had receivers Clark and Freddie Solomon lining up in the backfield behind Montana. John Madden, in his debut as CBS's top analyst, drew squiggly white lines on a brand-new toy called the CBS Chalkboard—TV's first telestrator. "One thing about the Forty-Niners offensively, they never give you the same look," Madden blurted. "One back in the backfield, or two, motion, fake reverses—just about everything you can imagine comes out of this group of red jerseys." The Giants stayed close to the red jerseys, with Taylor sacking Montana to force a third-quarter punt. The 49ers led by 7, 24–17. Giants quarterback Scott Brunner, subbing for the sore-shouldered Simms, guided the visitors to the San Francisco 5-yard line. From there, kicker Joe Danelo lined up a 21-yard field goal. Danelo was 44 for 52 career inside 30 yards, automatic from 21. He pulled the kick off the left upright and watched it plunk straight down. Half an hour later, cornerback Lott read Brunner's eyes or his mind. Lott's second interception of the afternoon sealed the Niners' triumph, sending them to another date with Dallas.

"Next Sunday," said play-by-play man Pat Summerall, "don't miss the NFC Championship between the Dallas Cowboys and San Francisco Forty-Niners."

"That," Madden said, "is a *real* real big one."

They drove across the Golden Gate and Bay Bridges, up and down the San Francisco Skyway and the Serra and Lick freeways, 60,525 fans bringing coolers, 49ers pennants, and a collective grudge to creaky old Candlestick Park. Several upper-deckers sported FUCK DALLAS T-shirts. The older ones remembered the 49ers' last trips to the postseason, when the Cowboys bounced them from the playoffs three straight times from 1970 to '72. Fresher wounds had been inflicted by Dallas's six-foot-nine Too Tall Jones. Early that week the Pro Bowl defensive end called his team's 45–14 regular-season loss to the Niners a fluke. "They didn't beat the real Cowboys," he said. "I didn't have a lot of respect for the Forty-Niners then, and I still don't." With Hollywood Henderson retired—after snorting his way out of San Francisco, Henderson signed with Shula's Dolphins, but broke his neck making a preseason tackle—Too Tall was Big D's big mouth. Of Joe Montana he said, "All you have to do against that guy is throw off his timing and you blow his game."

Asked about Jones's comments, Montana shrugged. But Walsh was livid at being slighted again, grumbling about "goddamn Dallas. They're so arrogant . . . I'm fed up with their bullshit." For a San Francisco team eager to prove it belonged among the league's elite, the 1981 NFC Championship was more than a grudge match. Walsh called it a vendetta.

As the Niners' Ray Wersching kicked off at 2:01 Pacific time, a four-year-old fan peered between grown-ups, looking along the sideline for number 16. The boy was Tom Brady, a preschooler from nearby San Mateo, who would later wear number 12 for the Patriots. He and his dad were there to cheer for the Niners and young Tom's hero, Joe Montana.

The retired Staubach stood near the Dallas bench in street clothes, clapping his hands for the Cowboys while Danny White led them nowhere. After their three-and-out, the versatile White did something Staubach never could. He punted. The league's only passer/punter pushed the 49ers back to their own 37. Young Tom Brady whooped as Montana, far thinner and slighter than his linemen, jogged onto the soggy Candlestick turf. Walsh's script for the Niners' first series called for a naked bootleg that sent the quarterback rolling to his right while Too Tall Jones, unblocked, bore down on him. Montana faked. Jones skidded past, reaching for him. Montana stepped forward and hit Dwight Clark for a first down, then turned to Jones and, looking anything but cool, yelled, "Respect *that*, motherfucker!"

Jones swore after the game that he didn't know what Montana was pissed about. Doubly flummoxed by the Niners' play-calling, a function of Walsh's unpredictable script for the first quarter, Jones could only flash back to October's no-respect blowout, when "things started happening so fast that we couldn't get control of the game." On the Cowboys' second possession, Tony Dorsett took a handoff from White, cut back, and slipped on the soggy turf. As safety Dwight Hicks flew by him, overrunning the play, Hicks's heel somehow got inside Dorsett's helmet and gave him a nasty lick in the left eye, knocking him out of the game. The Dallas drive stalled. Rafael Septien came on to try a 44-yard field goal. Connecting from that distance in a title game would be a feat for any kicker, particularly one with a hernia. Not that Septien knew he had a hernia. The Cowboys' team doctors had told Landry about it but said kicking wouldn't worsen it, so Landry, figuring that what the kicker didn't know wouldn't hurt the team, said nothing. Septien split the posts to cut the Niners' early lead to 7–3.

Scoring early seemed to give the Cowboys a measure of control they'd lacked in October. After a 49ers fumble, White threw a fast-ball strike to Tony Hill, the ball meeting Hill at the left-side pylon for a 26-yard touchdown. Dallas 10, San Francisco 7. Staubach, Landry, and the blinking Dorsett watched Montana's 20-yarder to Clark put the 49ers back on top. A crucial pass-interference call on Lott and a 5-yard dash by Dorsett (reentering, red-eyed) made the halftime score Cowboys 17, 49ers 14. The Niners retired to their double-deck dressing room—offensive unit on top, defense below. On the upper tier, a hooded-eyed Montana sank into a chair under a sign that read I WILL NOT BE OUTHIT. He was thinking of more than his team's 3-point deficit. At 3:30 Pacific time, Montana was worried about losing his life. During pregame ceremonies, the team's security detail had told him about a phone call to the stadium. The caller said he was coming to the game to shoot Joe Montana.

When the security team told him about the call, Montana nodded. He put his helmet on and headed for the field.

Neither coach gave a halftime pep talk. Landry was no talker, and Walsh knew that no speech would make his players more determined than they already were. They knew what was at stake—a first-ever trip to the Super Bowl. They knew about the death threat to Montana, too. As if protecting him from Too Tall and the Doomsday Defense weren't enough, they had an assassin to worry about. Montana, who'd confirmed the threat to his teammates once the news started going around, joked glumly that he didn't want to run any more naked bootlegs. Maybe he should just stay in the huddle in the second half or run quarterback sneaks—use the other guys as human shields.

"Anybody want to trade jerseys?"

Walsh spent the halftime break discussing tactics with his assistants. They decided to keep attacking Everson Walls, Dallas's rookie cornerback, who had led the league in interceptions. The 49er coaches saw that stat as a fluke. Watching film clips of every ball thrown Walls's way that year, they concluded that his 11 interceptions were a function of his vulnerability: Other teams kept picking on Walls, throwing his way, giving him more chances to pick the ball off. Sometimes he got lucky—an underthrown pass, a receiver who slipped and fell—and now and then he made a hell of a play. Still the Niners' coaches saw Walls as the Dallas secondary's weak link.

Landry paced the visitors' smaller, shabbier locker room while his assistants worked on adjustments for the second half. They all knew what was at stake for the Dallas Cowboys in the next thirty minutes of football. Vindication. Victory would be the penultimate step toward redeeming what Henderson called their tragic loss in Super Bowl XIII, the game that made the Steelers the team of the '70s. Today's second half could be the start of Dallas's decade.

Montana and White traded third-quarter interceptions. Were

they nervous? Both denied it later, but those two turnovers made for a total of six in forty minutes of play. This was no classic; it was a messy battle marked by fear, adrenaline, strategy, and sudden chances. After White's interception gave San Francisco the ball at the Dallas 13, Walsh ordered Montana to keep it on the ground. "No more mistakes." Four running plays led to a 2-yard touchdown by Johnny Davis that gave San Francisco a 21–17 lead. Another Septien field goal cut the lead to a single point going into the fourth quarter.

The Niners kept picking on Everson Walls. Freddie Solomon turned the Dallas rookie sideways for a 21-yard completion. But when running back Walt Easley fumbled, it was Walls who dove on the loose ball. Dallas drove to the Niners' 21. White looked for Doug Cosbie, the tight end Dallas had picked instead of Montana in the '79 draft. Hacksaw Reynolds, counting on help behind him, let Cosbie go. A hearbeat later, Reynolds saw White's pass going by—straight to Cosbie, who stepped into the end zone to put the Cowboys ahead. Dallas 27, San Francisco 21. The game's fifth lead change left Candlestick as quiet as the waters of the bay. There were ten and a half minutes to play.

After Septien's kickoff, Montana looked around the 49ers' huddle. Guard Randy Cross, who'd been fighting the flu, leaned over and threw up. Several Niners recoiled. They groaned. Montana shut them up: "Listen. We are gonna score."

Montana hit Clark for a first down at the San Francisco 35. Next he spun a tight spiral toward Solomon, covered by Everson Walls, on the right sideline. Solomon had a step on Walls, a clear shot at a 40- or 50-yard gain, but the ball was half a step behind him. Walls grabbed it at the Dallas 27—Montana's third pick of the day, Walls's second interception. Picking on Walls was looking like an epic mistake. For the first time, the Cowboys had clear control of the game. A short drive and a field goal would give them a two-possession lead in the fourth quarter. Landry tried to milk the clock, but on third-and-5

White threw behind Doug Donley. Incomplete. White stood with his hands on his hips, shaking his head. Unlike every other quarterback in the league, he stayed on the field while the punting unit came in. The quarterback/punter boomed a high spiral that pushed the 49ers back to their own 11. Montana led the offense onto the field. One more possession. Trailing by 6, the Niners were 89 yards from the red-painted end zone, a little less than a city block. It looked farther. The clock read 4:54.

Landry and the Cowboys went to a modified prevent defense with six defensive backs. Walsh crossed them up with running plays—Montana handing off to Lenvil Elliott, a smallish, little-used backup whose main asset was his work ethic. Walsh had cut Elliott in the preseason, then re-signed him after he rehabbed from knee surgery. A tenth-round draft pick out of Northeast Missouri State College, Elliott was thirty years old. He had carried the ball 7 times all year. Now, in a do-or-die series in the last four minutes of the NFC Championship, Elliott punched through the line for 6 yards. On second-and-4, Montana found Solomon for a first down. Then Elliott barreled right for 11 yards. Elliott swept left for 7 more. That gave him 24 yards on this decisive possession, 5 less than his regular-season total. An offsides call got the 49ers across midfield at the two-minute warning.

Walsh had Jones and the Doomsday Defense reeling. During the commercial break he called yet another handoff to Elliott, but this one would be temporary. On the first play after the two-minute warning, Montana tucked the ball between Elliott's hands. Too Tall and the rest of the Cowboys' front line pursued what appeared to be another sweep—until Elliott handed off to Solomon on a reverse that went to the Dallas 35. On the next play, Montana hit Clark at the 25. He hit Solomon at the 13. "With one minute and fifteen seconds left in the game, a field goal means nothing," CBS announcer Vin Scully said. "It's touchdown or bust." Seconds later, Solomon beat Walls in the end zone. For the second time on a do-or-die drive, Montana missed him. His humpbacked pass flew over Walls, receiver Solomon, and everybody else. Walsh jumped up and down in frustration. "I thought that was the championship right there," he would say. "We were never going to get that open again."

Second-and-10 from the Dallas 13: Elliott swept left, pressing the ball to his hip on what would be the final carry of his NFL career. He broke two tackles before three Cowboys dragged him down at the 6. It was third down. Fifty-eight seconds to play. Walsh called time-out. As Montana walked toward him, the coach said, "We're going to call a sprint option. Dwight will clear." Montana nodded. "If you don't get what you want," Walsh cautioned, "simply throw the ball away." The play's full name was Brown Left Slot Sprint Right Option. Diagramming it for the offense before the game, Walsh had predicted the Cowboys would fall for it. "This is great when they're tired, they're confused, and they want to get back to Dallas. This'll knock their ass off," he said. Solomon was the primary receiver, Clark the safety valve. Walsh told Montana to keep Clark in mind: "Get ready to go to Dwight. Got it?" Montana didn't answer. He was sauntering onto the field as if he had all the time in the world.

In the huddle, ten teammates leaned in to hear. "Brown Left Slot," Montana said. "Sprint Right Option."

With the field and the season down to 6 yards of mud, Landry finally ditched his prevent defense. The Cowboys reverted to their usual 4-3-4, hoping to pressure Montana or sack him. And from the moment center Fred Quillan snapped the ball, the 49ers' sprint-option play began falling apart. Primary receiver Solomon slipped, throwing off everyone's timing. He was out of the play. Montana rolled right, gaining time. The stadium clock clicked from 00:56 to 00:55, and a decade of NFL progress shaped each player's path. The play began at the left hash mark, aligned with the goal's left upright in accordance with the hash-mark rejiggering of 1972. Montana's blockers clawed the Cowboys' front four with open hands. The Niners' receivers went unjammed into their patterns. Dwight Clark made his way onto the red-painted grass of the end zone shadowed by Everson Walls.

Rolling right, Montana faced a wall of white jerseys—Too Tall Jones, tackle Larry Bethea, and linebacker D. D. Lewis—closing him into a shrinking space near the sideline. Montana pump-faked. Jones went for the fake, his eighty-eight-inch wingspan going straight up until his arms cast shadows like goalposts. Montana drifted right, waiting for Jones to come down. Had he thrown then, Too Tall could have blocked or intercepted the pass. Montana held the ball while Dwight Clark slowed and stopped in the back of the end zone. With Walls all over him, Clark spun and ran the other way along the end line while Montana, moving to his right with no escape route, spent a second waiting for him to clear. A second was all he had. Pinned to the sideline, Montana was out of room and out of time, but still alive. The play was pure Walsh geometry, Clark arriving directly behind the spot Solomon would have occupied if he hadn't slipped. Montana didn't have to turn his head to see Clark. Still hearing Walsh say, *Dwight will clear,* he saw a red jersey moving from left to right in the back of the end zone. Leaning backward, Montana flung a too-high ball that pulled Clark off his feet just as Bethea drove Montana to the turf. Clark jumped higher than he'd ever jumped. Walsh stepped sideways to get a better look. Thousands of fans stood on tiptoe, craning to see, and four-year-old Tom Brady burst into tears. All the grown-ups were blocking his view.

14

AFTER THE CATCH

At the apex of his leap, Clark got the fingers of his left hand on the ball. That was enough to stop the pass, but not to control it. He juggled the football for a split second, the ball floating weightless for an instant until Clark clamped it with both hands and brought it to earth. . . .

Montana lay flat on his back, looking at the sky. Like Bradshaw after the Immaculate Reception, he never saw his biggest throw caught. "But I heard the crowd roar, and that had to be good."

A pair of fans in the cheap seats hoisted a bedsheet scrawled in Niner red: AMERICA'S BRAND-NEW TEAM. But Dallas had another chance. After Clark's fingertip grab and Ray Wersching's extra point, the Cowboys trailed by a single point, 28–27. There were 47 seconds to play. They needed to gain about 45 yards to get into field-goal range.

Danny White clapped his hands. "Here we go. Let's get it done," he said. If White sounded sure of himself, his teammates didn't all share his confidence. In spirit, at least, the Dallas huddle still belonged to Roger Staubach, who stood on the sideline in street clothes, holding a microphone, waiting to do postgame interviews for CBS.

At the snap, White dropped back to his own 15. He shot a bullet to Drew Pearson, running a deep slant. Pearson, who'd caught Staubach's Hail Mary in the 1975 playoffs, pulled the ball to his chest and crossed midfield. One man, rookie cornerback Eric Wright, stood between him and the end zone. *"Caught by Pearson,"* Vin Scully told 69 million viewers. In the next instant Wright snagged Pearson with one hand, grabbing the neck of his jersey and yanking him down—a horse-collar tackle, outlawed in 2006 but still legal then. *"Wright had him by the shirt or he's gone!"*

The clock showed 00:38. With a first down at the San Francisco 44, the Cowboys had plenty of time to gain the 4 or 5 more yards that would put them inside Septien's range. As the herniated kicker made practice kicks behind the Dallas bench, General Manager Tex Schramm hoped the Cowboys had the right man under center. But he doubted it. For all his talent, White lacked Staubach's contagious leadership quality, his magic touch. As Schramm later told the *Dallas Morning News*, "If Roger had thrown that ball" on the previous play, "that guy probably never would have gotten Drew Pearson." It sounded crazy coming from the executive who helped computerize NFL scouting. Such spooky action-at-a-distance couldn't turn a football game, could it?

On the next play, White fumbled. Maybe Tom Landry should have had his quarterback in the shotgun, giving White a few more heartbeats to duck the rush, but to Schramm and other Lone Star loyalists the fumble seemed fated. It wasn't Danny White's day. Defensive end Jim Stuckey fell on the ball for the 49ers.

Montana ran out the clock. He raised both index fingers as young Tom Brady and sixty thousand other Niners fans hooted and cheered. Then Montana pulled his helmet lower on his head, as if it might repel an assassin's bullet. He tucked the ball under his arm and sprinted through the red-painted end zone to the safety of the Niners' double-deck locker room, where one party was on the bottom tier and another on top.

Rookie broadcasters Staubach and Terry Bradshaw were to conduct postgame interviews for CBS, with Bradshaw assigned to the winning team and Staubach the losers. But Staubach wasn't about to ask his old teammates how it felt to lose the game of the decade—that task fell to Bradshaw, who found the Cowboys "screaming, cussing, throwing helmets." Landry, stoic in defeat, spoke of how close his team had come to a sixth trip to the Super Bowl. "Sometimes time runs out," he said. Only after the TV lights dimmed, after defensive end Harvey Martin called the Cowboys' disappointment their worst ever, worse than their "tragic" loss in Super Bowl XIII, did Landry evince a bit of bitterness. "The Forty-Niners are not a better team than us, but the game ended at the right time for them," he said. Five years later, when his own life was threatened by a crank caller, he coached a game in a bulletproof vest. By then the Cowboys were also-rans, a team stepped over by two NFL dynasties. Not until the '90s, after Jimmy Johnson replaced Landry, would Dallas rise again.

The 49ers advanced to Super Bowl XVI: a rematch against Paul Brown's Bengals. Clark's grab in the NFC title game was already capitalized as The Catch by the time they flew to Detroit for the first Super Bowl played north of the Mason-Dixon Line. Six weeks after leaving Cincinnati one up on Brown, Walsh behaved as if he knew destiny was on his side. Revealing an antic streak some of his players didn't know he had, he met them at the team hotel disguised as a bellhop and yanked their luggage off the team bus. When the bus got stuck in traffic on Super Sunday, he announced that the game had started without them: The equipment manager was coaching, and the assistant equipment manager was playing quarterback. "And we just took the lead, seven to nothing!"

A record 110 million Americans tuned in Super Bowl XVI from the Silverdome in Pontiac, Michigan. Diana Ross sang the national anthem—a hint of future spectacle as pop stars began capitalizing on the game's growth. "It didn't feel like a game. It was a *time*," recalls Reggie Williams, who was making his Super Bowl debut for the Bengals. "I remember thinking about Vietnam, and the college kids shot at Kent State—the country changing so fast—and here I was at the Super Bowl. Then this skinny, little, tiny person shoves me. It's Diana Ross. So small and glittery and beautiful, and just *disdainful* of us football players. 'Let me by!' she says. 'I gotta get out there and sing.' And she goes to the twenty-yard line and waits, and she starts, '*Oh, say can you see . . . ,*' and I stood there singing my damn heart out."

Walsh called a trick play on the 49ers' opening drive: a handoff to halfback Ricky Patton, who handed off to Freddie Solomon on an end around. Just as Williams and the Bengals closed in on Solomon, he lateraled to Montana, who hit Charle Young for 14 yards and a first down. The flea-flicker was contagious confidence in action, and more. It was Walsh's way of flipping the bird at Paul Brown, who always liked to run a surprise play before the opponent got settled. The Niners took a 7–0 lead. They went on to win their first Super Bowl, 26–21. Two years after finishing the 1979 season 2-14, a year after going 6-10 in 1980, the San Francisco 49ers were Super Bowl champions, and Walsh was two up on Paul Brown.

Looking back, players, coaches, and fans all saw Montana's pass to Clark in the NFC Championship as a turning point. With one immortal Catch, Montana launched a new and different dynasty. The Steelers' and Raiders' hairy-chested brand of '70s football was on the way out, eclipsed by a cooler, more efficient NFL embodied by Walsh, Montana, and the 49ers. Less than a decade after the Immaculate Reception, the most colorful era in sports history— pro football's raging, reckless, hormonal, hairy, druggy, drunken, immortal adolescence—was over.

The NFL banned stickum in 1981. Human adhesives Fred Biletnikoff and Jack Tatum were retired by then, but Lester Hayes, Tatum's stickum-fingered successor in the Raiders' secondary, saw his interceptions dip from 13 to 3. Bengals quarterback Ken Anderson was the league's Most Valuable Player, making it two MVPs in a row for West Coast Offense passers. "The Browns' Brian Sipe won the year before," recalls '78 MVP Bradshaw, "and Sipe didn't have enough arm to break a windowpane! Suddenly Anderson's going twenty for twenty-two against our Steelers defense! I marveled at that. The West Coast Offense was the modern approach, and pretty soon Montana and Walsh are going to take it to a whole 'nother level. It was a new evolution, the start of what we see today."

In 1981 the Giants' Lawrence Taylor, who would remake the outside-linebacker position in the '80s, claimed the first of his three Defensive Player of the Year trophies. The league's Byron "Whizzer" White Humanitarian Award, named for the Supreme Court judge who once played for the Chief in Pittsburgh's backfield, went to Franco Harris. No longer hitchhiking to practice, Harris was now earning $350,000 a year, more than triple White's salary as an associate justice of the US Supreme Court, and giving tens of thousands to charity. In 1984, after his eighth thousand-yard season, Harris turned down the Steelers' offer of $560,000 for another season, and they cut him. He signed with the Seahawks for $385,000 and played out the string in Seattle, looking too shiny in the Seahawks' bright silver and blue. Ralph Wiley of *Sports Illustrated* described him "trotting onto the field as he always has, gingerly, like a man late for an appointment with his podiatrist." Still floating behind the line as if testing a force field, he was a step slow to the hole. He carried the ball 68 times in 1984, his final season, gaining less than 3 yards per try, never once crossing the goal line. "I liked Seattle, liked the fans, and I was in great physical shape," Harris recalls today. "But there was a mental thing going on . . . I couldn't picture myself breaking Jim Brown's record in a Seattle uniform." Franco Harris retired with 12,120 career yards, only 192 short of Brown's all-time record.

Phil Villapiano was gone, too. Ten years after the Immaculate Reception, the linebacker who covered Harris on that play was earning $200,000 in his fourth season with the Buffalo Bills. One more year at that level, he figured, and he was set for life. Villapiano kept getting stingers, and his left knee was shot—"like Jell-O and Silly String"—but others had it worse, and he still loved the game. Not that he was crazy about where the game was going, with all the platooning, overcoaching, and passer-protection rules that turned the quarterback into football's version of a designated hitter. What Villapiano loved was the hunt, the adrenalized *charge!!!* He got off on sprinting downfield, looking for someone to hit while sixty or seventy thousand fans howled and millions more watched on TV. What straight job would ever match that? He spent most of the 1983 season re-rehabbing his knee, abusing Cybex machines for hours on end, and reported to the Bills' training camp in Fredonia, New York, in 1984 only to be told he'd been replaced. He never played another down.

That was the year the Raiders won their last championship. After Al Davis beat the NFL in court, Villapiano's old team took up residence in the Los Angeles Coliseum, site of the first Super Bowl. With Flores as head coach, Plunkett at quarterback, and Madden in the booth for CBS, the Raiders won their third Lombardi Trophy, putting Davis's renegades second only to the Steelers' four, but launching the age of the fly-by-night franchise earned them the apparent wrath of the football gods. The Raiders haven't won another Super Bowl since. Their brief reign at the LA Coliseum was celebrated by the league's drunkest, brawlingest fans, setting the tone for the rest of the '80s. "Pro football was still king, but its imperial sense came crashing down," wrote Michael MacCambridge, "foreshadowing a decade of discontent, litigation, owner infighting, player discord that would lead to two strikes and numerous drug scandals, and myriad charges that the game itself had grown too corporate, too violent, too boring."

Television companies found the game violent and exciting enough to pay the league $427 million from 1982 through '86, boosting per-team TV revenue from $5 million to $13 million a year. With the disparity between baseball's haves and have-nots multiplying, the NFL maintained competitive balance by splitting TV money equally. Green Bay, Cleveland, and Cincinnati could compete with the New York teams thanks to the revenue-sharing deal Pete Rozelle hammered out with the owners in 1961. The league's TV revenue would double again before the '80s were out. Rozelle basked in praise from owners whose lone gripe was that he'd lost to Davis over the Raiders' move—and some of them were starting to think that wasn't such a bad precedent.

On a snowy night in March 1984, fifteen Mayflower moving vans rolled past a few cold, bedraggled Baltimore Colts fans. Colts owner Robert Irsay, following Davis's example, was moving his team without permission from Rozelle, his fellow owners, or anyone else. Weeks earlier Irsay swore that he had no plans to move, but could if he wanted: "It's my goddamn team!" Now, after thirty years in Baltimore, his team slipped out of town under cover of darkness. Six hundred miles later, Baltimore's pads, cleats, helmets, playbooks, first-down chains, Ace bandages, 256-kilobyte IBM computers, floppy disks, and office furniture were the property of the Indianap-olis Colts. From then on, the all-volunteer Baltimore Colts Marching Band spent twelve lonely years playing the team's fight song (*Drive on, you Baltimore Colts / Go in and strike like lightning bolts*) at parades, school fairs, and other teams' games. One Sunday when the Colts played in Indy, the band assembled at Memorial Stadium and played for forty-eight thousand empty seats.

Four years later the Cardinals moved from St. Louis to Phoenix. The Raiders slouched back to Oakland in 1995, while the Rams filled the void in St. Louis by moving there, leaving Los Angeles without an NFL team. In '96 the Browns shifted to Baltimore and became the

Ravens, taking the field at Memorial Stadium as the long-suffering Colts Marching Band, forevermore known as the Marching Ravens, stomped out a welcoming tune. Cleveland got an expansion Browns team in return. Dwight Clark, Cleveland's general manager, proved to be no catch as an executive. The new Browns went 5-27 in the first two years of their reincarnation. A year later the Houston Oilers moved to Memphis, where they spent a season before jumping to Nashville as the Tennessee Titans. In 2002 the league granted Houston an expansion franchise called the Texans, a name that had gone unclaimed since 1953, when the original Texans moved to Baltimore. A twenty-year game of musical stadiums had confused longtime fans and left Al Davis staring darkly ahead while a Tampa Bay team coached by Jon Gruden, the coach Davis had dumped the year before, crushed his Raiders in Super Bowl XXXVII. Still stuck on three titles, Davis was two down to the golden team across the Bay.

The '80s belonged to the 49ers, who won their second Super Bowl in 1985, over Shula and the Dolphins. Four years later, with Montana leading a last-gasp 92-yard drive, they edged Cincinnati 20–16 in Super Bowl XXIII for their third championship. "We played Walsh and the Forty-Niners five times, including two Super Bowls," says the Bengals' Reggie Williams, "and lost every time. Paul Brown *hated* that." In 1989, Walsh abruptly retired. His vaunted intensity burning him up from inside, he had begun overcoaching, constantly second-guessing Montana—shades of Chuck Noll and Bradshaw, though Bradshaw was never heard to mutter, "Fuck you, you white-haired cocksucker." Walsh handed the reins to defensive coordinator George Seifert, a move he would regret. The white-haired mastermind felt left behind as Montana and Seifert closed the decade by leading the 1989 Niners to a second straight Lombardi Trophy, their fourth in nine years. Montana was the league's Most Valuable Player as well as Super Bowl MVP, the first since Bradshaw to win both awards in the same season. So efficient were the smooth, scripted, well-funded (in an age before salary caps) 49ers that their record on the road during the '80s was better than any other team's *home* record. Meanwhile the Steelers grew as rusty as Franco Harris's knees. Pittsburgh surrendered its mojo after Bradshaw and Harris retired in 1983. Noll and the Rooneys weren't sure which quarterback they wanted in that year's draft. By the time their turn came—twenty-first in the first round—all the top passers were off the board. Stanford's John Elway went first overall. Todd Blackledge from Penn State was gone, too, along with Miami's Jim Kelly, Illinois's Tony Eason, and Ken O'Brien from the University of California at Davis. A young *Pittsburgh Press* reporter, John Clayton, told Dan Rooney, "You've got to take the Pitt kid." He meant Dan Marino. Clayton swore that the Pittsburgh-born University of Pittsburgh quarterback was far better than the sixth-best quarterback in the draft. Noll agreed—until he learned where the tip came from. Clayton had cost the Steelers a late-'70s draft pick by reporting that they'd broken a league rule by wearing pads in an off-season workout. Noll called Clayton a spy; he wasn't about to take his advice. And so, with its first-round selection in 1983, the team that had cut hometown boy Johnny Unitas drafted Texas Tech tackle Gabriel "Señor Sack" Rivera instead of Marino. Rivera would record 2 career sacks while Marino won 147 games, threw for 61,361 yards and 420 touchdowns, set 31 NFL records, and made the Hall of Fame. The Steelers would close the twentieth century without another title before adding two more in 2006 and 2009. With six Super Bowl crowns they lead the all-time list. But of all teams with more than a single Super Bowl appearance, only the 5-0 Niners have been unbeaten in the ultimate game.

The philosophy Bill Walsh developed in Cincinnati and San Francisco came to dominate the modern game. George Seifert, Mike Holmgren, Sam Wyche, Jim Fassel, and Dennis Green—all Walsh assistants—added reams to Walsh's playbook when they became NFL coaches. Other names in Walsh's growing coaching tree include

Pete Carroll, Tony Dungy, Jon Gruden, Steve Mariucci, Sean Payton, Mike Shanahan, Andy Reid, Ray Rhodes, and Mike Tomlin. Many helped advance Walsh's West Coast Offense, which never held still long enough to be precisely defined, evolving into a concussive sort of speed chess in which quick-thinking passers dissect defenses designed to disguise themselves before and after the snap. "The league changes faster all the time," says Gruden, a Packers assistant under Holmgren who went on to coach the Raiders and Super Bowl–winning Bucs before joining *Monday Night Football*. Gruden has relished watching Peyton and Eli Manning, Tom Brady, Aaron Rodgers, and Drew Brees, along with their coaches and offensive coordinators, matching wits with modern defenses. "Is today's game ten times more complex than in the seventies? It might be ten times more complex than in the *nineties*. That's why it's practically impossible for a rookie QB to master an NFL offense. If you think of how the X's and O's will be spinning around in ten years . . . it's scary!"

It's likely that pro football will still be America's favorite sport in ten years, when an aging Lady Gaga levitates into the halftime show at Super Bowl LVII. Old-timers may grumble ("You didn't see us buddying around with the other team, none of that garbage," says Bradshaw), but today's NFL is more popular than ever—almost twice as popular as any other American sport. ESPN's coverage of the annual scouting combine in Indianapolis draws more viewers than the Masters or the Indy 500. The nineteen top-rated TV programs of 2010 (and twenty-eight of the top thirty) were NFL games. An NFL game was the number one TV show in all seventeen weeks of the regular season. In February 2010, Super Bowl XLIV between the "small-market" Saints and Colts became the most watched TV show in history with 107 million viewers, eclipsing a twenty-seven-year-old record set by the final episode of *M*A*S*H*. In February 2011, Super Bowl XLV between the "small-market" Packers and Steelers set a new record with 111 million viewers—a record that stood until the Giants-Patriots Super Bowl of February 2012 broke it. Super Sunday viewership has gotten so rabid that Animal Planet breaks ratings records with a bit of counterprogramming called the Puppy Bowl, featuring dogs rolling around an AstroTurf field. The $427 million TV contract that made headlines thirty years ago has been dwarfed by a deal signed in 2009, surpassed in turn by one that could bring the league $20.4 billion by the end of 2013, not counting $720 million per year that Verizon pays to be the official wireless provider of the National Football League, $700 million per year from official beer sponsor Anheuser-Busch (as teams reap millions more for pouring rights in their stadiums), and other revenue torrents as pro football's net worth swells like the pre- and postgame shows.

Seventy-eight years after Art Rooney paid $2,500 for Pittsburgh's NFL franchise, his son Dan's net worth was $150 million. That made Dan Rooney the *poorest* NFL owner. Fifteen of the other thirty-one were billionaires. Players got richer, too. Walter Payton's $475,000 salary, tops in the league in 1980, was eclipsed by Montana's $4 million in 1990, Patriots quarterback Drew Bledsoe's $8.5 million in 2000, and Peyton Manning's $15.8 million in 2010. (Due to salary-cap quirks, Manning made almost $12 million less than Ben Roethlisberger's 2008 salary of $27.7 million.) In 2011, Montana fan Tom Brady made $18 million. Salaries accounted for 30 percent of league expenses in the 1980s, surpassed 50 percent in the '90s, and neared 60 percent in 2010, when the owners decided they'd had enough. When their bargaining agreement with the players' union expired, owners locked players out of training camps before the 2011–12 season, demanding a bigger slice of a $10-billion-a-year pie. Among their demands: a longer season. After four months the owners and players reached a new collective bargaining agreement that will last through 2021. Both sides made concessions, and for the first time player safety was a significant issue. The regular season remained at 16 games, with decreases in full-contact practice and a $1 billion fund for retired players.

Many of the men who helped build the modern NFL got no part of the pie. They were its ingredients. Darryl Stingley, who lived for thirty years after being paralyzed going over the middle against Jack Tatum and the Raiders, privately called Steve Grogan's throw "a shitty pass," but Stingley didn't blame Grogan. He blamed NFL owners. "The owners are making a nice buck allowing violence to be a major part of the game," he wrote. "No way they're going to put a lid on their money-making machine. They'd rather pay the hospital bills." According to his coauthor, Mark Mulvoy, the longtime managing editor of *Sports Illustrated*, the league paid Stingley's bills in order to avoid a lawsuit. "The league flew him around in a private jet outfitted with medevac equipment," says Mulvoy. "The last thing Pete Rozelle wanted was *Stingley vs. the NFL*." Stingley died in 2007.

Thirty years after making the Super Bowl matter, Broadway Joe Namath limped on a pair of artificial knees. The Oilers' once-unstoppable Earl Campbell was confined to a wheelchair at the age of forty-five. After two knee replacements of his own, Johnny Unitas played golf in the years leading up to his death in 2002, age sixty-nine. Unitas used his left hand to wrap the useless fingers of his right hand around the grip of a club, then strapped the deadened fingers in place with Velcro. Johnny U's frequent target John Mackey, the first president of the NFL Players Association, didn't try to play golf. After a ten-year career that led to his selection to the Hall of Fame and the 1960s All-Decade Team, Mackey would slip into premature senility. Jack Kemp, the Bills quarterback who became a congressman and cabinet secretary, once called Mackey "the smartest man in the room," but Mackey lost his bearings as he aged. Seeing the Indianapolis Colts' Marvin Harrison wearing his old number 88 on TV, the fifty-three-year-old Mackey shouted, "That's not me!" Retired players' health benefits expired after five years, and his NFL pension of $1,950 a month didn't begin to cover his rent and medical bills. After spending her husband's savings to pay for his care in a nursing home, Sylvia Mackey sold their house and went back to work as a flight attendant. Finally she shamed the NFL and NFLPA into creating what they call the 88 Plan. Named for Mackey's unretired number, it contributes up to $88,000 a year to nursing-home care for retired players suffering from dementia or Alzheimer's disease. As part of the deal, the league stipulated that there was no proof the ex-players' dementia had anything to do with their NFL careers. Mackey died in 2011.

After decades of celebrating headbanging hits, from Cosell's halftime highlights to *SportsCenter* clips, the NFL now funds research on the damage pro football does to its players. New, improved helmets will provide limited help because concussions occur inside the head, when the brain strikes the inside of the skull after a sudden stop or shift in direction. As Cris Collinsworth, the Bengals receiever turned TV analyst, told the *New York Times*, "We're talking about the very essence of the game. You try to teach toughness and to hit hard, and to be safe—there's a contradiction. The fundamental question is, do you want your kids playing football? That's the scary question. . . . I think we're talking about the survival of the game."

As part of a pathbreaking *New York Times* investigation, Alan Schwarz tracked down retired safety Dave Duerson. In 2010 the fifty-year-old Duerson, a four-time Pro Bowler who helped the Bears win Super Bowl XX, was living in Florida, despondent, convinced that football had cost him full use of his mind if not his soul. On February 17, 2011, he sent a text message to his family, saying he wanted his brain donated to the Boston University School of Medicine, which studies brain damage in football players. Then he lifted a shotgun to his chest and pulled the trigger. Duerson's suicide note asked that his brain be donated to the NFL's brain bank. Pathologists at the university's Center for the Study of Traumatic Encephalopathy found lesions in his brain—brown, tangled tissue showing repeated trauma. Duerson's was the fifteenth NFL brain they had dissected; they found similar damage in fourteen of the fifteen.

According to the Associated Press, in May 2012 more than 1,000 former players were suing the NFL. They charged that "not enough was done to inform players about the dangers of concussions in the past, and not enough is done to take care of them today." Among the big-name players involved in suits were Packers All-Pro Mark Chmura, Bears Super Bowl quarterback Jim McMahon, and Alex Karras, the Lions tackle who went on to join Howard Cosell in the *Monday Night Football* booth.

League spokesman Greg Aiello declared, "The league has long made player safety a priority, and continues to do so."

Thirty years ago, Roy Blount told readers of his shock at seeing the Steelers' hands up close. "On the backs of their hands and their knuckles, many had wounds of a kind I have never seen on anyone else," he wrote, "fairly deep digs and gouges which were not scabbed over so much as dried. They looked a little like old sores on horses." Many had wounds that were harder to see. Blount was haunted by a breakfast meeting he had with center Ray Mansfield in 1973, after the Steelers lost to Oakland in the playoffs. "My neck hurts so bad sometimes I think about killing myself," Mansfield said. He was thirty-two at the time. "I know I'll be a cripple by the time I'm fifty. But if that's what it takes, fuck it."

Mansfield retired in 1976. Twenty years later, still ambulatory but aching from head to both heels, with soaring blood pressure and a family history of heart attacks, he went hiking in the Grand Canyon. "I'm going to die in the Canyon," he'd told his son. At some point that day, after pushing what was left of his limits on a cliffside trail, Ray Mansfield, fifty-five, sat down and died.

"It wasn't a suicide," says Blount, "but he was in constant pain. . . ."

Searchers found Mansfield's body the next morning. He was sitting with his back against a rock, facing west, toward the spot where the sun set the evening before.

Epilogue

THE LAST LATE HIT

On February 11, 2001, Three Rivers Stadium collapsed. Pittsburgh's Controlled Demolition Company set off a series of dynamite charges that brought down the thirty-one-year-old ballpark in a controlled implosion. As a crowd of about twenty-three thousand watched from nearby Point State Park, the stadium's concrete walls shivered and fell inward in a growing cloud of amber smoke and dust. Fifteen yards from the implosion stood Heinz Field, the Steelers' gleaming new $281-million home.

The team saved a few items from Three Rivers. Among them is Franco Harris's old locker, displayed in the new park's vast Coca-Cola Great Hall. Sometimes fans admiring the locker will turn and see Harris himself looking over their shoulders. Now reconciled with the team that cut him in 1984, the Most Valuable Player of Super Bowl IX acts as a goodwill ambassador for the team and the city of Pittsburgh. He also runs a bakery—the Super Bakery, which makes doughnuts, muffins, cupcakes, and cinnamon buns fortified with his "MVP formula" (minerals, vitamins, protein) for schools and hospitals throughout Pennsylvania and much of the Northeast.

Harris is bulkier than he used to be, his chocolate-colored beard showing flecks of gray, his belly overshadowing his belt. But his legs work almost as well as in his playing days—a happy consequence, perhaps, of avoiding unnecessary contact.

"I've held up pretty well," he says. "I loved the art of running, not running *into*. For me it was about vision, anticipation, being one thought ahead of the defense." Still mentally nimble, he jokes with old teammates, remembering their wives' and kids' names, keeping tabs on ex-Steelers and even a Raider, Phil Villapiano.

Former wild man Villapiano somehow survived stingers, rat turds, red juice, Jell-O knees, a fight with Hells Angels, and a decade of headbanging hits with his mind and body intact. "Franco kept his brains by avoiding contact. I just had a thick skull," he says. He has surgery scars on his left knee and left hand, but can still hit a golf ball 270 yards. As a member of the last generation of players whose NFL careers didn't set them up for life, even if they made All-Pro, Villapiano needed another line of work. He found it in the arcane field of global logistics, and he became a vice president of Odyssey Logistics, a firm that coordinates shipping all over the world. "Madden always told us to prepare for life after football. Nobody did, but I found I could help manufacturers move freight. And I can't tell you how many guys from the old days I've heard from—most of them asking for a job."

Not Harris. "Phil! How you doing?" Franco said when they visited Heinz Field for the first time. It was September 15, 2002, a year after the implosion of Three Rivers Stadium.

Villapiano introduced his son. "Franco, this is my boy, Mike."

"Hi, Mike. How old are you?"

"Eight," the boy said.

Harris walked them around Heinz Field, with its weatherproof Kentucky bluegrass, heated from below to a constant turf temperature of sixty-two degrees, and its JumboTron flanked by mammoth

Heinz ketchup bottles that pour red rivers when the Steelers drive into the "Heinz Red Zone."

"What's your favorite team, Mike?"

"Raiders!"

"C'mon, let me show you something." Harris led peewee leaguer Mike down a ramp. They were gone for fifteen minutes. Villapiano wandered the grounds, gawking at the perfect turf, the luxury boxes, and the spotless concession stands selling garlic fries, Cajun peanuts, and craft beers. Finally he saw Harris waving at him with a big, cheesy smile, Franco pushing Mike toward him. Mike had a Steelers hat on. A Steelers jersey, number 32, hung from his shoulders to his ankles. His black-and-gold Steelers gloves clutched a Terrible Towel inscribed in black Sharpie: *To Mike, Remember the Immaculate Reception, 12/23/72.*

"Dad, check it out," the boy said. "Go, Steelers!" Franco was standing behind him, grinning.

In 2009 Harris's son, Dok (short for Dokmanovich, his mother's maiden name), ran for mayor of Pittsburgh. "I'm glad he's running for office instead of running with a football," his father said. Dok finished second in a three-man race and may run again in 2013.

The following fall Mike Villapiano, then a senior quarterback at Rumson High School in New Jersey, led the Bulldogs to the state championship in their division. He ran and threw for all 69 yards of the Bulldogs' game-winning fourth-quarter drive. "Mike's a hell of a kid," said Phil, nodding toward a life-size painting of Mike in the family's living room. "Will he wind up at a Division I college? Hell if I know." A late bloomer in high school, Mike lacked the two- and three-year stats other prep passers racked up. His NFL DNA meant nothing to college coaches, who didn't know or care that Mike's dad had won a Super Bowl ring and been to four Pro Bowls. Villapiano sent DVDs of Mike's highlights to dozens of colleges, where they joined stacks of similar DVDs on coaches' desks. Mike spent the winter working out with former Giants quarterback Scott Brunner in an all-weather bubble in northern New Jersey, strengthening his arm, honing his footwork. He ran wind sprints in hopes of trimming a tenth of a second from his 4.8 40-yard dash. He guzzled protein shakes and quarts of chocolate milk. Harvard, Stanford, North Carolina, Rutgers, and Colorado expressed interest in him, but nobody offered a full ride and a clear shot at the number one quarterback slot.

"College coaches ought to be ashamed of themselves," Villapiano said. "They lie. They lead kids on. One of them told Mike, 'Bring me a state championship and we'll talk.' So Mike did it, and the coach e-mails him, *Great job, Michael. Way to go.* That's the last we ever heard from him."

Mike Villapiano spent the 2011–12 season at quarterback for Connecticut's Cheshire Academy, hoping to attract the attention of a big-college coach. He could fire the ball 50 yards on a line. "All you need is reps," his father told him. Repetitions: the countless dropbacks, reads, and releases that might get him to Division I and finally the NFL. The odds were against him, and every play held physical risk. He and his father had discussed concussions.

"I've been dinged a few times," Mike said. "It's part of the game."

His dad hated the thought of Mike's getting hurt. "It's a risk. You play through it," Phil said. When Mike got dinged—probably concussed—during a high school game, the two of them talked about what Mike should do. Sit out a few plays? A few games? He couldn't win games or scholarship offers sitting on the bench. So Mike didn't tell his coach. He didn't tell anyone. He went back in and led Rumson to a victory. As his proud dad put it, the boy's got some Raider in him.

Today there's a statue at Pittsburgh International Airport, a life-size black-and-gold figure bending to make a shoestring catch.

"As you can see, I was a lot thinner then," Franco Harris said not long ago.

Harris, sixty-one, and Phil Villapiano, sixty-two, were talking football. They mentioned the current Steelers and Raiders—advantage Harris—and the NFL veterans their age who are sick or dying. "That head-injury stuff," Harris said. "Phil, we've all got it."

"Maybe. What are you gonna do? Keep going."

Soon they were ribbing each other about the Immaculate Reception—the busted play as well as the statue. "We're coming up on forty years," Harris said. "That's a long time to be thinking about one play."

"Yeah, but we keep it alive. You know, if you'd been running hard, you wouldn't have been where the ball bounced to."

"Look at the tape. We left the backfield side by side. If I was loafing, how'd I get to the ball first?"

Villapiano pointed at the statue. "Let me tell you something," he said. "One of these days you're going to go to the airport and that Franco Harris statue won't be standing there. Because I *tackled* it."

A Note on Sources

The Last Headbangers represents two years of research on the NFL in the 1970s. While working on the book I came to believe that the league entered a pivotal era with Franco Harris's Immaculate Reception in 1972, an era in which new rules, television, aggressive marketing, a special generation of players and coaches, and a changing America combined to help pro football dominate the sports landscape. In my view the game took on its modern form in the '70s, and what I consider "'70s football" ended with Dwight Clark's 1982 touchdown grab, now known as The Catch, ushering in a more corporate, scripted, and regulated version of the sport, exemplified by the great 49ers teams of the '80s.

A great perk of my work was dozens of talks with players and coaches I watched on TV while I was growing up, as well as writers, broadcasters, and others who knew them. Those talks were full of pleasant surprises (Roger Staubach's not a stiff after all!) and distress at the physical and spiritual toll the game took on many who played it. I also relied on contemporary newspaper and magazine accounts (many from Sports Illustrated, where I used to work), TV and radio broadcasts, official and unofficial websites, including pro-football-reference.com, and a small library of books on the game then and now.

Throughout *Headbangers* I have put original material in the present tense. If a line reads, "Bradshaw says . . ." or "Shula remembers . . ." or "Villapiano shouts . . . ," he said it to me. Quotes from other sources are attributed in the past tense.

Acknowledgments

The players come first. Sharp, funny, excitable, and endlessly quotable, the man Howard Cosell called *Vil-a-pi-anno* has to be the NFL's least retiring retiree. This book wouldn't be nearly as lively without Phil Villapiano. I'm grateful to him, his wife, Susan, and their son, Michael, for their time and hospitality. Note to college coaches: quarterback Mike Villapiano's got a big heart like his dad, and more arm.

Villapiano's old frenemy Franco Harris was helpful, as were Harris's teammates Terry Bradshaw and Andy Russell. Roger Staubach taught me more about leadership in two conversations than most men could tell you in a month. I was lucky to huddle by phone or in person with players including Reggie Williams, Joe Montana, Conrad Dobler, Tom Flores, George Blanda, Ken Stabler, Dan Dierdorf, Jim Otto, Matt Millen, Cedric Hardman, John "Frenchy" Fuqua, Gerald Irons, and Ben Davidson. Others who shared memories and insights with me include Don Shula, Roy Blount, Brian Billick, Al Michaels, Jon Gruden, Dr. Rob Huizenga, Don Ohlmeyer, Alan Schwarz, Mark Mulvoy, Dick Friedman, Dennis Lewin, Michael Lombardi, Bill Chastain, Dave Newhouse, and Carol Doda.

I've been a Michael MacCambridge fan for years. MacCambridge's *America's Game*—an invaluable read for anyone interested in sports history—became one of my football bibles, along with Blount's *About Three Bricks Shy of a Load* and David Harris's *The League*.

Tom Mayer is the Montana of book editors, razor-sharp, unflappable, unbeatable. Many thanks to Tom, Denise Scarfi, and their colleagues at Norton. Thanks also to Jim Levine and his colleagues at the Levine Greenberg Agency, and to Robert Chong at Getty Images and Annie Pratt at US Presswire for their help with photos.

Most authors rely on family and friends to help them through the years it takes to write a book. For me that group features Ken Kubik, Luis Fernando Llosa, Steve Randall, Patricia Cook (win for her, Colts), Tom and Kelly Cook, Jeannette Miller, Bob Broderick, Christina Bloom, Allison Burnett, and, most of all, the brilliant and beautiful Pamela Marin and our home team, Calloway Marin Cook and Lily Lady Cook.

Select Bibliography

Belichick, Steve. *Football Scouting Methods*. New York: Ronald Press, 1962.

Bernstein, Ross. *The Code*. Chicago: Triumph Books, 2009.

Billick, Brian. *More Than a Game*. New York: Scribner, 2009.

Blount, Roy, Jr. *About Three Bricks Shy of a Load*. New York: Little, Brown, 1974.

Bradshaw, Terry. *It's Only a Game*. New York: Pocket Books, 2001.

Carlin, George. *Braindroppings*. New York: Hyperion Books, 1997.

Chastain, Bill. *Steel Dynasty*. Chicago: Triumph Books, 2005.

Cosell, Howard. *I Never Played the Game*. New York: Avon Books, 1985.

———. *Like It Is*. New York: Pocket Books, 1975.

Frum, David. *How We Got Here*. New York: Basic Books, 2000.

Gunther, Marc, and Bill Carter. *Monday Night Mayhem*. New York: William Morrow, 1988.

Harris, David. *The Genius*. New York: Random House, 2008.

———. *The League*. New York: Bantam Books, 1987.

Huizenga, Rob. *You're Okay, It's Only a Bruise*. New York: St. Martin's Press, 1994.

Jaworski, Ron. *The Games That Changed the Game*. New York: ESPN Books and Ballantine Books, 2010.

Layden, Tim. *Blood, Sweat and Chalk*. New York: Sports Illustrated Books, 2010.

Lombardo, John. *Raiders Forever*. Chicago: Contemporary Books, 2001.

MacCambridge, Michael. *America's Game*. New York: Anchor Books, 2005.

Maraniss, David. *When Pride Still Mattered*. New York: Simon & Schuster, 1999.

Millman, Chad, and Shawn Coyne. *The Ones Who Hit the Hardest*. New York: Gotham Books, 2010.

Myers, Gary. *The Catch*. New York: Three Rivers Press, 2009.

Richmond, Peter. *Badasses*. New York: HarperCollins, 2010.

Rooney, Dan. *My 75 Years with the Pittsburgh Steelers and the NFL*. Cambridge, MA: Da Capo Press, 2007.

Stabler, Ken. *Snake*. New York: Doubleday, 1986.

Stingley, Darryl. *Happy to Be Alive*. New York: Beaufort Books, 1983.

Travers, Steven. *The Good, the Bad, & the Ugly*. Chicago: Triumph Books, 2008.

Wexell, Jim. *Tales from Behind the Steel Curtain*. Champaign, IL: Sports Publishing, 2004.

Yost, Mark. *Tailgating, Sacks, and Salary Caps*. Chicago: Kaplan Publishing, 2006.

Index